Shark Infested
Custard

Shark Infested Custard

The Golden Age of Television

ROBIN BROWN

Weidenfeld and Nicolson
LONDON

Published in Great Britain by
George Weidenfeld & Nicolson Limited
91 Clapham High Street
London SW4 7TA

ISBN 0 297 81072 3

Printed in Great Britain by
The Bath Press, Avon

In fond memory of
Robert 'Bob' Heller,
documentary-maker

Chapter One

We stood like sombre Bisto Kids in the iron cage of Victoria Station. Annette was sullen. She had been all but dragged here from the Shangri-la life of a white colony where the air was hot and throbbing. Tiffany and Lisa, our two little girls, were stunned by the cold and the noise. They remembered a sunny playground and a warm tranquillity broken only occasionally by exploding bombs. As for their father, I was stateless, jobless, and penniless. Slime-green trains slid into the station through thick cloud resembling a wet blanket of porridge hanging across the end of the station. It was January and, bar a sweater each, we were dressed for the summer that never ends in high middle Africa.

'Every cloud has a woolly lining,' I joked. A smile from any of them would have warmed my soul.

Annette shivered instead.

'They're catching their deaths,' she hissed, pulling her honey-gold, goose-pimpled offspring in the direction of the buffet and against the grey tide of commuters. Seven-year-old Tiffany resisted, suddenly crying out: 'There's Annie!'

Lisa, five, followed her pointed finger and howled with delight.

'Annie!'

I spun round in anguish, wildly searching for that small chunky figure with the big banana smile who I knew was quite capable of crossing countries and perhaps even oceans if the mood took her. She was, after all, remotely related to the Kings of the Matabele, Mzitlikaze who threw people off high cliffs, and Lobengula who had gout from drinking too much champagne.

Giddy with disorientation, I could think of only one thing: if it was Annie Mutesa, would she still be carrying our gun?

Meanwhile the children had disappeared in the direction of Smith's bookstall and Annette searched the crowd frantically. (Unlike me she had spent a lot of time with the children, but the fact that the cold might be causing them to hallucinate seemed not to occur to her.)

Inevitably, there was no gun-toting nannie. The few blacks around were either doing menial jobs just as they had in Shangri-la, sweeping out the trains and emptying waste baskets, or they were posing as white railwaymen and collecting tickets from commuters who appeared not to notice this subterfuge.

We walked closer to the news-stand and I half-expected Annie to leap from her hiding place among the *Playboys* and *Penthouses*.

Then suddenly we saw what the children had seen. All across the bookstall racks were magazines featuring Annie Mutesa on the front cover. Wearing her smart nannie uniform, she was holding Lisa, who in turn was holding the large pink plastic doll we had used to smuggle sterling out of Shangri-la.

'There is a God!' I cried jubilantly. 'We made the cover story!'

'Annie!' Tiff cried again, confident for the first time since we had stepped off the *Comet*.

I grabbed a magazine and thumbed quickly through it. There were sexy pictures of Annette with her hair done like a Barbie doll, taken through the bomb screens of our bedroom window in Bulawayo, with my caption about the gun she had to keep in her bedside table, and pictures of our neighbours. All 2,000 words of the article I had written about the demise of Shangri-la were there, faithfully reproduced, and they had even used my title 'Living Through A Crisis!'

I was transfixed with delight, not just that the article ensured money in a British bank account, but more with the vindication headlined there – we had lived through the crisis. England was awful, the winter climate was unspeakably awful and Victoria Station was just simply unspeakable, but we had survived. We had made the transition from a flawed paradise to a place that other people appeared able to tolerate. It appeared there was life after death.

I thrust the magazine (it was the now-defunct *Woman's Mirror*) down to the children. Lisa studied it for a moment, stroked the paper, then burst into tears; a one-dimensional Annie Mutesa was simply not enough and it confirmed her babyish instincts that a real, and absolute, change had taken place.

Annie Mutesa was very nearly the last person we had said goodbye to in Shangri-la, after the most frightening and dangerous journey of her life carrying our gun.

She was a cousin of the Matabele revolutionary Joshua Nkomo, then languishing in a concentration camp called the Place of Skulls. Shangri-la was in turmoil. Ian Smith had flown us to cloud-cuckoo land by declaring the country unilaterally independent from Britain, history and reason.

From their concentration camps the black leaders were directing their pawns and knights in games of bloody internecine chess to see who would rule Shangri-la when the white ostriches finally suffocated.

With great sadness, I had decided not to stay for the last act of this farce. I was emotionally exhausted from keeping one foot in both camps, and Annette had bags under her pretty eyes after a year of sleepless nights behind the bombscreens of our bedroom windows.

We said our first goodbye to Annie Mutesa at our home in Bulawayo. It was very sad. She had never quite believed we were going until the *Mirror* sent a photographer to take her and Annette's picture for an article I was writing about the trauma of leaving Shangri-la. The photographer broke the news to Annie that we would be living in England.

Annie turned to me and said: 'You're runnin' away Baas – you?'

'Yes, I'm running away.' I replied, 'Does that surprise you?'

'Not much,' Annie grunted. 'You all have to go sometime.'

That's why I had originally kept Annie on, even after the police had warned me of her political connections. She could be relied upon to tell me straight where I stood with the people. She was always more one of the people than one of us.

Friends of ours born and bred in Shangri-la found this the most difficult of the revolutionary paradoxes. Would a Boy or a Nannie who had been part of their family all their lives murder them in their beds if so directed by Mr Nkomo? They could not believe it. Annie Mutesa left me in no doubt. She admired me as a white liberal, I think she loved me a little because I so obviously shared her love of Africa. But when it came to the moment of them or us, Smith or Nkomo, Annie would have taken Nkomo's orders.

Anyway, this all proved to be an exaggeration. Hardly anyone was murdered in their beds when Mr Mugabe took over Shangri-la.

It was not just Annie who made it difficult for me to leave. A very senior representative of Mr Smith's government summoned me to a meeting in a railway carriage in the Bulawayo sidings. I went quaking, convinced I was going to be eliminated as an enemy of the people.

Behind drawn wooden blinds in a leprous yellow light, I was told that Mr Smith did not understand my decision to quit the controllership of a television station at the tender age of 27 and felt strongly that I was setting an unfortunate precedent for the young executives of Shangri-la by opting for the 'Yellow Route'. The Yellow Route was that taken by white cowards.

How would I like the Bulawayo South constituency? How would I like to be a Member of Parliament?

A member of Mr Smith's party?

Indeed.

They let me out when I said I would consider it.

I went home and later Annette and I sat in bed looking out into the purple African night through the petrol bomb screens.

'I think we should leave sooner rather than later,' I said. 'I think the Government is losing its grip.'

So we went in three weeks and it was many months before I heard down the guava vine that the offer had been genuine, not that it would have made any difference. By then about the only thing I knew for sure was that Mr Smith's Rhodesian Front was destined to be one of history's shortest lived political parties, and that the country he ruled, Rhodesia, my Shangri-la, was going to vanish off the world map.

Three weeks is not long to wrap up your whole life. Our possessions weren't much of a problem; we packed quite a lot of treasured items into a huge, rough-slabbed mahogany box and sold the rest. When the big crate arrived in England the wood turned out to be worth more than its contents, and somehow mukwa stools with woven kudu hide seats and sisal rugs did not look that good in Putney.

The real difficulty was living with the reaction of our friends for three weeks. During the past year on television, I had been using my evening news magazine to make defiant, hopeful and liberal noises. When it was announced in the papers that I was taking the yellow route, our friends treated us like aliens from another planet.

One of the more coherent ones took me on one side and explained that he felt betrayed. 'All the times we watched you on television defiantly interviewing Smith and van der Byl and Lardner Burke about their lunatic policies, it meant we didn't have to take them that seriously. And now we do.'

'I'm not a clown. I meant you to take them seriously,' I told him.

'Jesus Christ!' he said, and made his own departure arrangements.

Others tried to talk me out of leaving by commending me on my courageous crusade. Our Jewish family doctor said the situation was similar to the Thirties in Nazi Germany. That genuinely shocked me and more or less confirmed my decision to leave as soon as possible. Resolutely Jewish, however, he opted to stay; thankfully Robert Mugabe was not Adolf Hitler. After Independence my doctor friend seemed to grow bored and went to South Africa.

My secretary came to me and said: 'I never, never, thought you would quit when the going got tough.'

Knowing that your personal secretary never really understood you was another sobering thought.

The more belligerent of our friends came and sharpened themselves on us, like carving knives against steel.

'We are going to see it out to the end,' they would say over big glasses of gin.

We felt obliged to say goodbye to everyone at a series of ever more sad parties. 'This is a last-ditch stand,' some of them said.

I demanded to know what that actually meant. It sounded glamorous, perhaps if I could understand I too would stay and make a last-ditch stand.

'We'll go down fighting,' they declared.

'What for?'

'Civilized standards.'

That one just reduced me to silent despair. In the event hardly any of them became killers in the name of civilized standards; most of these last-ditchers put the moment off by going to South Africa.

Annette tried various ways of staying, but none of these worked out. She left me briefly and went to live with her most determined girl friend. The girl friend confessed that she, too, was thinking of leaving. Annette finally came home and we auctioned all our left-over bits, said our tearful goodbyes to Annie Mutesa, and went to stay with my mother in Salisbury before boarding the plane for Great Britain.

I was unemployed for the first time in my life. We had long discussions about where we should go. Great Britain? The Huge Vast Continent of the United States? The Mega-Island of Australia? The Union of Soviet Socialist Republics?

'If we have to go then it must be Home,' Annette said. We had married very young in England and her father had given her a small sum of money for a ticket home which I knew she still had.

My mother who had been born in England nodded her agreement. Anywhere else was unthinkable. I reviewed the several introductions I had been given by journalist colleagues and decided the most powerful were the English contacts.

Of these, unquestionably the most promising was a card I had been given by an English naturalist. In those days David Attenborough was beguiling television audiences with his famous trick of reaching down holes while giving a loving and enthusiastic description of the creature that was about to bite his hand off.

As a youth I had developed a great passion for natural history but this interest had rather lapsed by the time David appeared as a guest on my *Tonight* show on television. We did it live and David had to wait while I interviewed one of Mr Smith's awful Cabinet. I never set out to be gratuitously nasty to these people but rarely ended up being otherwise.

In the hospitality suite later, I asked the question which David must have been asked a thousand times: had he ever been seriously bitten by anything?

'Now and then,' he replied, looking round the room where others from the programme were being given drinks. His eyes came to rest on the Cabinet member. 'They tend to bite if you worry them too much.'

I followed his gaze. 'There are some creatures here that could get quite nasty,' he added and gave that famous smile. Later he gave me his card with the very kind offer that I contact him, should I need to head for the hills.

'What about you? I asked my mother. The question confused her. She had come overland to Africa and had never been anything but Afro-Anglo. As Africa became more troubled she came overtly to recognize that the traumas of that journey had somehow cauterized the Anglo influence. By the time we of the next generation came to the conclusion that it was time to leave Africa, she was entrenched. The nicest compliment I can pay the Zimbabwe revolution is that they recognized my mother's position and allowed her to stay on as a 'Madame', because essentially they understood that her racism was benign. I think it was also overtly recognized that ordinary Boys and Nannies were as confused by the speed of change as she was and that in a funny kind of way they needed each other in the transition.

What is certainly significant is that my mother never even considered leaving, and her relationships with her black servants changed only in that each became more respectful of the other. My mother learned to curb her racism and the black people with whom she associated came to respect her as a determined woman who really was going to stay. She could be depended upon, and therefore would be allowed her occasional outbursts of racism. She was also good for a bandage, or a shilling, or a lift to the hospital when a little black baby was dying.

As Annie Mutesa pointed out in the end, I was not.

We left Annie to her revolution, but only after the most bizarre second and final parting. Annette and the children were away saying yet more goodbyes to their friends when there came a sharp knock on my mother's back door. She gingerly opened the top half (all doors were opened gingerly in Shangri-la in those days), inspected what was outside and hastily summoned me.

'It's a native woman for you,' she said with great suspicion. 'I don't think she's from round here.'

I walked round to the back and there, swathed in a kaffir blanket, was a shifty-looking Annie Mutesa.

'Quickly Baas,' she cried, scurrying off into the big clump of bamboo that divided my mother's house from her servants' quarters.

'What the hell are you doing here, Annie?' Even in those days, Matabeles from the south rarely travelled alone to this Shona stronghold of the north. For a wild moment I concluded she had decided to come with us!

She reached inside the blanket and took out a gun – Annette's little .22 pistol.

I snatched it from her.

'You shouldn't have this Annie, you know that!'

'It's the Madame's gun, Baas. She's going to need it over there 'mong them devils looking after my children.'

The whole of our short life in Shangri-la was encapsulated in the sentence. 'The Madame's gun' neatly defined the state we had reached where young white women habitually kept a pistol in their bedside tables. 'Over there' was a sombre description of Britain, the power across the water which had imposed a century of colonialism on Annie's people – those 'Devils'. And finally there were 'her' children; quite clearly from her tone she saw us as kidnapping them. Tiffany, who had spent her days wandering in our big garden among the chickens, the citrus grove and the big acacias huge with technicolour bouganvillea, checking in now and then with Annie Mutesa for Mazoe orange fruit drinks and lunch; baby Lisa, who had been an active crawler and liked to spend her time lost in the deep green clumps of agapanthas, eating slugs. Annie tolerated this as long as she knew which clump was occupied and only bothered to clean her up once a day for Annette's midday inspection. Annie was fiercely protective. Once Lisa crawled in front of a vegetable seller's bicycle just as he moved forward to show Annie his wares. The tyre ran over Lisa's foot, causing her to scream. I arrived just in time to stop Annie beheading the Boy with a meat cleaver.

'We don't need the gun, Annie,' I told her, 'and you definitely should not have it.'

In fact the gun was a certain death warrant for Annie and any of her race, and she must have known it. Caught with it, her trial would have been swift and the death sentence mandatory. In those dark days death was mandatory even for throwing stones.

The gun had gone missing during the nightmare of our move and as I had possessed it illegally, in common with most whites, I had put the matter out of mind. Privately I suspected that Annie had procured it for the revolution, and even more privately I allowed the subscription.

She explained that it had been jammed at the back of the drawer of the bedside table we had given her, along with other items of furniture. I could not comprehend why she should have taken so outlandish a risk to return an object which, loaded or not, would have been a very attractive gift to some of her friends. I decided it was simply because, for the time being at least, Annie still felt bound to us. I felt vaguely ashamed.

Then she revealed the true purpose of her journey. Wistfully she asked: 'The children not here, Baas Robin?'

There it was in a nutshell. She had risked her life and made a hazardous sortie into enemy territory for one last look at the children.

'No Annie, they won't be here today,' I said as firmly as I could. We had only just calmed down the children from the last anguished parting.

'Okay Baas. I'm going now to get the bus.'

I gave her rather a lot of money which she accepted without any particular show of gratitude and departed, a sturdy, indestructible chunk of Africa, armour-plated with stoicism. We never saw each other again, nor corresponded. It is hard to pass messages between different planets.

I said nothing to Annette or the children about the visit as I was feeling guilty about the gun.

As Smith's cloud-cuckoo land government was doing everything it could to stem the outflow of capital down the Yellow Route, and our total allowance was £300, we spent our last evening in Shangri-la stuffing Lisa's pink plastic doll with illegal British currency and still trying to persuade my mother to think ahead. A black revolution was hardly the place for a middle-aged widow who felt that every black man should not only be called Boy but also be treated like one.

She was a secret admirer of Ian Smith, not least because for the last year good old Smithie had been telling the white settlers that they did not need to think ahead. We would do it for them.

My mother fought me off with Smithie slogans.

'We'll not give up without a fight,' she avowed.

'Nonsense. When the going gets really tough most of them will go down to South Africa. What's the point of all the killing if the outcome's inevitable?' I argued.

'That's what the Americans were saying in 1939,' my mother retorted. 'Where would Britain have been if she'd accepted defeatist talk?'

Having studied the racist ways of most British immigrants to Shangri-la, I had often wondered whether Britain might actually have prospered under Hitler, but this suggestion would have made my mother genuinely angry.

She enjoyed patriotism. She and her family had come out here in 1947 by mistake. A journey that began as a holiday-style adventure to escape the awfulness of post-war Britain turned into a nightmare of heat, dust, danger and disease. The oasis of Shangri-la, a British paradise in the centre of Africa, seemed to welcome them just as they were at the end of their tether.

My father, Leonard, soon began to recognize it as the mirage it was but, fortunately perhaps, had died before the crunch came. My mother remained covertly nervous of everything, but grateful, and when Ian Smith came along she was quite happy to fly with him to cloud-cuckoo land along with eighty per cent of the white population.

We, the Young Turks of White Liberalism, took the Yellow Route and went Home, even though Britain, the country from which our parents had fled in horror and disgust might as well have been another planet. It was high in the northern hemisphere; we were low in the south. Its climate was dominated by cold and rain, ours by heat and droughts, its social structures by ancient feudalism, ours by an egalitarian if elitist hegemony. There one's home was one's castle, and tame deer ran on the lawngrass of the park; here we lived outdoors alongside a wilderness still teeming with wildlife. The single act of going Home contained so many elements of paradox that none of us expected to arrive there sane; and indeed the refugees who arrived at Victoria Station on that dark winter's morning perhaps were a little mad.

I had anticipated this and before we left had applied for an immigration permit to the United States, but it was by no means certain it would be granted. There was the added complication that I was completing a novel that would have put me in jail under the new laws Smith had introduced. One way or another we had to go Home.

Bye-bye mother! (was she so calm because she thought me a coward?) Goodbye Brother Peter! (I can hardly bear to look you in the eye because you may well die in the coming war). Bye-bye Shangri-la. (The nightmare that I am the citizen of a vicious illusion is confirmed by the cold light of day).

At the airport the Customs Officer took the little doll Lisa had washed that morning and gingerly placed it to one side while he gave our luggage a cursory inspection. The doll dripped.

'British Customs are taking a hard line with foreign immigrants,' he grimaced in a friendly fashion. 'They have a drug crisis being fuelled by foreign immigration.'

'What are they smuggling?' I quavered.

'Heroin and opium,' he said fiercely. 'And some new stuff called marijuana worth a fortune. Don't let the little girl carry the doll through, that's a favourite method.'

I emptied the doll of its meagre sterling when we were airborne, secretly regretting not having stuffed it with dagga – marijuana –

which could be bought for next to nothing on any Shangri-la street corner. We dried the notes by sticking them to the Formica panels round the window. The BOAC air hostess smiled understandingly and gave Lisa a Junior Jet Club Passport to make up for the beheading of her dolly.

Having survived the space warp of arriving Home, we went to stay with my in-laws. They lived in what seemed like a brick refrigerator ventilated by a wind tunnel leading up to the Sussex Downs.

Annette's father was a careful man. He had always worked for the post office, beginning as an incredibly menial labourer, when his mother sent him off every Monday to dig holes in roads provisioned with a week's supply of Cornish pasties. I visualized him living in one of those little tents repairmen put up over the holes. In Shangri-la, Annette used to tell the story of the pasties rather proudly, but I had always treated it as apocryphal because where we lived those pasties would have been bright green and crawling with maggots by Wednesday at the latest. A few days in her father's company, however, convinced me the tale was true.

By the time we came home Albert Wheeler had risen to the position of foreman and he was still being careful. While we were struggling with the train-changes, he spent the time at home fixing rubber pads to the sharp edges of furniture, which he had decided were at head height for the children. The foam rubber on the dining room table he had actually nailed into the wood. The red brick house, much of which he had built himself, was apparently full of danger. There were dangerous open fires in two rooms to which the children were attracted like fireflies; dangerous electric fires in the bedrooms which were only switched on briefly before the children went to bed. He always came up to see the children to bed and became very agitated when we found it difficult getting them to undress as far away from the fire as possible.

The beds themselves had one single habitable landing spot, that which was warmed by rubber hot water bottles. Albert spent a lot of time teaching me how to squeeze the air out of the bottle necks before screwing in the plug to avoid them exploding and scalding the children.

The house was cleverly planned to provide the minimum amount of heat required for human survival. Little hottish areas could be reached by moving quickly through the freezing parts. The kitchen was hottish. There was a hot belt round the parlour fire, and on feast days another round the sitting room fire. A pipe down the wall provided an impression of heat in the bathroom. But running the gauntlet of the cold in the early mornings, which I had to do when I started going up to London to hunt for work, was grizzly.

My withdrawal symptoms from Africa, in particular, African

temperatures and African light, were at least the equal of any heroin addict's.

Albert's heart was in the right place. He loved the children. When a day or two of warmish weather, apparently called summer, arrived later that year he built them a boating pond and a boat. The pond was two feet long and about an inch deep. The girls would climb into their little boat and it would instantly (and safely) ground. The girls rocked back and forward perfectly content with this illusion of boating and Albert glowed with secure satisfaction.

My mother-in-law, Ivy Wheeler, was a strong woman of considerable intelligence who respected Albert for his carefulness without apparently recognizing that she had been lobotomized by it. Or perhaps she was too strong to let me see that it was an idiosyncracy she had accepted. Ivy was not at all careful with the children and took them everywhere, and they thrived on it. Patcham Women's Institute, the Mothers' Guild and Ivy's Painting Circle must have seemed very exciting to two little white Africans who had rarely travelled outside the wilderness of our back garden, other than to Annie Mutesa's clandestine political meetings in her smoky kia.

She never once complained about the upheaval to her and Albert's careful life. Admittedly I was not there a lot, I was out looking for work. It was warmer.

I first tried journalism, even though I had just fled a successful career in television; one look at British television had produced in me a deep and dreadful inferiority complex. In Shangri-la I had produced my 'Tonight' show (half an hour live every night) with two other people. We went into the tiny studio, interviewed the guests, presented regular diary items and cut the films. There were no trade unions, no restrictive practices, and nobody to tell us how very ordinary we were. It was lovely.

Almost the first show I saw on Albert's television was a repeat of *That Was The Week That Was*. Albert watched it avidly, announcing every few minutes that the participants should be locked up or shot, 'particularly that Bernard Levin' I simply gaped; the show was so slick, intelligent, fast, daring, technically innovative – brilliant!

The credits confirmed my feelings of inferiority. Apart from the dozen of technicians you could actually see on the set, the credits confirmed a huge production staff; you had to be a good reader just to manage the roller-caption for the writers.

I was simply not in that league, so I took a handful of letters of introduction I had garnered from visiting journalists and tried Fleet Street and its fringes. It soon became crystal clear that I was not in that league either.

Deep and absolute depression began to descend. Our tiny fund of cash was running out. My novel *When the Woods Became the Trees* had made it to number nine on the Books and Bookman Bestseller list and for a while we were aglow with the euphoria of imminent fame and fortune; it had been nominated for the American Pulitzer competition.

Our hopes withered in the weak northern light and a year later, despite good reviews, total sales weren't even enough to meet the mortgage deposit on a house.

Life became tense in Patcham. It was impossible for any of us to keep up Albert's standard of carefulness. A job was imperative. I reached to the bottom of my battered suitcase for any introductions I had overlooked – and came up with David Attenborough's card.

It was ridiculous to think anything could possibly come of it. We had met just once, more than two years previously, and in the interim David had quit the field for the prestigious post of Controller of a whole new television channel, BBC2.

What the hell? I wrote a short letter making a joke about having to fight my way out of Africa, hence the state of the card, and posted it along with several more reasonable requests for work on papers like the *West Sussex County Advertiser*.

David wrote back almost by return inviting me to come and see him. That night on the box some angry politician claimed that being on British television was like swimming in shark-infested custard.

I said nothing to Albert about the interview but spent a lot of time on my shoes that morning before catching the train to Shepherd's Bush.

'You off somewhere special?' he asked.

'Swimming,' I replied, my mind elsewhere. 'Shepherd's Bush.'

'That's where they have them race riots,' Albert pointed out. 'Just you be careful.'

I smiled. Race riots and swimming were the two activities on which I really was something of an expert!

Chapter Two

Coming down the road from Shepherd's Bush Green I observed the graffiti of racial conflict wherever I looked. The tube station was daubed with slogans calling for the public burning of someone called Enoch Powell. Blacks (belonging to a tribe I had never met) lurked on every corner; they had bulges on their heads which I assumed to be a kind of cerebral elephantiasis. These monstrous brains were encased in vast Andy Capp hats and they were dulling the pain of their affliction with dagga rolled in long cigarettes of brown paper!

Maybe England was not so foreign as I had feared!

I ventured to ask directions from one of the Big Brain tribe, mainly to see if I could identify a tribal accent. He waved loosely northwards and sung me a tuneless calypso.

'Are you Africans?' I inquired politely. There had been many British possessions in Africa and I assumed these big brains were from the white man's grave regions of West Africa – the exotic Gold and Ivory Coasts, Chad, Dahomey and Upper Volta – all very wild and woolly to us high-savannah types.

'Yer gottabey yoken maan,' the Big-Brain sang. 'Us am Rastas from the West Indies stuck he in dis orrible ples.'

'The Rasta tribe from the West Indies!' I exclaimed with some excitement. I had heard of these people. They were not actually Indians at all but the descendants of African slaves. I was talking to my first evolved slave!

'No, maan, no,' the Big-Brain said patiently. 'Forgit that tribal sheet. Is Rasta Re-lee-jun from Ethiopia.' He took off his cap and shook out about three cubic feet of African hair, tightly rolled and incredibly greasy. 'Dreaaadlocks,' he cried fiercely.

The cold English winter breeze cut through his dreaded (or was it 'braided'?) locks and he quickly put his cap back on again.

'Church of Ras Tafari, God Emperor of Ethiopia.'

'You mean Haile Selassie?'

'Right maan!' he was truly impressed. 'De Lion o' Judaaah.'

'I am from Africa myself,' I told him.

'You got any money, chief?'

But I was used to handling beggars.

I smiled formally, said: 'no sorry, not today' and fended off his attempts to sell me 'ganja dope' while carefully measuring the distance I still had to cover to reach the BBC compound. Unlike some of the dagga-addicts we had learnt to put up with in Shangri-la, however, he of the dreadful locks was not particularly abusive.

The BBC police made no attempt to confront these Rastas. They stayed behind high mesh gates, sallying out from a military-style guard house to admit people who could produce credentials such as my card from David Attenborough. I felt a warm rush of familiarity — it was just like Shangri-la.

Inside the building was even more daunting; it was almost as big as the city I had last lived in, and Kafkaesque in its layout.

The BBC security may have been effective against the Rastas but it was lamentable once you were inside the gate. I was neither frisked nor asked to lodge my weapons, although thanks to Annie Mutesa I was not carrying any, of course.

Within minutes I was lost. Again I had a warm reminiscent flash of Africa as I got hotter and hotter. I tried to note landmarks but ended up walking in a circle. I made one complete circuit of the building and, when it became almost certain that I was starting on my second circle, I started marking doors with my felt-tip and would probably still be doing so to this day had not a kindly secretary emerged just as I was about to mark her office door. She deduced I was lost and asked me whom I was trying to see.

'David Attenborough.'

She looked at my felt-tip, at my very narrow trousers (flares were just becoming all the rage) and at my sun tan.

'He's the Controller, darling. I think you'd best report back to Reception before you get into deep trouble.'

I made the call from her office and when it was confirmed that I really did have an appointment with the Attenboric Eminence she gladly took me there in person.

David's office was very impressive and shaped like a huge piece of cheese. I began to feel out of my depth. David was seated at a desk in the distance down the broad end of the cheese I could only just recognize him. The office was so big he apparently did not realize I was there for a moment; then that sunny voice rang out.

'Come on in, old chap! How good to see you!'

I stood there not really believing it was him until I realized that he was in his shirt sleeves – and there was a rip under the arm.

David has never been much concerned with his appearance but many years later when he was Sir David Attenborough and I was producing *Nature Watch* in competition with his programmes at the BBC Natural History Unit I reminded him of that meeting and how his ripped shirt broke the ice.

'Most of my shirts got like that,' he recalled.

One is not supposed in books like this to indulge in hero worship. Heroes are supposed to be understated, but I've never seen the point of this. David Attenborough, Peter Scott, Konrad Lorenz, John Lilly, Miriam Rothschild, Roger Payne and a host of others involved in natural history are all special people of our time and the rest of the world can't hurt from being reminded of it.

In naming these people it also means that I don't give the impression that all who swim in the television medium become sharks. Suffice it to say that David Attenborough is the most consistently sincere, level-headed person I know in television and he proves that it is possible to be powerfully motivated and, in a sense, ambitious, without the need of a large dorsal fin. I do suspect he saw a fin growing when they made him Controller of BBC-2 but he has always claimed he quit because he liked making programmes better.

He pulled down the arm with the torn sleeve and looked me over a little. I had done none of the right things like preparing a CV or rehearsing a presentation on the kind of programmes I wanted to make. David did not seem to mind. We talked a little about Rhodesia and he suggested I had made exactly the right choice. (I was convinced I had been mad giving up a huge hacienda, five servants, two cars and my job as Controller of Programmes, albeit in a little place called Bulawayo.)

Then he completely dumbfounded me by inferring I might be qualified to work on a new BBC series about popular science.

'I haven't exactly been living at the frontiers of science,' I pointed out. 'Just at the frontier.'

'You're a reporter and I think you could do it, and you're quite an experienced presenter,' he said kindly. I could not suppress a short laugh. My *Tonight* show had attracted quite a large audience by Rhodesian standards but mostly to see what new trouble I could get myself into.

I have no definite evidence that his offer was for the famous and now very long-running *Tomorrow's World*, but I think it might have been. We spent a little while longer discussing the BBC – 'you'll find it quite colonial in parts' – and then his next appointment arrived and in due course I received a more formal invitation to attend a Board for a position in the features department.

Events had moved on by then and I never took up the offer but I shall always be very grateful to David for encouraging me to believe

I could survive in British television and I am sure my eventual decision to move into full-time natural history film-making was influenced by the respect I have for him and his work.

I was dissauded from joining the BBC by my literary agent Ursula Winant, who was a tall, cultured spinster. She had an extraordinary simpering manner which disguised the fact that she was really as tough as old boots.

Ursula had a slight guilt complex about me because she thought she had tempted me to abandon my homeland, bring my little beauties to Siberian England and suffer unemployment, for a novel that was not actually doing too well.* Ursula was also having to compare her lack of real success with my book to that being enjoyed by Wilbur Smith. By comparison with Wilbur's first novel *When The Lion Feeds* mine was doing terribly and Wilbur was still squatting in Africa, soaking up the sunshine and writing his next best-seller.

Ursula had discovered Wilbur and me under the same Central African bush. I was a young reporter on the *Rhodesia Herald* and he a lowly accountant in the Income Tax Department. Writer-wise (as Ursula put it) I was much the more qualified.

But Wilbur's first five-figure edition sold out almost overnight. Ursula soon had film rights and several foreign editions sold on fabulous advances and Wilbur was rich. Every time I trotted in to ask how we were doing she almost died of embarrassment, which was kind but really uncalled-for. My novel was a political essay with literary pretensions, Wilbur's a bloody good read.

I was quite happy with Ursula's efforts. We got nice reviews including two columns in the *Sunday Times* by one of my heroes, Elspeth Huxley; it made the lower half of the *Books and Bookmen* Bestseller list and Ursula soon presented me with a paperback deal. For a beginner from the backwoods it was sensational, but Ursula could hardly look me in the eye as Wilbur Smith grew ever more rich and famous.

She did suggest that things would improve if I became more Wilbur-like. She said my writing reminded her of early Hammond Innes, but she could sense that I really wanted to be Graham Greene. I might not make that, (she hinted) and, given the number of mouths I had to feed, I should not burn any bridges into television.

By way of compensation she set up all manner of publicity venues for me and got me invitations to publishing parties where I met the authors of 'good' books and the type of people who go to publishing parties for good books. They definitely put the TV world into a more acceptable light.

One of these parties was for Tony Firth's first novel, *Tall, Balding, 35*. It was an incredibly well-written book about nothing — almost

* *When the Woods Became the Trees*, Michael Joseph

as if Tony was testing his word power. I was both impressed and depressed; if Tony was the benchmark then I did not even have the vocabulary to write a good book, and my concept of a story was positively florid. (Time has confirmed that!) Tony also worked in television somewhere and Ursula was his agent too.

But everyone seemed to like my book and I met a lot of literary lions including, as it happened, Hammond Innes. Ursula thought I was beginning to move in what she called 'the right circles'. Nevertheless I was very surprised one day to receive a letter from Robert Heller, Head of Documentaries, Associated Television, Marble Arch. It appeared I had been recommended by Tony Firth. Why?

Robert Heller was an almost diametric opposite of David Attenborough, who is tall and very English. Robert 'Bob' Heller was short, powerful, with a huge bald dome of a head, and quite obviously not English. He was an American in voluntary exile.

His office was quite ordinary compared to David's huge hexagon at the new Television Centre, and rather than put me at my ease Heller appeared intent on terrifying me.

When I was shown in he was reading a newspaper upside down, or so it appeared. He peeked over the top of huge owl glasses and asked me if I could read Chinese.

'Er no,' I confessed, thinking how much I suddenly liked the idea of working on a science programme. 'Apart from English the only language I can read is Afrikaans.'

'Well that makes you something of a specialist,' Heller observed without apparent irony. 'I ask because I don't read Chinese too well myself and there is something in here I need to know.'

'I wouldn't know which end to start,' I joked feebly.

Heller looked at the up-and-down type and hiccuped a token laugh. 'That's pretty good,' he acknowledged. 'Tony told me I should read your book. I read it. You write a little like Salinger.'

I wisely kept my mouth shut. (My book was subsequently compared to Salinger's *Catcher In The Rye,* particularly by American reviewers, which at the time of meeting Heller I had never read.)

I also did not know that Bob Heller was something of a legend in the television world. He was intelligent, very well educated, and (the legend had it) had been a Vice-President of a major US network. He became caught up in the McCarthy purges and fled to Mexico where he ran a *ranchero* retreat for other intellectuals who had suffered the same fate.

He was brought to England by Sidney Bernstein to open up a documentary department at Granada TV (documentaries have been that station's proudest tradition ever since) and was poached to ATV by Lew Grade. These larger-than-life characters, the front-of-house showmen like Grade and Bernstein and the behind-the-scenes players like Heller, were just becoming a real force in Britain when I went for my interview. Television was still a new and exciting challenge for them.

Their genesis also explains, I think, why ITV has always fought shy of being regarded as an artistic medium like the theatre or even cinema. It was started by showmen for commercial entertainment purposes and audience numbers were always paramount. In most countries where this happened, particularly America and Australia, entertainment television (soaps, quiz and game shows) soon entirely dominated the schedules because programmes were paid for directly by advertisers who demanded nothing but the largest possible audience. The bulk of the output was dross.

British television was saved from this by 'regulation', a word I don't much like but which appears to be vital to the preservation of quality television. When ITV began there was already a highly regulated quality channel setting precedents – the BBC – run by moguls with incredible power. The only analogy I can think of for the autonomy enjoyed by Lord Reith was the case of J.Edgar Hoover. Moreover, the BBC had very definite intellectual and artistic pretensions; in fact it was a circus of performers in which you survived if you were a politically adept tightrope walker or a good juggler.

So ITV when it began, although conceived as a more proletarian channel than the BBC, had its output regulated by the IBA (the Independent Broadcasting Authority) and the IBA insisted that a good part of that output should be quality factual programmes, music and drama. Very soon well-funded ITV programmes – Lord Thomson had described the franchise as 'a licence to print money' – were competing with the BBC.

The BBC licence fee, which in those days the viewers paid almost gratefully, was sufficient to run a vast empire with money left over to fund expensive programmes. They indulged in wonderful experiments, like *That Was The Week That Was*, which played like an electric storm round the outer limits of artistic and political taste. Such shows, which were highly popular, employed artists and intellectuals (Milly Martin, Bernard Levin *et al.*) on the same bare set. In fact most of the people on that particular set had a degree.

This was what has been called the golden age of television. American and Australian producers look back on it just as nostalgically as we do because it was programmes from this era (*Civilization, The Ascent of Man, The Forsyte Saga, Upstairs Downstairs, Survival*) which showed America and Australia that there could be something more than candy floss on their screens and led, indirectly, to the creation of the national education channels in those countries.

It appeared that this television renaissance had the luck to flower in a uniquely liberated age – the Swinging Sixties – and that outrageous television programming was simply a reflection of that exuberant era. Looking at old editions of *That Was The Week That Was,* I sometimes wonder whether it wasn't the other way round.

One way or another it was all very transcendental and was eventually recognized as such by sharp-toothed creatures with degrees from places like the Harvard Business School. Public fascination, they astutely observed, was not so much in the message of television, but in the medium itself. An American called Marshall Macluhan was the first to voice this disturbing home truth – the reef on which all of television's artistic pretensions finally grounded.

It took another ten years of careful market testing to show that our audience, like all others, would watch what they were given and another ten to breed the television controllers who realized that to make expensive quality programmes was really to waste the shareholders' money. It will take at least another decade to prove them wrong but by that time British television as we know it – the best in the world – will be dead.

Robert Heller was a talent scout and was already employing young men and women who would go on to be famous documentary makers and film directors. These included Peter Collinson, Jack Gold, Mike Tuckner, Adrian Cowell, Kevin Billington, Chris Menzies, Tony Snowdon, Ken Loach, David Bailey, Brigid Seegrave and Germaine Greer. Tony Firth turned out to be a former President of an Oxbridge Union whose job seemed to be the processing of ideas for Heller. He occasionally produced an actual programme and when he left Heller's documentary department it was to run his own in Scotland.

Heller cross-examined me vaguely about my short career in television, in somewhat more detail about my reporting experience, and with rapt interest on the subject of African politics. Apart from Rhodesia-cum-Zimbabwe, it soon became evident he knew much more about the dark continent than I (I only knew about the white parts). At least he could not read Afrikaans.

There cannot be any other reason, apart perhaps from charity to a fellow political refugee, why he ended that interview with the hint of a job.

'If you can get yourself a union ticket,' he mused, 'I might have a little something here for you. Derek Hart's coming out of the BBC and he could use help.'

'I'll get one,' I assured him.

Heller gave a very grim smile. 'I don't want to put you down, but you apparently don't know what that involves. Have you ever been a member of a trade union?'

'No.'

'Well this one, the Association of Cinematograph and Television

Technicians – ACTT – is particularly tough. They run a completely closed shop.'

He saw my expression and sighed. 'I guess you don't know what a closed shop is either?'

'No, I'm afraid I don't.'

'Nobody gets to work anywhere in ITV without a union ticket. All the companies have signed an agreement to that effect.'

'What do I need to get a ticket?'

'Lots,' Heller grunted. 'There's a big queue of people waiting for a Director's ticket and not all of them are related to a union steward.'

'You're offering me work as a Director?' I tried not to gulp. At best I had assumed a reporting or research contract.

'You ran your own show out there in Africa, didn't you?'

'Sure,' I croaked. 'One a night.'

'Well this thing Derek wants to do is a kind of magazine series.'

'I'll get a ticket,' I assured him.

'To get a ticket you have to have a job in television, and you can't get a job in television without a ticket – right?'

'Catch 22,' I pointed out.

'Catch about 922,' Heller confirmed.

'Do I need one for the BBC?' I asked.

It was said in innocence. I would not have dared horse-trade with a powerful man like Heller.

'Are you under offer from the Beeb?' Heller snapped.

'Not exactly,' I squirmed.

'How not exactly?'

'David Attenborough has mentioned a new science series.'

'You know David?'

'A bit.'

'You get about,' Heller commented, 'for a new boy. We pay a lot better on ITV.'

'I will try to get a ticket,' I temporized. 'Unless it's impossible.'

Heller smiled. 'It's that kind of business – we expect miracles.'

He handed me a broadsheet, the magazine of the ACTT.

'There's an item in there I thought I'd save for you. Call me if you get lucky. You can tell them you have a contract with me if they'll give you a ticket.'

Looking back, I think there is a good chance that Bob Heller was constantly on the lookout for ways of bringing new blood into ITV, and that meant finding loopholes in the union's restrictive practices. He wasn't at all anti-union (at one time he must have been very left-wing) but I think he preferred American union practices where deals could be struck rather than the impregnable stone keeps in which British unions liked to live.

With me he thought he had found a loophole. The ACTT were

violently anti-Ian Smith and his oppression of blacks and the Union's General Secretary Jack Elkins had written a powerful condemnation in the news sheet promising special help for media people who refused to work for the Smith regime.

It took me some time to find the item and even longer to realize its significance. It was not my qualifications that had impressed Bob Heller (and probably not my writing): I represented a loophole to the sacred keep. What the hell, I thought, there were babies to be fed in Brighton.

The head office of the ACTT was then in Soho Square. I stood in front of Jack Elkins' secretary's desk listening to her several excuses as to why it would be totally impossible for me to see the General Secretary, how union membership, especially for Director grades, was under a moratorium because of over-subscription and how they were not even handing out application forms, let alone tickets.

'Is the General Secretary here?'

'You can't see him!' the secretary said nastily.

I am not a small person. I reached down and picked up the corner of her desk and moved it to one side. I then reached down and moved her on her wheeled chair to the new location. I strode across to the General Secretary's door and, when it stuck, I quite consciously but with no great force, kicked it open.

'This won't take long,' I promised his secretary, who was by then reaching for the phone.

Jack Elkins was actually very nice.

I pointed out that I was a political refugee of sorts, showed him copies of write-ups about my novel which suggested that I would be locked up if ever I went back to Rhodesia, and told him of Bob Heller's job offer. I rounded this off with a bank statement showing we had £72 left in the bank.

He said he would put my application before the appropriate committee at the earliest possible opportunity – some several weeks hence. I told him I was sure Bob Heller would not wait that long.

'We're obliged under rule to submit applications to the shop stewards of the company where you will be working. ATV has a very strict shop and a big waiting list.'

I told him my only other alternative was to work as a journalist and as Ian Smith's declaration of independence – UDI – was very topical I would be obliged to write about what had happened to me up to and including the present.

'I'm actually claiming political sanctuary within this union,' I told him.

I left clasping a temporary membership card as a Director-member of the ACTT. That little piece of paper was literally worth a fortune. By the time the ATV shop got round to considering permanent status almost six months later I had made two programmes. The magic formula had been met: I had a job in ITV, had proved I could hold it; they confirmed my ticket. I am not particularly proud of this episode but if you create an impasse as daft as a closed shop you force people to find ways round it.

My new dorsal fin was so little I couldn't even feel it.

Chapter Three

The series I was given to make with a presenter called Derek Hart was entitled *The Champion Makers*.

I had not the vaguest idea who Derek Hart was, but Albert was astounded when I mentioned the name. I felt embarrassed and asked him who he was. The veil of suspicion that always seemed to hang over Albert's face whenever we talked slipped back into place.

'Have you really got a job working with him?'

I showed him the contract that had arrived that morning in the post.

'Well I never,' he said. 'And you know how to do this sort of thing, do you – direct television programmes and such like, with people like Derek Hart from *Tonight*?'

'What do you think I've been doing at RTV?'

'Yes, well, that was Africa, wasn't it?'

And he was right!

It seemed I had been contracted to direct 10 half-hour film programmes with the ace reporter from the BBC's most successful current affairs show.

But there was no turning back, and Annette and I had to find a place of our own to live if there was to be any hope of saving our marriage, which had been under great strain ever since we left Shangri-la.

The in-laws had certainly had enough of us. Albert was rapidly running out of padding for the furniture. The children had apparently learned the law of the jungle in the agapantha beds of Bulawayo and could be 'little tigers' according to Ivy, who did not share Albert's view of them as fragile blonde dolls.

We started to examine the London evening papers for flats, which made very gloomy reading indeed for a young family in 1967.

London was apparently still entirely feudal. All the best bits were owned by ancient families like the Westminsters who did not sell their houses but granted chunks of time in them for extraordinary sums of money. A lease on any of these tenancies in Westminster, Belgravia or Chelsea cost at least four times as much as any house in Africa. Additionally, you had to pay something called 'key money' to an agent and sometimes a fee for 'fixtures and fittings'.

One property we inspected had been stripped bare; even the wallpaper appeared to have been removed. But I was told that the 'fixtures and fittings' were £1,000.

There weren't any, I pointed out. The agent indicated the single lightbulb and gave me a tight smile.

We quickly abandoned any hope of living in Central London and slowly began working our way out into the slums. I have no conscience about describing Clapham, Battersea, Wandsworth, Fulham and most of the boroughs fringing the feudal areas as slums at that time. In fact they were suburbs of *kias* – dirty, run-down, cramped cottages for workers. But even they cost at least twice as much as a good bungalow in Africa.

I hit psychological bottom when my bank manager suggested I was wasting my time looking at either Westminster leaseholds or Fulham freeholds. I could not even afford a slum!

Our only option was to rent and this was even worse because the landlords of London had two pet hates – children and blacks – and they advertised this quite openly.

My first phone call in response to an advertisement for a flat offered for rent in Chiswick went something like this:

'Are you a couple?'

'Yes, a married couple with two young children.'

Long pause.

'And you're not from this country?'

'What makes you say that?'

'Your accent is not of this country.'

'We're from Africa.'

'I'm afraid the property is no longer available.'

'To Africans?'

'Yes, I'm sorry. And anyway we don't take young children.'

I put the phone down in shock. I had never come across racism quite that raw, even in Ian Smith's Africa. We had at least been secretive about it and even our worst racists had certainly not hated children as well.

And then, as always happens when the going gets tough for me, He who controlleth Fate, grinned. (I don't actually believe in the advertised God who has always seemed both vindictive and limp. My deity never puts in anything but benign and effective appearances, albeit rarely.)

I answered an advertisement for a nice-sounding flat in Putney, the annexe of a house, in fact, with two bedrooms, sitting and dining room, its own entrance and the use of a big garden.

The house was on the busy Upper Richmond Road and was very grand. It had a large front door, an elegant hall and wild floral wallpaper climbing up an impressive staircase. From the hall I could see into a lavish dining room with gleaming antique furniture and a sideboard groaning under a great weight of silver.

Brenda Nixon came to the door like a tornado. She was smoking at least one cigarette, talking to at least two children and a workman, and, from the state of her apron, had been baking bread.

'Uh come in for uh God's sake!' she roared – further proof of an impending miracle.

She talked and smoked so much she had to make short pauses to take deep breaths which ruined the punctuation of her sentences. I was shown into a large sitting room with huge sofas and chairs, and rich antique curtains drawn back from wide French doors leading out into a beautiful garden. I grew ever more convinced that I had come to the wrong place and then, the longer I sat there, ever more worried that perhaps I had come to the right place.

A small boy, eternally smiling, came in through the French doors, sat at my feet and held my hand. My embarrassment prevented me from realizing for some time that he was mentally retarded. A rabbit then came in and sat on one of the sofas, chewing slowly and watching me carefully. It was followed by a girl in a loose dirndl dress and a great deal of hair.

'Alice,' I said, thinking aloud.

'Sue,' she corrected. 'Have you seen my mother?'

'Thataway,' I pointed.

'Right, don't tell her you've seen me, I'm bunking school.'

A Siamese cat stalked stiff-legged across the room and then climbed straight up the curtains as if gravity did not apply.

Eventually Brenda came back in with two huge cups of real coffee and grinned at the boy and me with great affection.

'You've met Guy,' she smiled. 'He's autistic.'

'We haven't actually met,' I corrected. 'He hasn't said much.'

'When he does, you won't get a word in edge-ways, will he darling? Where are you from?'

'From Brighton actually,' I prevaricated warily.

'My brother-in-law is a priest at a school in Rhodesia,' she said without artifice. 'If you're a Robin Brown from Rhodesia, which you sound as if you could be, I've read your book.'

'What!' She was the first person I had ever met who had admitted this. I was not even sure Annette had read it from cover to cover.

'*When the Woods Became the Trees*?'

'Yes!'

'I think you could be a good writer,' Brenda said, giving me the first criticism of any kind outside of the reviews. 'Do you want to look at the annexe?'

'I do,' I said with great feeling. 'But I think I should tell you we have two young children.'

'Wonderful,' said Brenda. 'That's just what we were hoping for. I've got lots too so we won't be short of baby sitters, and I've got an American washing machine. The annexe is a bit basic but you'll want to get some things of your own and if there's anything you really need we're bound to have something in the house.'

Needless to say I thanked our lucky stars and we moved in. The advance on the rent was £78 but Brenda happily accepted my £72 and we arrived to find a big basket of groceries from her in the little kitchen. She was very worried that I should have somewhere decent to write, and gave me a Queen Anne desk from the heirlooms in the house as a present. She is the only person I have been able to take expensive presents from gracefully simply because she gave things away all the time with great and obvious pleasure. In time she gave away everything and now lives in Devon in a house she recently gave to her eldest daughter who has made a life's work of looking after children like Guy.

Her husband Cecil was another entirely nice person, in fact the Nixons are unquestionably the nicest people I have ever come across.

In their case it came directly from God. Cecil was an Irish Catholic from an aristocratic family. Brenda deliberately projected a shady past – including being a secret agent during the war – but I deduced from their great hoard of heirlooms that her family had been 'good' as well. Brenda's first husband had been killed in the war. Like everyone she met, Brenda loved him dearly but she was not a person to waste her enormous capacity for affection on the dear departed.

She joined a very raunchy London set and had a very exciting war. Her flat was a kind of staging post for excitable young men and women on their way to do or die.

Tall, languid, exquisitely-mannered Cecil was an officer in the Gurkha regiment, neither raunchy nor excitable. He was steady, kind, moral and very good and Brenda had the sense to marry him when she realized that Cecil was actually very open to exciting ideas. They had four children of their own as well as Trish from Brenda's first marriage.

From the beginning Cecil was a challenge: could she convert him to socialism? Brenda's socialism was a cocktail of her own making. She lived surrounded by such intellectual cocktails. She was a powerful Catholic convert and never questioned that faith, but she also believed in a mystical and mathematical logic to the universe.

She taught me that rocks have souls (through the way crystals reform their structures to some divine law), that the most primitive creatures on our planet have obvious intelligence even though they have no brains (the proven ability of planarium worms to sulk) and a lot of other fascinating junk.

As the bottles of expensive brandy emptied in the twinkling gloaming of the silver candlesticks, Brenda also tried to talk Cecil and me into a belief in Communist Russia at its worst. During the Bulganin and Brezhnev oppressions, Brenda sliced through our repugnance at the obvious death of human rights and freedom of expression and movement and demanded that we acknowledge the basic goodness of Marxist principles.

None of us had been anywhere near Russia. We resisted Brenda invoked quantum physics. Cecil fell diplomatically asleep I lured her off into the mysteries of the origins of human life but we always grounded on Brenda's unswerving insistence that God be given his due.

Most of it was pure serendipity. Brenda, I think, wanted a provable mathematical framework for the God she believed in so fervently, and structured Goodness (hence her socialism). I was interested in the scientific origins of life which meant our basic tenets were opposed. We got nowhere other than to become good friends.

It soon became clear to me that Brenda and Cecil were naturally charitable. They were the first of this rare species I have ever met. My charity, like that of most people I know, has to be tweaked. Brenda and Cecil's house always had a refugee or two to enliven the big dinner table; middle Europeans, black Africans (Brenda was entirely colour-blind), little old ladies from the retirement home in the Upper Richmond Road, one or two of the workmen who had grown old trying to finish the jobs in the house, and of course us, the resident refugees.

Quite a lot of this came from having Guy. Brenda had been told he was a cabbage, that she should forget him and place him in an institution. This suggestion did not go down well.

Instead the Nixons explored what our society had to offer this little boy from whom innocence shone like a strong beam of light and who thrived on his family's love like a flower thrives on sunshine. It did not offer a lot.

They kept him at home until eventually they discovered the Rudolph Steiner Schools, managed to obtain one of their rare places for Guy, and became very involved with the enlightened end of training and boarding facilities for the severely mentally handicapped. Guy 'the cabbage' is still a child in a man's frame but he can read and write, has an encyclopaedic knowledge of popular music, travels on his own on public transport, and remains an active and much-loved member of the Nixon family.

Moreover, he believes in God. Whenever I see Guy I am forced to concede that if he can believe in a God, given the hand he was dealt, so should the rest of us.

So, with the considerable help of the Steiner system, Guy strengthened the Nixon family and liberated their charity, their love and their beliefs. The bonds of family are said not to be what they were in our society; perhaps because we do our best to eliminate such paradoxes.

The Nixons were just what I needed. They proved that a happy family could exist under the grey porridge of British skies. I put surburban Brighton behind me for ever and dived into the custard.

Day One on my first real location. There was Derek Hart, a little ball of determination, ready and waiting to introduce *The Champion Makers*. There was Louis Wolfers, Britain's leading documentary cameraman, surrounded by half a dozen huge silver boxes, the contents of which were mostly a mystery to me.

My main contribution to that series (which was supposed to explore the true grit of heroes) was to turn it into something much more trivial. Derek wanted to discover what drove Mr Universe. I went to see a Mr Universe at his gym in the East End and quickly realized that what drove him was insecurity, narcissism and a mindless addiction to exercise. Derek, fresh from serious reporting on *Tonight*, was quite taken with this Freudian approach to begin with, but I knew in my heart that it was not the custard our audience wanted.

I pointed out to Derek that there was also a Mrs Universe (a former Miss Great Britain) and two little blonde Miss Universettes rolling the big weights across the floor of the gym. Mr and Mrs Universe did their muscle-bulging routines together to the theme tune from *Exodus*.

Derek's eyes began to gleam. Without really realizing what I was doing, I introduced an anti-hero sub-plot into *The Champion Makers*. Anti-heroes created by new-wave writers like Alan Sillitoe, John Braine and John Osborne were very much the vogue at the time. It was also the beginning of an exploration of human eccentricity which I have pursued ever since and which has largely supported a long career in television.

But here at the very beginning I was confronted with the need to prove myself as a Director.

Derek said: 'I'm ready.'

Louis said: 'Ready, governor.'

The sound man said: 'Sound ready.'

The sound assistant held up the clapperboard on which was written: *The Champion Makers* Dir: Robin Brown.

My career was about to begin; I had only to give the command and everything I had dreamed of becoming out there in the backwoods of Africa would come true.

Unfortunately I did not know the command! I had never seen a clapperboard, nor had I the vaguest idea how all this gear worked. Without going into too much technical detail, the very basic camera equipment we had used on my news-gathering sorties in Rhodesia had not required a clapperboard; the cameraman had simply started his camera and given me a wave.

I gave a wave.

Louis paused a second.

I added an encouraging nod.

He hunched down and pressed the necessary button, crying: 'Mark it!'

The sound assistant smashed the hinged board together within a centimetre of Derek's nose. Derek didn't even blink. He smiled into the great void, saw five million people and spoke his Introduction.

This, I thought, is insane, I have since always hated directing, although I love film-making.

There are two kinds of directors. Those who love directing - and it massages the ego more effectively than any occupation I know - plan strange movements of the camera that take hours, sometimes days, play with lenses, angles, framing and so on. This is mostly a total waste of time if you are making television documentaries, and this kind of director is very often using documentaries to become a drama or feature film director.

I have honestly never wanted to be either of these because both of these approaches involve a considerable sacrifice: you have to entirely escape reality. But there are some people who like it and don't mind (or, more accurately, don't notice) what they become. You also have to mix with actors, which is a little like living in a world suffering a permanent Africa heat mirage.

As I progressed into what was called Dramadocs (the dubious re-creation of reality using 'true' stories in which 'real' characters are played by actors), I came to suspect that a desire to act is a mental condition that has much in common with autism. The very good actors use the stage a bit like a Steiner School, live forever within its protective ambience, and seem real by playing 'real' well. The very bad ones get addicted to the rich custards like television, grow old and cynical in it, and eventually became as retarded as Guy but without his innocence.

The other kind of director is the one who simply chooses a good cameraman and lets him get on with it. Louis Wolfers was one such and once he had got used to the idea that I was the only silent director in the era of sound films, he got on with it and produced camerawork that was always much better than if I had attempted to impose my untrained eye on his experience and craftsmanship.

Quite a lot of these cameramen have gone on to become directors, indeed famous directors like Chris Menzies and Ernest Vince. I like to think that my studied neglect contributed to their success.

I did, however, keep a very careful eye on content and on what was actually going on, and I think I can say that I become a good director in the cutting room, which is where the rough outline that has been gathered in the field is crafted into the finished product. I decided I was entitled to this immodest conclusion after I worked out how many thousands of hours I have happily spent buried in windowless, smoke-filled, sweat-smelling, panic-suffused editing rooms in places like Birmingham and the back alleys of Soho.

We had some really wonderful times making *The Champion Makers*, particularly so for me because I was such an innocent and knew so very little about the peculiar British.

We went to Northumberland to film leek growers.

'Why?' Bob Heller grunted when I showed him the treatment.

'They feed them on special recipes, blood and Guinness and sit up all night in the bitter cold guarding them against the Phantom Leek Slashers.'

'Go to it.' said Heller.

By now I had proved the series enough to justify a Researcher, Brigid Seegrave, and we went together to Manchester to talk to a Mr Ace who ran the last Flea Circus in Britain. Mr Ace's title of champion flea trainer of the world had, understandably, never been challenged.

Halfway through the interview, which was conducted in his caravan at the Manchester Zoo Park, he showed us how he fed the 'artistes' – by lining them up each day on alternate arms! Brigid confessed to an uncontrolable itching all over her body and fled the caravan.

I stayed long enough to ask him why his Flea Circus was the last of a long tradition dating back to medieval times, and back came his priceless answer:

'Fitted carpets.'

He repeated it in context when we came back to film the programme.

'We use human fleas because of the feeding problem,' Mr Ace smiled like Dracula. 'And of course human fleas are a highly threatened species. All our artistes died in the terrible winter of 1956 and we were forced to go on a kind of a safari to the back streets of Liverpool. We were very polite about it, took trouble to explain, but you have no idea how difficult people got even though we were offering very good money.'

Derek, almost biting through his stiff upper lip, said: 'Yes, I can see the difficulty, but how do fitted carpets come into it?'

'There's a little nature reserve round the walls of rooms with fitted carpets where the Hoover can't reach,' Mr Ace revealed. 'But it's difficult finding the right kind of house — one that would have artistes — that could also afford fitted carpets. We found Goliath in a house like that.'

Goliath was his Champion, a flea that Mr Ace had trained to pull a miniature state coach across the tiny stage of his circus in a hut in the Zoo Park. When we filmed Goliath straining across the stage it was just a black speck that moved a charm-bracelet coach about an inch. The cameraman subsequently enlarged this with special lenses and when I saw the rushes I nearly threw up. Mr Ace had somehow tied fine fuse-wire round the waist of an object like a pus ball with huge, muscled legs that jerked convulsively. Each jerk (the poor creature was actually trying to jump) moved the dead weight of the charm-bracelet coach forward a centimetre or so until the flea collapsed with exhaustion.

One of our viewers wrote in to complain that it made her think of Christ hauling his cross to Calvary. I thought Bob Heller might enjoy this, but he always took viewers' letters very seriously and suprised me with the observation that he thought the Flea Circus show had 'raised some weird questions.'

Then we went to the Ram Brewery in the heart of the then slummy Wandsworth to film a story about their champion Shire horses. This was a much more pleasant programme to make; the huge Shire horses were lovely, but in their way no less bizarre.

'Why are you still using cart-horses to pull drays round London?' Derek asked.

We had been out with one that morning and knew that the drays with two sturdy Shires puffing away in front of them created little pockets of traffic jams all over the borough. Interestingly, it is the only time I have ever seen motorists in a traffic jam smiling. Looking at beautiful animals was apparently good for the spirits, a fact I filed carefully away for future reference.

To our surprise the Ram Brewery man did not confirm that it was simply good publicity. The brewery had been serving Wandsworth for a long time and a lot of the pubs they owned were quite close together. They had done expensive time and motion studies and found the horses could do the round as efficiently as lorries. Moreover, because the horses were so nice to look at, their constant stopping and starting did not annoy Wandsworth people (the customers) as much as awkwardly-parked lorries.

In other words, all those thousands of cars out there filling the Thames-side air with lead poison were totally unnecessary. Wandsworth had been built to be served by horses and carts. Derek made this observation and the Ram brewery man replied: 'I suppose you could be right. Cars have invented their own problem, haven't they? If people did not have to go long distances we would not need cars at all.'

Bob Heller stopped sucking his teeth when he saw this in the rough-cut.

'Don't get carried away with social comment.' But he left the line in, observing only that if we wanted people to take on serious stuff like that we had to give them time to think about it, and therefore he suggested that the pretty trotting-horse sequence following the interview needed to be lengthened, with only background noise over it. Heller was also a good teacher.

It got even more romantic when we filmed inside the building where the drays and horses were kept. Outside cars swirled round the South Circular; inside we had travelled back a century. The place was all wood and hay, and little old men in big boots and stained leather aprons loaded wooden barrels onto the drays or did things for the horses.

There was a complete blacksmith's shop where a smith, built like one of the beer barrels, hefted the huge hooves of the giant horses between his knees, pared hunks off the frogs like slices of cheese, buffed the edges with big files, scorched hot shoes onto the hooves to test for size, and then nailed them home with nine square-sided spikes.

Throughout this process, up close to the roof, huge black and white horses' heads stared down on us Lilliputians through limpid eyes fringed with film-star eyelashes.

'Do you ever get kicked?' Derek asked, standing well clear.

'Nay lad,' the smith said. 'I'm here to prove it. You'd only need to be kicked once by one of these beauties.'

We busked our way through the first few programmes together, with Louis taking care of the technicalities and delivering exquisite pictures. By the time Bob Heller saw them and had grunted near-approval, we had emulsified into a companionable unit. My ability to spot a strong story held up, Derek's BBC experience was invaluable and Heller would spot immediately where the structure was wrong.

Heller was a superb Executive Producer; he was tough, politically adept, devoted to the work above family and friends, expert in public affairs at home and abroad, and able to see into the future. He also had to know, with absolute conviction, whether a film was right or wrong structurally, editorially and for the consumer – and if wrong, how to fix it. Bob's stable of directors had plenty of energy and very strong views of their own but he kept us in line with a fine goad of terror, the main sting of which was the hint that he was always a little disappointed.

I think he probably was. He once told me that he believed you could actually edit a film down to one perfect frame. We worked to time slots of about 25 minutes, 38 and 52 minutes, so we were left with thousands of imperfect frames, which Bob had to live with when he reluctantly approved the finished 'fine-cuts.'

Most of all, Bob Heller had the courage of his own convictions. The best test of these I ever saw followed Adrian Cowell's appointment. Adrian Cowell is the leading environmental film-maker of our age, and Heller contracted him to make the first of many trips into the Amazon, accompanied by Chris Menzies and Ernest Vince who were then cameramen.

Adrian's real purpose was to record the destruction of the world's most important rain-forests, long before the international conservation movement started to worry about them. He has managed to keep that film record going for more than a decade and it is already a unique series of films, known collectively as Decade of Destruction. The Duke of Edinburgh recognized Adrian's crusade with the prestigious Conservation Award at the Wildscreen '88 Film Festival. I was there collecting the prize for Environmental Journalism for a *Nature Watch* programme, and it came as no surprise to hear from Adrian's wife that he had had to rush out and buy a suit for the occasion!

To give Adrian's conservation film better audience appeal, he had agreed with Heller that it should have an adventure-expedition theme. Adrian would search out a tribe called the Kree Nakore which had never been contacted by white folk as a thread through his report on the destruction of the Matto Grosso and the devastating impact it was having on aboriginal tribes. The film was called *The Tribe that Hides from Man*.

Bob Heller knew that this was going to be very expensive and take a long time. The average time spent shooting a one-hour documentary in those days was four to six weeks.

Adrian was gone for months, a fact Heller kept to himself while continuing to send great swatches of film, an aeroplane, portable refrigerators (for storing the film), medicines (Adrian contracted almost every kind of malaria known to man) and reinforcement film crews into the jungle.

Back came miles and miles of film showing leaves.

To bolster his nerve, Bob used to invite us to sit with him in the viewing theatre when he was running these rushes.

'Can you see anything?' he would demand hollowly.

'Nice jungle, Bob. Looks like he's hand-holding the camera walking down that path.'

'That's it?' Bob cried. 'Jungle and paths? Looks like he just keeps running in the hope maybe he'll catch a glimpse of a goddam Indian.' (Which is exactly what was happening!)

After many months the accountants went to see Lew Grade and Lew told Bob to bring Adrian home. Bob said Adrian would come home when his film was finished and staked his job on the decision, although by then he must have known that Adrian was probably never going to film the tribe.

Nor did he. Throwing aside most of the jungle path footage, Adrian structured a fascinating portrayal of the perfect symbiosis between pristine jungle and pristine people – so much so they could be invisible if they chose. The various attempts to lure the tribe into a meeting were meticulously filmed and each near-contact was a nail-biting experience. Adrian recreated an incident where one of the tribes fought back against the settlers raping their forest. From then on the audience sat on the edge of its seat waiting for the dark green veil of leaves (that Bob had virtually counted individually) to part and the poison arrows to fly. There were some exquisitely sympathetic views of forest/Indian life and the film was a huge success, winning among many others the Italia prize, Europe's top documentary award.

No small part of that was due to Bob Heller's skills as a film fixer. Adrian had a huge amount of footage to cut down to one hour and we all get lost. Heller would sit through the viewings of rough-cuts sucking his teeth if he generally approved of what you were doing. Some very strong-minded film makers have quailed when Heller suddenly stopped sucking.

Finally the fine-cut was approved, and Bob was heaving visible sighs of relief when Adrian announced that he was not only going to write, but also intended to read, the narration.

This was very unusual in those days. You hired a star with a famous voice to read your narration (known in America as 'the Talent'). Moreover, there was no way Bob could veto the decision on the grounds of it being an ego trip (as he would have done with most directors making the request) because Adrian was the most self-effacing man. Bob knew Adrian wanted his complex story simply and factually stated and he did not trust anyone else to narrate it.

So Bob let him have a go and then, for once, lost his nerve.

Adrian's delivery gave new meaning to the expression 'dead-pan'. Each complex sentence was delivered as a series of short, peculiarly-punctuated phrases. Nowadays this kind of narration is quite often heard, particularly on serious documentaries where the film-maker does not want a rich voice imposing itself on the stark quality of the pictures.

I could tell how alarmed Bob was when he, a man of abundant moral courage, passed the buck to me.

'He's sitting in there doing it,' Bob said in a hushed, horrified voice. 'He can't hear what he sounds like, which is a schoolmaster spelling it out for a bunch of kids. I want you to get down to the dubbing theatre, and every time you hear him doing it, or saying something you don't understand, put your finger up.'

It was not a task I relished but Bob's anxiety was palpable.

'It's not his fault, he's been swinging in his hammock stewing over the words,' Bob said, wild-eyed. 'It's probably brilliant but I can't understand half of it – what do you think all those Kansas City milkmen are going to think?'

A Kansas City milkman was Bob's imported model for the hypothetical viewer to whom our narrations had to be comprehensible.

I demurred 'You're asking me to make an enemy of one of the people I admire most in this business.'

'I'll risk that!' he said. 'Adrian knows you don't grind axes – yet. Just look him in the eye and tell him what you think honestly. It's important to the film.'

I should have refused, but there were still those babies to feed and we had begun to think we might just be able to afford a slum.

In fact Adrian was very understanding about my intrusion, and Bob did have a point. I think Adrian actually wanted to deliver his own words in that very slow style because he knew some of the concepts were difficult, even for our local milkmen.

So I did what Bob asked and every time Adrian came out with something I did not instantly understand I held up a finger and the Dubbing Mixer stopped the tapes and I told Adrian why. During that process I grew to like Adrian's style of delivery – and Bob never thereafter raised any objections to him doing his own narrations – but we did de-mystify the script somewhat, and as I have said, it went on to win every documentary prize there is.

It also marked the end of my apprenticeship.

Chapter Four

I now faced the biggest hurdle there is in the television business, the jump from freelance director of other people's ideas to producer-director of my own. This was the big pond where the Golds, Billingtons, Loachs, Tuckners and Cowells swam, and finding a subject that would tempt Heller into giving me one of his precious one-hour network slots became an obsession.

Bob was keen for me to continue making *Champion Makers* but, somewhat to his suprise I think, I firmly turned this down and told him I was determined to make an hour show.

'Are you ready,' Bob mused dubiously, as if inspecting the stub of my new dorsal. 'People who run before they can walk usually just skin their knees – in here you can also starve to death.'

'I'm ready.' In fact I had decided that if Heller refused me a slot, I would take my idea to the BBC. He seemed to sense that.

'Okay,' he said. 'Here's what we'll do. If you can write on a single sheet of paper an idea that I think will make a network hour, you can direct it – with Peter Batty as your Producer.'

Fair's fair. To keep a television audience interested in serious material for 52 minutes is the most difficult challenge on television.

Peter Batty was a newly-arrived Producer/Director from the BBC, where he had had a great deal of experience on network current affairs programmes. And I think Bob Heller might have had a double motive. He was visibly nervous of Peter, suspecting, I think, that he might be a contender for his job. If I failed dismally Peter could be responsible, and the chances of my achieving a big success that would improve Peter's position were remote.

Some weeks later I delivered my single sheet of paper (a few sheets in fact). Under the title *Kangaroo Valley* were several vicarious paragraphs about how the London suburb of Earls Court had been invaded.

'You're telling me the colonials are taking Earls Court back!' Heller questioned. 'There's a ghetto down there?'

'A place of wanderers and lost souls,' I confirmed. 'I stayed there briefly.'

Why on earth Earls Court?'

'It centres round a place called the Overseas Visitors Club. It's the focal point of the Grand Tour that young white colonials feel impelled to make when they come of age. Most of them completely underrate the culture and climate shock and end up hiding in the OVC greenhouse where the central heating is turned up all the year round and they keep the Fosters and Castle lagers chilled. Even the brave ones prefer to find a room not too far from the OVC, hence Kangaroo Valley.'

'Weird' said Heller, biting. I had not, of course, overlooked the fact that a film concerned with exiles would be of special interest to him.

'It get's weirder, I assured him. 'You can only live happily in Kangaroo Valley if you are frightened of England. If you go the other way and start liking the place, as the brighter ones do, it means you've made probably your first objective assessment of home. So the place is crawling with Aussies who've discovered there is something more to life than sun and surf, Canadians who've learnt not to put maple syrup on everything, and some very screwed up South Africans.'

'What's wrong with them?'

'They've discovered black is beautiful. Actually the Aussie girls have a problem in that direction too. There are one or two with dusky babies who are not at all sure they can get back into Australia. So Kangaroo Valley is also a refugee camp and home for a few permanent exiles.' (The most famous of these at the time was John Pilger, whom Heller also later talent-spotted; he commissioned Pilger's first series of television reports.)

'What do the locals think of all this?'

'They don't understand why the rest of the world can't see they've been invaded.'

Bob sucked his teeth.

'Aren't there any Champions down there – surf-board riders, scuba divers?'

'No,' I said firmly.

'Okay, we'll go with it if Peter buys it.'

Kangaroo Valley was really rather a success. Peter came and looked around the district with me and made the inspired suggestion that as the back streets of Earls Court had not changed much, it might be possible to film an introduction which evoked the tranquillity of a place that had once been a garden suburb of the West End. Then we would cut to the bold, brash Kangaroo Valley scene.

We managed that very well by hiring a rag and bone man with a horse and cart to wind down those narrow streets calling his wares, carefully framing out anything modern like television aerials. We did a crunching jump cut from that to the throbbing heart of a Kangaroo Valley party, bouncing with sexy South African girls learning the thrills of miscegenation; bawdy, boozy Aussies telling wonderful jokes, and long-haired Yanks playing pass-the-parcel with sausages of cannabis.

We also discovered a ghetto within the ghetto, which made Heller very pleased. During the war there had an earlier club in Earls Court for Polish airmen. Many of them had bought the scruffy Earls Court tenements cheaply after the war and had chopped them up into tiny cubicles when the transient colonials began to reoccupy the areas. For rooms just big enough for a bed and rucksack they were charging twice the going rate for inner London.

This first long production taught me that you had to know some artistic direction to sustain a film of this length; until then I had really regarded television films as stories in pictures. Subtle points of the story are best suggested pictorially. Emotional poignancy, for example, can only be properly evoked by pictures, not words. Journalists, many of whom aspire to film direction, are very bad at it until they learn this important difference.

The film attracted a great deal of interest from the Press, and Bob Heller was as happy with write-ups and reviews as he was with ratings and awards. A question was asked in Parliament about why foreigners had been allowed to take over part of London and an Australian spokesman prevaricated when asked whether the Australian girls with coloured babies would be allowed back into Australia, which made another headline. When the news agencies carried the story abroad, mothers of Australian girls in London wrote by the hundreds ordering their daughters home before anything unpleasant like that could happen.

The film sold well in the former colonies, and soon thereafter Heller offered me another network slot and a staff Producer/Director position. As the ACTT still had ITV in the iron grip of an absolute 'no redundancy' agreement, this amounted to a well-paid job for life. We were in a position to indulge in serious slum-hunting.

Annette had not got on as well with the Nixons as I had although they were extremely kind to her and the children. She found Brenda's metaphysics boring and never got involved in these abstract debates.

We chose to move to a derelict area of Fulham in the gentile shadow of the Hurlingham Club. A lot of poor media people had realized the potential of these robust Victorian cottages. We had Michael Gough, Roland Curram, Sheila Gish, and Rodney Bewes of *The Likely Lads* as our immediate neighbours, and we went to nice parties never, of course, forgetting to bring a bottle of wine.

As everyone was living in various states of slummery the conversation either ignored the subject of living conditions altogether (quite often parties were held in half-demolished rooms), or applauded the cunning of the conversions. Michael Gough took all the ceilings out of his house. The borough surveyor made him put the top floor ceilings back and warned that he was lucky the house had not collapsed. Mick took them out again a few weeks later and the house is still standing. The Currams lined their excavated fire-places with a rainbow of non-matching Victorian tiles which could be brought cheaply in ones and twos. We discovered that insulating cork used in ships could seal damp plaster; moreover, it could simply be nailed up because the nail heads were hidden in the cork's coarse grain. We passed many a happy evening engrossed in such money-saving trivia.

That brief interlude of domestic togetherness was interrupted by Annette very nearly dying. She was pregnant again and something started to go wrong just before we were due to move into our half-finished slum in Bettridge Road.

Annette was getting thinner by the day, I was busy at work and moving day was almost upon us. We assumed the problem was morning sickness but when Annette's weight was reduced to anorexic levels she was sent to St George's Hospital where it was discovered her blood was all but leeched of the trace elements vital to life, and she was admitted that same day.

Something dreadful was completely blocking Annette's intestinal tract. The doctors could not tell us what it was but it had to be a growth of some kind. Moreover, it was going to be desperately difficult to diagnose because of the pregnancy and X-rays could do nasty things to the foetus. In any event, an operation was going to be inevitable as the blockage was simply preventing her getting any nourishment. There was at least a 50/50 chance that the trauma of the operation would cause Annette to miscarry.

My side of the equation was as follows. I had exchanged contracts on the slum and paid the deposit out of the only cash we had. We had a mortgage agreed but because the house was a ruin, £1800 of this was retained until we finished the work, so I had borrowed that money on an expensive bridging loan. I was half-way through the editing of *Kangaroo Valley* which would miss its transmission date if I did not put in eight hours a day. Without Annette I had somehow to look after the little girls.

I went round to see the Nixons in a state of extreme self-pity, looking for an excuse to drop out of the whole enterprise. They simply climbed into their overalls and suggested we start painting straight away.

I have forgotten to report that the Nixons loved painting. It was a kind of companionable therapy for them. They painted everything in sight with great alacrity: huge areas of wall, woodwork, fiddly windows, even furniture. We went to their shed, loaded up with great quantities of painting equipment and went to the slum that very night. They painted the kitchen a rather peculiar green, assuring me I would feel much better when it was done.

I didn't, but it did prove that slums really do respond to a coat of paint – and it convinced me that I could not live there with the girls until at least a part of it had been done.

I phoned Ivy Wheeler and she very generously suggested that Lisa, who was not yet in school, come and live with her until we knew more about Annette. We both realized this could be a very long time.

With Tiffany I went to see my other best friends, Pat and Brian Emmerson. Brian and I had grown up together in Shangri-la and he had been my best man. He too had now quit Africa permanently and was working on his own slum in nearby Putney. Brian's slum was considerably more advanced than mine and he offered us his spare bedroom. This had bare walls, bare floors bare windows and a wonderful, new, raw, central heating radiator.

Every day I drove Tiffany to her school in Fulham and she was picked up at 3.45 by a jolly local child-minder. There Tiffany waited until I could come for her, eating great platefuls of baked beans, fish fingers, Angel Delights and chips; food which she had never been allowed in such quantities before. After that I went house-painting or raging at the builder, a self-confessed Polish bodger.

'I do basic work at cheap price, Meester Brun. That's what you want, hey?'

That's all I could afford. What he failed to add was that he would only turn up for work if I kept constantly on his back. Eventually, however, we had a peculiar network of pipes running about the place which mostly produced hot water, a central heating system which flushed the radiators if you bled them permanently and electric light. We even discovered a second bathroom, buried like a mummy's tomb beneath a collapsed ceiling in what I had assumed was a bedroom. Half-way through this work the builder went up on the roof and condemned it.

He knew I could not afford a new roof.

'You want I do a basic job on the roof jus' to tide you over hey?'

'How basic and how much?'

'I charge you for repairing slates but I don' use slates, jus'a' labour.'

'What will you use?'

He hauled in a sheet of ancient lino we had ripped up from the hall.

'Old lino!'

'Cut it up into slates. Cost you nutting. Lasta cupla years, maybe more.' (In fact they lasted almost four years!)

My brother Peter had become an engineer with Central African Airways and flew to London on a free ticket. He spent a few days working with me on the house and then began a series of frantic attempts to get home. He never actually mentioned the slum but when he started accepting stop-over trips via Lisbon which actually involved two abortive journeys, I concluded it was that.

Every day, morning and evening, I went to see my wife, who was by now dying as the focus of everyone's attention. St George's was a teaching hospital and for the young gynaecologists she was certainly their most interesting case. She was on a drip feed (and stayed on it for many weeks) and her gaunt face was the colour of grease-proof paper. But although her body wasted, both the baby and the suspected tumour thrived.

She was almost permanently surrounded by groups of students and specialists who were trying to work out how they could do that vital X-ray. Eventually a special lead corset was built and pictures taken of the intestine through narrow ports well clear of the foetus, or so they hoped.

'We have a modicum of good news for you.' her specialist told me after they processed the negatives. 'It looks very like an impacted ulcer rather than a tumour. The ulcer would have burst and then healed over, closing the intestine. However, when that happened, she must have been in terrible pain. Unless she has an exceptionally high pain threshold, it would have knocked her out.'

I explained where we had been living. It was a place where exceptionally high pain thresholds, mental and physical, had been a requirement of survival. But she had never complained of the agony he was describing.

'Women have a higher pain threshold than men,' he said with what I thought sounded vaguely like an accusation. 'That may help her through the next stage. We have to operate, and the sooner the better because she is not getting any stronger. In her present condition her chances of keeping the baby are not high.'

'Are you suggesting an abortion?' I asked, having thought about this, especially after the tricky X-ray problem. I had not been able to stop thinking about Guy Nixon: but this unborn child was more than usually important to me. Annette had been happy with the pregnancy, happier than she had been in a long time. I had allowed myself to think that when we had a proper home, that happiness might encompass me.

'No,' he said to my surprise and relief. 'I don't think that's a decision we have to make. We'll be ready for the eventuality but I think we'll leave the event to her and the Almighty.'

I trusted Annette's survival instincts and I was pleased he had not mentioned God, although I had secret suspicion that the Nixons had been doing a lot of praying behind my back.

Victoria Nyanza Brown was born on a sunny June day at St George's Hospital, healthy, lusty – and with all her toes, fingers, and brain just where they were supposed to be, although it would not have mattered a damn if that had not been so.

Annette survived the operation minus a short section of intestine and recovered fast once her body could refuel.

Through all that time I leaned on Bodger the builder more heavily than could the Tower of Pisa.

'This house has got to be finished for my wife and the baby to come home to.' I told him virtually every day. 'When it is I can also go and get my other little baby who I have hardly seen for three months. You've got children I know.'

'Loverly children me!'

'You have just three weeks to avoid them becoming orphans.'

Annette was genuinely amazed by the transformation of the house, and the extensive finishing and furnishing still to be done filled her time and bred a sense of purpose and commitment.

Wisely, we had determined to make the break with white Africa absolute and by the end of that year virtually all our friends were English from the little media ghetto that was blooming in Parsons Green. There was actually another ghetto of former white Africans spread loosely over the old colonial retirement suburbs of London – Putney, Wimbledon and Richmond – but attending a couple of their soirées made us so sad we never went again.

These dyed-in-the-wool ex-colonials were known as the When-we's – because of the way their conversation inevitably lapsed into a lament on how much better Africa had been 'when we were running it,' or the good life 'when we had four servants,' or 'when we could afford to go on holiday to South Africa twice a year.' The truly sad when-we's were the Liberals who also indulged in gloomy nostalgia about 'when we really thought there was a chance of a multi-racial future in Central Africa.'

Really they had not left Africa at all. They were very like the inhabitants of Kangaroo Valley and had simply exchanged the white greenhouse of Rhodesia for a very leaky one of their own making in Wimbledon. Quite a lot of them fled back eventually to sunny black Zimbabwe (where they now constitute a when-we secret society) or got stuck half-way in the worst limbo of all in places like Malta.

Bob Heller probably saved me from that too.

He had been very understanding about Annette's illness and my homeless state.

'I don't care what hours you work or when you work them, just so long as the film makes its transmission date.'

Peter Batty had sent me to a very experienced editor in Hammersmith, Len Trumm, who could just about bear to have me around for a maximum of two or three hours a day. I assumed that this was a reflection of my inexperience, but in fact Len was quietly cutting two films at the same time and he liked to get rid of me before his other director arrived.

One day we overlapped and I found myself shaking hands with James Bond! Len's other documentary was about the Scottish shipbuilding industry and was being directed by Sean Connery as an intellectual break from film stardom. Thereafter we often had meat-and-two-veg lunches in Len's local pub where I came to realise that 007 was a very pleasant, modest man with strong political convictions.

But Kangaroo Valley came and went and it was time to present Heller with another good idea. I had come to the conclusion that that meant going abroad. In the big league you had to be an expert and the only place I could claim any expertise was Africa. Adrian had South America, Hellier owned a raft of British experts, so Africa it had to be.

Africa was then and is now the most bloody awkward, downright dodgy place on earth to make serious films. It has more diseases, fewer hospitals, more mortality, less government, more corruption and the least law of any country on earth - and I speak as one who loves the place.

I knew it was about the worst time I could have chosen to be away, usually in places where you couldn't even find a phone, but I convinced myself I had no option if I wanted to hold on to my place in the big league even though I knew it wasn't true. There were lots of home-based magazine shows that would have welcomed a qualified newshound with an established reputation as a director.

The fact is my dorsal fin was well and truly grown and when my early inquiries into the film that was eventually called *The Animal War* came up positive, nothing really would have stopped me.

Heller also knew a good story when he saw one and within a couple of weeks or so of my showing it to him I was on my way to the hinterland of Tanzania to begin properly what has turned out to be my life's work.

The cameraman was Mike Whittaker with Dick Pope as his assistant and we were looked after by a young Production Assistant, Julie Stoner, on her first television trip out of England.

Mike and Dick were extremely experienced world travellers, in fact international gypsies at that time. They had about ten silver boxes packed by the legendary Pandora and from them they would extract all manner of creature comforts including a portable stereo music system with dozens of tapes (a decade before the Walkman). Dick, who was a Vegan, even brought his own food, a huge sack of muesli; this was a mixed blessing as we found plenty of food in the wilderness but very little water, and even Dick couldn't digest dry muesli. He nearly starved to death.

An artistic documentary cameraman (he later founded a special drama-documentary unit at Granada), Mike had the marvellous ability to remain unruffled under any circumstances. He could also sleep anywhere and at any time. We hired Land Rovers in Nairobi and drove south. Mike promptly fell asleep with his neck resting gainst the metal frame, untroubled by the pot-holes and corrugations.

For Julie it was total baptism by fire which she survived magnificently simply by forgetting she was a girl. We became a unit in every sense of the word, sharing the hardships and the laughs, the rough roads and the danger, as one. Julie's great moment of triumph was at a tiny bank in the Tanzanian town of Arusha which was refusing to change our money because sterling was suffering one of its regular crises. We were about to strike into the heart of the Serengeti where there would be nothing resembling a bank, so the whole expedition hung on young Ms Stoner getting money out of that bank manager. Sitting outside in our Land Rovers we felt like the Hole in the Wall Gang while the locals watched with increasing suspicion as Julie – and for that matter anybody else – failed to reappear.

There was a lot of ribald comment about her powers of persuasion when she returned with several thousand pounds of vital currency, but Julie had simply worked her way to the head of a large queue and announced that she would not move until the transaction had been completed, effectively bringing the business of the bank to a grinding halt. Any one of us would have been arrested!

Everyone on the crew was rather kindly assuming that I was the African expert and it is true I had been this way before as a young boy, but since that early safari I had lived in the white greenhouse of Rhodesia. Kenya and Tanzania were black Africa and some very powerful teachers had spent a lot of time conditioning me to loathe and fear countries run by blacks.

This now proved very difficult to believe. The blacks at Nairobi airport were polite and helpful. Most airport staff get very impolite and unhelpful when they see our multitude of equipment.

Outside was the same gaggle of boys desperate to be helpful that I remembered from my youth, but their entreaties to travel in the world's most unsafe taxis (since replaced by a Government company operating Mercedes) were efficiently brushed aside by a smiling black representative of the safari company we had hired.

Nairobi is, in my opinion, the most exciting town in sub-Saharan Africa because of its cosmopolitan mix of 'ex-pats' (it has a huge diplomatic community), smart black 'wabenzi' (the fat-cat local businessmen and politicians who drive Mercedes 'Benzies') and the street peasants who are extremely poor but very jolly with it. It would not surprise me at all to see Humphrey Bogart and Ingrid Bergman ordering the pianist at the Fever Tree Cafe to 'play it again, Sam.' Nairobi has a Casablanca feel to it.

This general air of raunchiness must be a special pollen in the local air. In the colonial days Nairobi was famous for white mischief. Nowadays its black mischievousness is quietly envied by most Pan-African nations and it is the most popular venue for their conferences.

Useful bits of the colonial legacy have been kept. We stayed the night at one of them, the Norfolk Hotel, where the nostalgia of Kenya's white-mischief days is used to flavour excellent service and fine food. On the wide balcony of the Norfolk an egalitarian crowd of diplomats, politicians, safari guides and tourists sip sundowners against the traditional evening display of a flaming sunset while they receive their briefings on what they will see in the Mara and the Tsavo game areas.

You walk to bed through a courtyard housing a collection of Model-T safari cars and two huge aviaries full of stridently coloured local birds to rooms that are still sprayed nightly against mosquitoes. That bitter-sweet antiseptic smell finally brought echoes of my boyhood journey rushing back.

When we set out for Tanzania the following morning my memories had thus been sharply primed and, sadly, I was soon seeing (or rather not seeing) evidence of how much had changed in the twenty years I had been away.

On our original journey to Shangri-la in 1947* we had driven in a second-hand war-surplus Dodge desert command car from Mombasa on the Kenya coast through three primitive African countries.

On these northern plains of Kenya and Tanzania the herds of game had been a continuous frieze across the horizon. Now, at best, only patchy silhouettes etched the view.

The story of a war of attrition on the plains game of East Africa which I had pieced together from some East African When-We's was apparently true: the African holocaust had started.

It was the beginning of the tragedy that has since reduced Kenya's national herd of 170,000 elephants to 8,000, and 20,000 rhino to probably less than 200 (in the wild) in 20 years.

Twenty years ago a man called Eric Balson was among a clutch of East African game wardens putting their futures at risk with warnings that this was happening. Yes, the great disaster particularly affecting black rhino and elephant which has made the headlines recently was first warned of twenty years ago!

Now Eric was waiting for us (I prayed) at the end of the new tarred

* *Bye Bye Shangri-la* (Weidenfeld and Nicolson, 1989)

highway we were presently navigating – down the Rift Valley, across the border into Tanzania, to Arusha.

Arusha was then still a spick-and-span town set in high hills of dark green and livid red flame trees. I use the past tense because nowadays there is little that is spick-and-span in Tanzania apart from the Masai world's most dramatic savannah wilderness. If it is possible for whole countries to become ghost towns Tanzania is that, but equally the country is proof positive that 'civilization' destroys wilderness. We may one day have to decide which we need most.

As a person who loves Africa I still regard the contemporary collapse of Tanzania as a tragedy. It was the epicentre of the African revolution where a saintly teacher much loved by his people attempted to shrug off an unsightly Jacob's coat of German/British colonialism and build a new, model, black Jerusalem.

Julius Nyerere is rightly revered by African leaders (and by myself) as the father of the new Africa. Few of those leaders (nor myself) can bring themselves to spend much time in Julius Nyerere's new Africa because the dream has lapsed into the dark, not the new, age. The doors of once prosperous Arusha swing in a wind of inexorable poverty. Togetherness, *Ujuma*, collapsed fifteen years ago, the economy thereafter. Now even hope seems to have gone. Valuable animals, especially those with tusks or horns that can be sold for hard currency, are illegally hunted ('poached' is too much a euphemism) to extinction.

Eric had been given the job of catching the poachers and the men who funded them.

It was something of a surprise to find Eric looking so like a Wild West sheriff. He wore a floppy wide-brimmed felt hat, dusty khakis, and had a pistol strapped to his belt. He had a Deputy sitting guarding his truck, a coffee-coloured, aloe-eyed young man holding a well-oiled Lee Enfield service rifle. His smooth face appeared to have no muscles and he looked me over with passive indifference as if he had no interest in anything other than targets for his rifle. This turned out to be uncomfortably close to the truth.

'I'm sorry about all the fire power, 'Eric apologized. 'But I'm rather having to watch my back at the moment.'

Chapter Five

Eric Balson was, I think, nearly the last white man in Africa to believe that the wildlife holocaust that started in his time could be stemmed. He also knew he would be putting his life on the line if he became involved.

He came from a long tradition of men who had devoted their lives to the fight for the rights of animals, starting with Captain Arthur Ritchie who set up the East African Game Parks in the Thirties and which has on its roll of honour people like George Adamson, John Owen, Myles Turner, David Sheldrick, Peter Jenkins and Bill Woodley, to mention just the ones I've met.

All these wardens fought a very good fight and David, George and Myles died doing it. Bill Woodley and Peter Jenkins are still in harness but I cannot believe that they have lived in hope this last decade.

In 1971 Eric Balson still thought there was a chance because his commission to break the poaching rackets in Tanzania had come unsolicited from Julius Nyerere's government. In those days the wardens did not believe blacks cared as much as whites, indeed there are many who still don't and quote Africa's recent record to prove it. This racial attitude is wrong; African conservationists care, but unlike the colonial wardens they have to operate in the real world of contemporary Africa. Eric Balson occupied momentarily a unique position of a foot in both camps: the authority of the colonial warden backed by the mandate of a black government.

Balson had launched a two-pronged attack on the game racketeers who at this time, when it was still legal to sell game trophies in shops in Nairobi and Dar-es-Salaam, were dealing in everything – antelope and zebra skins, ivory, elephant footstools, hide, tail-hair 'good luck' bangles, rhino products, and big cat skins, particularly leopard.

First he spent night after night going through years of import permits for these products and soon began to spot anomalies, particularly with licences to export products from Kenya out of the Tanzanian port of Dar-es-Salaam.

Double-checking the Kenya licences, he found that large numbers of these, certifying the spoils from thousands of animals, were from certificate books stolen in Kenya.

The traffic was incredibly convoluted. Illegal ivory from both countries was being taken across the borders and validated with questionable documents. Prior to Balson's activities, customs officers at, say, Nairobi airport clearing shipments of ivory from Tanzania would not bother to check the Tanzanian-issued certificates of ownership, and vice-versa with shipments out of Dar-es-Salaam.

Early in 1971, Balson made his first arrest of a trader bringing ostrich skins into Tanzania on permits from an out-of-date, cancelled Certificate of Ownership book. The book had been issued to a Nairobi tourist shop who would give out a certificate on a legal purchase. But the business had gone bust and the certificate book returned to the Game Department and cancelled.

Soon after this arrest an attempt was made to run Eric down in broad daylight, and from then on his pale-eyed Masai rode shotgun wherever his Bwana went; Eric himself began to pack at least two handguns.

He also tried to tackle the trade more directly by setting up a network of informers. These dubious characters would creep into Eric's garden after dark and the armed Askaris would fetch Eric to talk to them. Using this information Eric would pose as a buyer, on one occasion actually meeting with leopard-skin poachers in a mountain cave. He remembered the occasion particularly vividly not so much because it was so fraught with danger but because the poachers proudly revealed how they were killing the leopards without marking their valuable skins. They were trapped and then killed with a heated spear thrust up the anus.

Eric set up ambushes to trap the dealers when they delivered the goods he had agreed to buy. His most spectacular coup at the time we met was a lorry-load of 52 rhino horn.

Shots were fired across his garden three nights thereafter. Undeterred, Eric set up another contact which this time produced a tragic bonanza of 286 rhino horn, including 70 very rare white rhino horn, with paperwork indicating that this horde had been poached in Uganda and the Sudan.

Eric did not of course realize that this horde would represent almost as many wild rhino, black and white, as would exist in the whole of Kenya, Uganda, Sudan and Tanzania three decades later!

The trader was convicted and sentenced to five years imprisonment, but the sentence was later quashed on the technical grounds that no expert was called from the Game Department to certify that the 286 exhibits before the court were actually rhino horns.

Eric's mission was palpably suicidal, and the longer we talked the more I became convinced the risks he was taking were pointless. Everything he was uncovering pointed to covert political involvement, indeed he had even received a letter from the Attorney General of Kenya, Charles Njonjo, warning him that this was the only explanation.

The Kenyan 'royal' family of Kenyatta was also being accused by the world's press of involvement in illegal ivory exports throughout the Seventies, but even when in September 1971 the Kenya courts acquitted three dealers whom Eric had named for the unlawful possession of 134 rhino horn, 734 elephant tusks and 11 leopard skins, he still believed Tanzania would reform if he could but identify the leading racketeers.

His naiveté held until a real Mr Big was caught red-handed, a commercial hunter related to the Prime Minister.

When Eric's contract became due for renewal shortly thereafter it was not taken up and he retired to South Africa in disgust, where the last I heard he was running a curio shop specializing in African carvings. Had he somehow managed to save that last shipment of rhino it would, today, equal the Kenya national herd.

When we finished our interviews about all these adventures I asked Eric whether there was any chance of us filming the activities of the one group of poachers with whom he had any sympathy. These indigenous hunters used bows and arrows; they sold the meat to the communities around the big game parks and represented no threat to the excess of antelope inside the sanctuaries. Eric used these hunters as trackers when he went after poachers and considered them a threatened species in their own right. They were easy prey for zealous Game Department guards who should have been concentrating on the motorized commercial poachers – who unfortunately tended to shoot back.

Eric suggested that we set up a camp at a spot just outside the Serengeti after we had filmed another legendary poacher-hunter, Myles Turner, and he would let 'some people' know we were there. It sounded very hazardous and I resolved only to try it if we were very short of material.

It was very hot and the great plain we had to cross to reach Myles Turner's camp at Seronera had been burnt to a black waste-land by bush fires. Oblivious to all this, the Land Rover with the crew forged ahead with Mike Whittaker's sleeping head bobbing up and down on the steel rim of the passenger door while loud music from the crew's stereo wafted back to Julie and myself in the truck behind. Julie looked very wistful and thereafter always travelled with the crew, ostensibly to play Travel Scrabble.

A stern young black game guard was manning the gate and he peered into the lead truck with open suspicion. A hand reached out and clamped a pair of huge earphones over his ears while expert fingers inside the crew truck turned knobs that injected his first loud fix of stereo!

He was transfixed! His inherent love of rhythm and beat was suddenly, traumatically, transfused with sounds the like of which he could never have heard before, and it reduced him to a jibbering, ecstatic string-puppet. Every day thereafter when we passed through the gate, he would demand another demon dose of the Grateful Dead or the Electric Light Orchestra, and I seriously worry about what became of him when we left.

Myles Turner was not at all pleased to see us.

He was a short, squat, exhausted evangelist who really did not want a film crew making a record of what he regarded as his wasted life.

'Look,' he said. 'It's all over. We're fighting an animal war here, and we're losing. There's nothing much left to make a film about.'

'So far as the British are concerned this is a unique place,' I told him. '"Serengeti Shall not Die" and all that.'

Myles laughed in a tired fashion.

'We collected 10,000 wire snares this month alone,' he said shortly, 'and the snares are nothing compared to motorized poaching using fast Landcruisers and automatic weapons.'

By evening he had agreed to let us accompany him on an anti-poaching patrol.

We started before dawn. Tea came through the hut door and there was a lot of noise from the Seronera vehicle compound. I dressed hurriedly in the wrong clothes; it was cold enough for winter woollies but I had only shorts and a shirt ready.

The crew glowered, holding me instantly responsible for the early reveille and the obvious fact that they weren't going to get any breakfast yet.

Myles's truck drew up outside our tents and his scouts started to throw our equipment into their truck. That got the crew moving.

'Let's go,' said Myles and the truck stormed off into the darkness, followed by two others.

It was the most nightmarish drive I have ever undertaken. We appeared simply to be crashing through the black bush at lunatic speed and without lights. I had just had time to scramble into the open back of Turner's truck and we were all now hanging on to anything solid while trying to sit on the silver equipment boxes to stop them flying out of the vehicle.

Mike, for once, lost his temper.

'This is bloody crazy,' he gritted. 'Nothing's going to work after this pounding!'

I did not care – we would all be long dead before that need arose.

I can only assume Myles had recruited drivers who could see in the dark. We crashed on, brushing under, round and through the low mopani and acacia trees, thumping through gullies and down boggy *vleis* and *dongas* until eventually after an hour during which we were never more than a second away from some violent collision, somersault or skid, they switched the engines off and we drifted to a halt on the edge of a wide plain to watch the sun rise.

'Lovely, isn't it?' Myles said. 'Not another sight like it in Africa.' And do tell your chaps to keep the noise down, old chap, or they won't see a bloody thing.'

'They are sorting out their equipment,' I said icily, adding: 'What are we hoping to see?'

'Poachers,' he said, 'It's our only hope of catching them red-handed. This is the time their trucks come in to pick up the loot and we can sometimes come down on them while they're loading.'

But this was not to be one of those sometimes. We sat in the icy dawn, Africa's most beguiling time, watching the great red-tailed hawks hunting small mammals scurrying home after a night's foraging; a hippo meandering guiltily back to his waterhole like Cinderella who had stayed too long at the ball; the light turning from blackcurrant juice to nectarine syrup to strawberry mousse; and a herd of elephants stalking out of the forest fringe to cross the plain while the day was still cool.

'Go in peace,' Myles said, almost to himself.

We spent the morning collecting snares, more than fifty in an area Myles had cleared only days before. They were simple steel lassoes set across the game paths and tied to loose, heavy objects like dead tree branches or large rocks. This technique meant big animals could never bring enough tension to bear to break them. Instead they dragged the tightening, cutting snares around until they died of exhaustion or loss of blood.

The snares were of a whole or split strands of steel wire rope – hawser – and we wondered where this sophisticated material came from.

'The Williamson's Diamond Mine,' Myles explained. 'Round here wire of this strength is more sought after than the damn diamonds.'

After two hours of this exhausting work, finding snares set wherever we turned, Myles spotted a full-grown Topi antelope lying dead in a snare – or so we thought. These are large, powerful animals with silky, russet coats, short horns and black leg markings. They have a habit of standing guard on top of termite mounds and only run when predators like lions are almost on top of them. Then they run very fast indeed.

This Topi had glazed, bluebottle eyes staring from its head and the snare was deeply bedded in its neck. Spume and blood were trickling from its mouth.

Myles approached the Topi very gingerly and had two of his field force free the snare. Then he sat in front of it, gently stroking its snout; a touching requiem which Mike filmed eagerly.

Suddenly the Topi came back to life. One moment it was lifeless, the next it was on its feet and running at full speed in a weaving pattern as if all the lions of the Serengeti were after it. It is the mark of a good cameraman that his reflexes and operating skills can cope with a situation like this. Mike was hand-holding the camera, yet somehow he managed to follow steadily the erratic blur of the Topi's run, altering both his focus and his aperture as the animal moved in and out of the light. He still had it centre-frame when it stopped, seeming almost to pose on the horizon against the strawberry-pink morning.

It is at brief moments like this that the trials and tribulations of making films become as nothing. Mike and I both knew without a shadow of a doubt that he had just shot the closing sequence of our film, so we very carefully checked the gate.

'Checking the gate' is field-television's most nail-biting ritual. Film stock sometimes leaves thin shreds, known as hairs, in the toothed gate behind the lens, creating a disfiguring line down the negative. Hairs have a devilish propensity to appear when a shot has been particularly special, particularly when there is no chance of a second take. This time we were lucky. No hairs.

But still no poachers. Myles, who saw things not visible to us mere mortals, started to sniff the air in one clump of snares and he and his men went rushing off into what looked to us like a thicket.

Behind this natural screen there was a complete al fresco butchery, with strips of meat hanging up to dry between two trees and a perfect little hut woven cunningly into the undergrowth. Inside we found the remains of a fire.

'They were here last night,' Myles said resignedly. 'How the hell did they get away from here without us seeing them?'

Soon after that, at our midday break, he tiredly gave us the title of our film.

'Tell the people back home that we're fighting a war here. An animal war. And you might as well admit that we're losing it.'

So that was the Serengeti – dying.

We had a week of nightmarish drives and never saw a poacher. Myles showed us an enormous pile of ivory tusks that he had captured or found abandoned. He also showed us the bows and arrows, tipped with deadly acokanthera poison, that the indigenous poachers used to kill elephants. I told him about Eric Balson's sympathy for the indigenous hunter and Myles agreed that tribes like the Wanderoba, who had always hunted elephant, had a strange empathy with their victims.

'This stuff would drop you in your tracks,' Myles said of the black acokanthera. 'We have to be really careful handling arrows. Just a scratch is lethal and it stays toxic for a long time. But it can take a day or two to kill an elephant and a Wanderoba hunter will just follow along, not harassing the animal until it lies down and goes to sleep for good. I've caught them sitting right beside the animal just waiting.'

He paused.

'I don't approve, you understand. Nobody gets away with killing my animals, but it's different to the bastards who creep in here with their four-wheel drives and blast the hell out of a herd with Bren guns.'

Myles Turner and I got to know each other a little over the years that followed. After the Serengeti, where he had been internationally famous and often showed royalty and heads of state around, he went to a saner job in Malawi where he evolved a wildlife management plan that continues to work very well. Eventually the East African crisis drew him back and he was working as an adviser in the lovely Masai Mara park when he suffered a fatal heart attack.

This came as a great shock to everyone, not least to those who knew him from his Serengeti days – although it has to be said that anyone who had been poacher-hunting with Myles, and knew how he could live on his nerves, may have been less surprised. Today I am very pleased to report that his son Michael is a member of our Nature Watch Trust which is doing what it can to mount a last-ditch rescue of Central African rhino.

In the months that followed our interview the situation in the Serengeti grew worse and worse. Ivory-poaching for the illicit Kenya market was said to have become virtually a state-licensed activity, indeed it was alleged in a report written by a leading East African elephant expert, Ian Parker, that Jomo Kenyatta actually gave permits to 'collect' what was called 'found ivory' (the product of natural mortality) to some of his ex-Mau Mau generals. Huge quantities of this 'white gold' were then sold to 'licensed' middlemen exporters, the largest of whom was Margaret Kenyatta, Jomo's daughter. Mrs Kenyatta – 'Mama Nginja' – was also named in Parker's secret report (which investigated the tidal wave of elephant poaching which swept over Kenya through the late Sixties and Seventies), and she certainly made no attempt to conceal her rapidly increasing wealth.

It is in my opinion totally unreasonable to think that Jomo Kenyatta did not know of the activities of his women-folk and other members of the 'royal' family, who were sometimes caught with crates of dodgy ivory when customs officers at Nairobi and Brussels (the favoured European destination) decided to do their job properly.

But it also has to be said that the world's leading conservationist, Prince Bernhardt of the Netherlands, must surely have been aware of the Ivory Connection when he made what I regard as the most bizarre conservation award of our century – the Golden Ark to President Jomo Kenyatta in 1974.

This award has always seemed to me to symbolize the Achilles heel of the conservation movement. It was made when elephants were being killed in their tens of thousands under the noses of the many conservationists-in-residence. It may be that effective conservation has failed this century because the movement did not recognize it was building up crippling layers of vested interests. I hope that is the reason.

Why, to take the classic case, did Prince Bernhardt not publicly withdraw the award when he learned what was going on. For years I assumed he did not really know, but I then discovered Parker's detailed report which was written at the request of Jack Block, Chairman of the Kenya branch of the World Wildlife Fund. Did it reach Europe? Parker confirmed to me, in writing, that it did; in fact he 'took back' a copy of it from the headquarters of WWF in Switzerland (Parker personally retrieved a copy from their offices well before the Golden Ark award was presented to Kenyatta.)

The contents of that report (I have one of the few extant copies) are utterly condemning of the Kenyattas, and also names leading politicians, senior members of the Game Department, politicians, police and businessmen. Why dig it up now? Well, had the Prince used it instead to provoke the international anger that was due, the poacher barons would have been forced to slow down their activities at the very least, and many thousands of elephants which Kenya now desperately needs to keep the national herd and its vital tourist industry viable, would have been saved.

Instead of this course, conservationists opted for the diplomatic approach. A low-key ceremony was arranged, and for at least another five years thereafter large quantities of ivory continued to leave Kenya by the back door.

It only slowed significantly when there was little heavy ivory left to be had. Just three months after the Golden Ark award, the United Africa Company, of which Margaret Kenyatta was Chairman and owner of 49% of the shares, was given a licence to export 1,250 baby elephant tusks.

Dr Iain Douglas Hamilton, Kenya's most consistent activist (a role which has caused the conservation establishment to send him to Coventry for most of the Eighties) did a calculation based on tusk weights in the middle Seventies and concluded that a ton of ivory represented roughly one hundred elephants. He then proved that in 1975 Hong Kong alone imported 515 tons of ivory, and concluded that as late as 1976 known ivory imports were indicating a slaughter of perhaps 400,000 animals and certainly no less than 100,000.

Those were extinction statistics, Iain warned. But only a decade later, when Kenya announced that its national herd was down to 20,000 animals (a figure many believe to be a great exaggeration), was he taken seriously.

Now it is too late. Kenya and Tanzania have safari-park numbers of black rhino and elephant. The story has a deeply ironical end. When Kenya finally recognized their rhino crisis and decided to fence Nkuru Park as a captive breeding sanctuary, it was a contribution from Prince Bernhardt which got the project started.

Myles Turner certainly saw all this writing on the wall way back in 1969 and there were people who said that the sadness and desperation drove him slightly mad. He went on almost endless patrols with his raggle-taggle field force (many of whom were ex-poachers) getting ever more angry and deadly. He should have saved himself the agony, like Prince Bernhardt.

Then, as happened to so many white wardens in that era, his contract was not renewed and he went off, poor and pensionless, to sleepy Malawi. But it probably saved his sanity.

We left Serengeti and ground our way through uncharted bush to Eric Balson's compass location, put up a couple of old tents in a section of dry forest just outside the park, and waited. Time went by. We ran out of food and ate pieces off a very smelly giraffe leg which some predator had obligingly dumped near our camp one night.

We got our water from a little bilharzia-infested river and one night Julie was attacked by a complete squadron of giant mosquitoes. She had packed a long-sleeved, ankle-length white nightie for just such a contingency (and, I think, for the contingency of having to share sleeping accommodation) and the following morning it was polka-dotted with great red splodges of blood where the mossies had lanced straight through it.

I was asked rather pointedly by the crew how long I intended to stay in this God-forsaken location 'that I had chosen.'

Nobody used the word 'we' at all.

Two long days later, I was sitting beside the morning campfire wondering how I was going to explain to Bob Heller what we hadn't been doing for the past week, when four very dangerous-looking people stepped out of the bush about four feet away from the fire. I was in no doubt that they had been sitting there watching me for some time.

They were armed with bows and arrows (not acokanthera-tipped, I noted with relief) and narrow-bladed throwing spears. One was a complete primitive clad in nothing but a leather loin cloth, Masai beads, a tacky scrap of leather worn as a cape, and filed teeth.

Their leader was a very tall skeletal fellow with a smile like Boris Karloff, and the others were lean-muscled teenagers. These three wore holey khaki shorts and string vests, more string than vest. They were my best examples yet of that small tribe of people who would kill as soon as look at you.

They squatted down on the other side of the fire and simply waited, staring, smiling now and then but never looking you in the eye, lightly weighing their bright, sharp spears.

Mike came out and gave them a good scowling.

'Would I be wrong in thinking these are friends of yours?'

'Eric put the word out.'

'They're poachers, aren't they?'

'Ex-poachers.'

'They don't look at all ex to me.'

With a shake of the head he went to get his camera.

We had a very bad time keeping up with our ex-poachers, who started at a run and kept it up most of the morning until they came across a big herd of wildebeeste. Then they spent about another two hours creeping up close to the herd until I really began to have sympathy for followers of the ex-poacher life.

They duly killed two wildebeeste, slitting their stomachs in front of the camera to dump great green putrid sacks of blood and guts at our feet. Mike started the shot on the telephoto end of his 10 × 1 zoom but rapidly pulled back, giving me a very dirty look.

I think we were probably inside the park boundaries by then and the whole time this was going on I expected to see Myles and his gun-toting maniacs come crashing up over the horizon. I was completely convinced he would have opened fire on us and I can't say I would have held it against him.

Mike probably would have applauded.

Then there was another three hours of carrying the heavy carcases back across the plain to a *donga* where they set up a butchery very like – in fact identical to – the one we had inspected so self-righteously with Myles a few days earlier.

Mike filmed all this without comment and he stayed quiet while back at our camp I paid our four villains for their time and trouble. Then, to my great relief, they vanished as anonymously as they had come.

'So what are you going to say when they ask you how you got this footage,' Mike said eventually.

'Luck.' I said shortly.

I was very tired and sensed that none of that would matter when we got back to the big shark pond.

And of course it did not. *The Animal War* was a terrific film and was soon nominated for the Goldengate Award, America's premier documentary prize. Bob Heller was delighted and my reputation as a champion of nature was secured.

So far as I know, however, Mike Whittaker never shot another natural history picture and it was some years before I went back to it. By then I and the children were not so hungry.

Chapter Six

Should I have hired ex-poachers to hunt illegally and then pretend they were real poachers? Yes. So long as the reconstruction was technically accurate (as indeed it was) the technique would be acceptable to most of my peers and verges on common practice.

It became such common practice in America that the broadcast standards authority there insisted such sequences be labelled 'a reconstruction.' The IBA in Britain has always regarded that as unnecessary; in fact my insistence on absolute technical accuracy – any spear-carrying villagers would have done – could be considered rather pedantic.

In truth, traditional ethical considerations or traditional interpretations of ethics do not play an important role in television. Indeed they wither like deciduous plants in a desert under the hot glare of competition. Let me hasten to add that we are not monsters, it is to do with an essential lack of reality in the medium in which we work.

My friend Allan Root, whose natural history documentaries set new standards of truth (in the television sense) once most astutely answered the question about ethics in natural history film-making with an honest response disguised as a joke: 'Ethics? Isn't that the county next to Sussex?'

This may come as no surprise to discerning viewers who have pondered the methods of investigative reporters, the sincerity of game-show hosts, the veracity of quizzes, or the extraordinary ability of newscasters to memorize whole bulletins.

However, I do hope it will come at least as something of a surprise that the most evangelically-inclined of us all, we of the natural history élite, also bend the rules much of the time. How we bend them, and more importantly why, is crucial to a proper understanding of television.

I never bend a rule without feeling guilt. I have killed a fair number of small animals, molested dozens, 'reconstructed' regularly, and have taken what we might henceforth usefully call the Prince Bernhardt Amendment if a point of principle ever looked liked jeopardizing a production. The production is everything; well, not quite everything, but sometimes we have to do bad to do good.

Most of my colleagues in the natural history film business regard our rough handling of nature and the subterfuges we employ as justifiable, provided the programme is evangelical for nature.

The animals we terrify and kill are martyrs to a greater conservation cause, and are most often the victims of very high (technical) standards. There is no other way to show you the interior of a busy beehive or an anthill than to stick fibre-optic lenses and lights inside them, even though that has much the same effect on the anthill as, say, Rommel sticking the barrel of his Panzer through your front window.

We further console ourselves that these animal martyrs have served the cause of nature well. There is a far greater awareness of conservation today than there was when I filmed *The Animal War* twenty years ago, and natural history films on television, especially the very high-grade product that was made in Britain until fairly recently, has been largely responsible for this. We have succeeded – there is a green revolution!

But this is not a book about morality, but about television. Have the conjuring tricks become con tricks? Increasingly television's ambition and hunger for higher ratings has pushed natural history film-makers into a competitive frenzy of whizz-bang picture sequences. That county next to Sussex is in danger of becoming our spiritual home.

Let me give you some examples. Take the lemmings myth. Lemmings do not commit mass suicide by throwing themselves over cliffs into the sea. The phrase 'behaving like a lemming' is a total misnomer. This nonsense owes its origin to a piece of mistaken observation by a long-since forgotten biologist. It is assumed that the one group of lemmings he saw engaged in this aberrant behaviour were probably just sick. An American film company got to hear about it, however, and etched it on record with their film cameras.

No, they did not travel to the Antarctic and film the biologist's lemmings committing suicide. They took perfectly healthy lemmings to a set in Canada and projected them over a cliff. The film was called *A True Life Adventure*!

And what about the deadly piranha? Did you know that piranha fish in the mighty river Amazon *don't* tear live prey to bloody shreds?

I only discovered that this exotic legend was nonsense two years ago when I went to buy some film from one of America's leading natural history film-makers.

The American television custard is a good deal more shark-infested than ours because of the need to satisfy hard-nosed advertisers. This film-maker was refreshingly open about his attitude of giving the customers what they wanted. He gave me a cheerful smile and told me the truth about piranhas.

But, I pointed out, we had just been looking at an incredible sequence of his in which a creature that looked like Rattie in *Wind in the Willows* had been devoured before our very eyes by a mass of ferocious piranhas. I had seen innocent Rattie attacked and stripped to the white of his bones in a gory shambles of frenzied piranhas before my very eyes!

'You can't have a film about the Amazon without piranhas,' he observed. 'Not in the States.'

'You reconstructed that!'

'In a 45-gallon petrol drum.'

'And the client okayed it?'

'Let me! They made it quite clear that they thought I was failing to produce the goods when we weren't able to film the live action. I told them piranhas don't seem to attack live prey but they wouldn't have it.'

'So!'

'I got a whole bunch of piranhas in half an oil drum and a bucket of blood from an abattoir and after we had filmed the coypu (Rattie) swimming down a bit of river we killed it, dropped it in the drum with the piranhas and blood, and slowly raised the drum up to the surface to make the fish thrash about. We stripped the carcase and filmed it back in the tank through various stages.'

Let me hasten to add that he is one of the most accurate film-makers I know and his telling me this story is a vindication of his honesty and openness. He would much prefer not to reconstruct scenes, but recognizes that his survival in a highly-competitive business occasionally depends on it.

He is not alone, but most of us prefer to confine our confessions to our own trade halls.

Another experienced colleague from a British ITV company had an uncomfortable moment at the Bath Wildlife Film-Makers Symposium when Eaumon de Buitlear (who is now Senator for the Environment in Ireland) asked whether a deer shown in a film of theirs was of a new, previously undocumented species.

'No,' he said. 'Why?'

'Because,' said Eaumon in his soft Irish drawl, 'the little deer the leopard is carrying appears to have a zip down its belly.'

It was admitted with understandable embarrassment that the deer had been gutted and sewn up for the film because the leopard in question was a very valuable star and they did not want it to get food poisoning. He did not reveal whether they, or the leopard, had killed the deer (the film of course implied the latter), nor was he asked because we all assumed the former.

This all happened in the course of a debate on ethics, during which others admitted dropping 'flying' snakes out of a drainpipe and confessed that their panther shots were done in a secret enclosure. A famous cameraman found it surprising that we did not all know that he keeps a miniature zoo of 'prop' animals for every big film.

The ornithologist/film-maker Jeffrey Boswell who was chairing the session on ethics produced an ingenious grading of creatures of varying sizes and cuddliness, starting with dolphins and whales, then chimps and gorillas, elephants and rhino and so on down to spiders and flies. His test question was something along the lines of: 'Stop me when you would be prepared to risk killing one of these to get a picture.'

It reduced us all to embarrassed, squirming silence and only when Jeffrey got down among the creepy crawlies did a few hands go up, whereas almost every one of us had bigger skeletons than that tucked away in our film cupboards.

I suppose my main concern in this context, is not the fate of these poor animals. We are a meat-eating species and exciting natural history films on television are a part of our diet which I suspect, were it put to the viewer-vote, few would give up.

I am more selfishly concerned with killing the golden goose of our credibility. I know for certain that natural history film-makers go to expensive, extraordinary lengths to reproduce reality with their prop animals, film sets and special equipment.

But what does their presence do to the reality? Are we creating a special television reality that is no more real than the fantasies made on studio sets, while still selling it to the public as the real thing? I am also becoming increasingly concerned, as the so-called green revolution becomes something more than a passing fad, that we are sanitizing the product, rubbing off the warts, disguising the fact that there is very little left of the pristine glossy wilderness you see in our films. Will it all have gone by the time we dare tell you about it?

I have not, as you may be forgiven for thinking, lost my way in a swamp of introspection. The success of the *The Animal War* made me what Heller wanted, a reliable producer/director of network-standard programmes, not a flash-in-the-pan.

That status, however, also provoked, indeed required, a dramatic shift of priorities. I was no longer a married man aspiring to be a television producer but a television producer for whom the world was suddenly my oyster. Into that scenario, somewhere, I had to fit a wife and children and it has to be said that I did not succeed very well.

I think I sensed this change as I flew home, exhausted, slightly malarial, malnourished but secretly jubilant.

All I wanted to do was sleep.

My little girls, who had been dressed like Judy Garlands and posed on the stairs for my triumphant return, went off to their play group, denim jump suits and noisy ways. My wife tried to get me to talk and found that even that did not work.

'What is Tanzania like?' Annette asked me.

'It's breathtakingly beautifully . . . awful . . . violent. The flame trees of Arusha are like a living fire . . . and they will kill anything, everywhere!'

'Who are they, Robin?'

'They have silver eyes and filed teeth . . . and you should see the animals. In the dawn they are like a frieze someone has strung around the horizon . . .'

And then my head would nod and I could see in her eyes that she thought I could not be bothered, when in fact I was pleased to be home, delighted to be back in sanctuary, but not capable of sharing any of it.

That is why television and marriage, both of them, require more intellect than I had then – that, and the fact that Bob Heller thought he had his priorities right.

On the fifth day when I was just beginning to surface and see my home as the place where I lived, and my wife had decided that I was genuinely not well, and the children had got used to their detached father being back again, Heller called.

After a brief conversation I carefully put down the phone. Annette waited in the silence.

'I have to go to Biafra.'

I can still see her face.

'Is this the way it's going to be?'

'Yes. This is it. This is what I do.'

She did not suggest I did something else. How could she? What I was doing was one of the most enviable jobs on earth. We had arrived. If the price of arriving was constant departures, so be it.

Biafra was the place where, after a night of madness in which several thousand Ibos were slaughtered by a ruling class called the Hausa, the Ibos broke away from the mother state of Nigeria taking the national oil wells with them.

In the civil war to get these oil wells back some six million Biafrans died of starvation.

Bob Heller sent me to Biafra to film the man who was doing his utmost to stem the starvation, Dr Auguste Lindt (of the Swiss chocolate family), who was the Red Cross special ambassador.

I was supposed to document a story of intrepid endeavour in which Dr Lindt directed the milk of western human kindness down onto starving Biafra, like pints of cream into a chocolate bar.

The reality was a farce, a slab of bitter-sweet that simply could not be told as it was, not to my audience and certainly not to my wife.

We flew out to Abidjan in the former French colony of the Ivory Coast. Abidjan at three o'clock in the afternoon looked like a swamp covered with huge buildings made of Weetabix. To my relief the airstrip was smooth and wide, fringed with tubby Hercules transports.

The city was comatose and we joined the siesta until nightfall, when the Weetabix buildings suddenly glowed with disco-lighting and loud rock and roll vibrated their slender structures.

The whole coastal strip was a vast nightclub!

At the heart of these swinging venues, through which slender black hookers fluttered their wares like exotic African moths, morose Swiss, Danish and Swedish pilots in silky aviator's overalls sat adding up their danger money.

We met the air crew with whom we would be overflying Nigeria to the Biafran capital of Enugu. The flyers were delighted to see us. Normally they flew with dried cod and dried cod is hard to frighten.

'The Nigerians do not approve of supplying Biafra,' they explained. 'So they will try and shoot us down if they can get one of their Saab jets in the air.'

Ha ha, they laughed, but not to worry because that was not very likely. The Nigerian Saabs were flown by Egyptians and even if the Nigerians could get the jets to start, the Egyptians would forget to take them up. Ha ha ha – yes?

There was also a Nigerian bomber flown by an Egyptian and we could expect him too. How else would he find Enugu – ha ha? They had an understanding with the Nigerian Egyptian bomber. They would let him follow them to Enugu, talking to him all the way because otherwise he would certainly get lost, ha ha, on the understanding that he would let them land on the Enugu airstrip lit by the lights of wrecked cars before he dropped his bombs.

There was no danger at all from these, they assured us, he had never hit the airstrip once. The main danger was the quality of the batteries in the wrecked cars alongside the Enugu airstrip. Sometimes the Biafrans forgot to charge them and several Red Cross planes had flown on to light up the jungle.

Also the Biafrans had an anti-aircraft gun which they occasionally got to work. Usually they fired at the Nigerian bomber, but if the lights from the cars were very dim . . .

We took off in total darkness. I have never been so frightened in my life. The plane was completely blacked out except for the sepulchral glow of muted cabin lights and once the sparkle of Abidjan had passed behind us the dark continent lowered itself all around us. We hung droning in the void while the pilots grinned, sipped their coffee and exchanged pleasantries with the Egyptian, who was indeed following us in a Nigerian Dakota loaded with bombs!

The landing was the ultimate nightmare in a not unadventurous life.

The pilots called Enugu on their radio and requested the landing lights. Two small orbs lit up on the ground an immense distance away and the pilots sighed and radioed the ground again.

Three more lights came on and then a couple more, but they were more like one of the constellations on a misty night than a flight path. Our pilots seemed satisfied, however, and began moving the many knobs, wheels and levers required to get a large aircraft to land.

Warning sirens and bright flashing lights started up all over the cockpit as we began our final approach and five hundred yards from the strip they turned on their searchlights, illuminating a small fat khaki patchwork aircraft directly in front of us.

'Bugger off Abdul,' the pilots roared, flashing their bright halogen wing beams – and he did, apparently apologizing profusely while we stormed by. Minutes later we landed with an agonized howl of brakes, tortured rubber and reverse thrusts. Several tons of salted fish, dried milk powder, the mad dogs of war, and five petrified Brits rolled off the tarmac into the oily grass with the crew hooting with triumph and marking up another huge payment from charity.

We were given sanctuary by the International Red Cross in the ruined city of Enugu.

I now know what the end of civilization is going to look like, thanks to that brief sojourn in Enugu. It will be populated by a handful of burocrats and aid workers going about their business as if nothing had happened – and opportunists. Our pilots were of that breed and Enugu was being run by them. Their tribal chief was a young Englishman who had sniffed us out by morning, announced very openly that while he was ostensibly a Red Cross driver he was also, in fact, a member of the ACTT with tax problems – a brother, ready to help out. He invited us to go for drinks at his house.

So far as I could tell, no one house in Enugu had everything working. If the electricity was on the water wasn't, if you had windows the door had gone missing, if the toilet worked there was no toilet roll, and so on.

Tony's pad was a rather elegant house where some rich colonial had once lived. Here little worked but a line of refrigerators and a row of the Red Cross nurses whose function appeared to be to open their doors and distribute largesse to an endless stream of visitors.

Like all opportunist feeders, Tony had got his priorities right and had looted all the surrounding houses for their fridges, which he had then wired up in lines and filled with food, booze and medicines.

As the primary source of exotic titbits, he was running an actual restaurant at the end of the world. The currency was barter. We did very well with our supply of English fags and tales of home and Tony plied us with an endless supply of beer, Pernod and Red Cross nurses who warned us, proprietorially, not to screw around with the black women because they were riddled with VD.

It was, in a strange, lovely, technicolour way, Armageddon, and I have ever since been convinced that the human race will not, as the pessimists suggest, vanish with a cry and a whimper. I think we will go out celebrating.

Dr Auguste Lindt arrived the following morning to prevent that happening immediately. The whole of Enugu stood by its bed and mentally saluted as this brisk, incredibly energetic 70-ish Swiss gnome flew in to check on the progress of his supply operation.

Drunks sobered under his patrician gaze, languid nurses stiffened to Florence Nightingales, Tony sat to attention behind the wheel of his newly-polished truck and I cried 'Action' much more loudly than was necessary.

Dr Lindt said 'Zergut!' and flew off to Geneva by way of Brussels, promising to be back that night with another squadron of aircraft. This is hardly an exaggeration. I was to learn over the next few days that it was unwise to let the august Lindt out of my sight if I wanted to make any sort of film. He had the most extraordinary capacity for air travel I have ever witnessed and one day literally did fly, unannounced, to Europe for a conference and was back in Enugu via Abidjan the following morning.

Tony had said something in his cups at the previous night's party that had seriously disturbed me.

'Total fuckin' waste of time and money, mate!'

'What is?'

'All this Red Cross bullshit. 'Part from the bloody canny Swiss that is. You tell me who's got the contract for all this flying?'

'You tell me?'

'Bloody Swissair, innit?'

'Somebody has to have the contract,' I pointed out.

'You tell me what for, mate?'

'To stop the Biafrans starving!'

'You can't.'

He had sobered suddenly. So had I.

'Is that right?' I demanded. 'This is all a big waste of time?'

'And money,' Tony nodded. 'Cept for the Swiss as I said.'

'That's not how it's perceived in Europe.'

'Perceived in Europe?' he mocked. 'Ask me where the perceived-in-Europe Volvo soup kitchens are – in the customs shed in Lagos where they'll stay until the war is over and somebody turns them into hamburger trucks. And it'll probably be done by a sharp little Biafran businessman. We're just making it hard for them.'

'I don't understand,' I said icily. What I actually meant was, had I projected myself into this hellhole for no good protestant-evangelical British documentary-maker reason? According to Tony I had, and by the end of the evening he had convinced me.

'The Biafrans can't win,' he pointed out. 'All Nigeria has of any value is its oil and they aren't going to let the Biafrans corner that. If you go up the hill behind here you can film the Nigerian army's crack unit, the Scorpion Battalion. They have tanks! They can come through here any time it takes their fancy. But what are they doing, they're sitting under the palm trees getting pissed while this place starves itself to death and we eke out the agony. All we're doing is putting off the evil moment.'

I woke up the following morning, smelt the seductive perfumes of the African dawn and rejected Tony's remarks as a boozer's gloom.

He had elected himself our official driver and we went with Dr Lindt to the Enugu hospital and filmed his inspection of the sad victims of civil conflict.

'Four of those lads blew themselves up trying to weld fins onto hand grenades for their home-made rocket launcher,' said Tony. 'Can you imagine – welding fins onto live grenades? Funny thing is it hurled such noisy, nasty missiles – because in the early days they had no fins – it sort of convinced the Scorpion battalion to hold back.'

'Fascinating,' I said waspishly. 'The hospital seemed very well run to me.'

'Right,' he agreed. 'And very clean and tidy, specially the outside which they painted with milk powder last week.'

'What!'

'Somebody forgot the mixing instructions and they thought it was whitewash. Things like that happen all the time. We've got about 300 tons of dried egg we don't know what to do with.'

'Why not?'

'Biafrans won't feed their kids eggs. They think it turns them into thieves. Somebody in Geneva didn't do his homework.'

'I don't believe any of it!'

We had stopped outside a big fenced compound. Dr Lindt was already striding down the well-ordered mountains of American grain and high-protein soup, Swiss milk powder, Swedish dried fish and, most bizarre of all in that climate but apparently very popular, British army blankets. We recorded an interesting conversation about nothing breaking through three layers of plastic bags no matter from how high it was dropped.

This I checked with Tony.

'Quite right,' he acknowledged. 'They've killed three people with them.'

'The air drops!'

'We're much better than Abdul, especially with the dried fish. Think of those bony edges!'

A week later, Tony swung open one of his fridge doors under instruction from a nurse and saved my sound recordist's life. We had been on the frontier filming the distant specks of the Scorpion Battalion when they appeared to make a move. By the time we had wrapped our equipment and worked our way back down the hill our Biafran driver had also spotted the Scorpions and made good his escape. We had a very arduous walk home through villages housing the ghosts of Buchenwald. All these skeletal people could spare was a little water, and by the time we reached Enugu Frank was in a very bad way with a mixture of heat exhaustion and diarrhoea. Tony's fridge provided sulphur tablets but Frank's condition quickly progressed to dysentery and we were advised to take him out as soon as we could.

Unfortunately, a spurt of activity by the Nigerian MiGs had temporarily grounded the transports. Dr Lindt offered seats in the light aircraft in which he would be travelling to Lagos for diplomatic talks about the airlift.

Somebody then pointed out that our presence in Nigeria/Biafra was illegal as we had flown in from Abidjan, and it was generally agreed that the officials at Lagos gave short shrift to illegal immigrants, especially those obviously sympathetic to the heroic Biafran stand.

'Then you will have not to exist,' Dr Lindt said calmly and quite seriously. 'We will file a flight plan for Abidjan for the plane, with a stop at the private side to drop me off. Then you just go on.'

And so we wafted illegally in and out of Nigeria at the height of the war by simply sliding down in our seats while the pilot spoke calmly to the tower and kept our two little engines running and Dr Lindt strode across the tarmac under a diversionary cloud of diplomatic immunity.

Sometimes it is wonderful just not to exist.

Back home and at the office I felt obliged to tell Bob Heller that the airlift was a farce.

'The series,' he pointed out coolly, 'is called *Man of the Month*. Dr Lindt sounds like the best one we've found.'

I reviewed the immense moment of relief I had felt when we took off from Lagos.

'Very much so,' I agreed, with feeling.

'So be it,' said Bob.

And so it was. The world did not get to hear of the success of the Red Cross's dried-fish bomb runs, the useless egg powder nor the chalky, milky walls of Enugu hospital. Ours was a story of human caring, not of extended genocide, and it was a moving success.

This was another story I had difficulty recounting to Annette and in any event she had silently – very silently – accepted my need for sleep after such trips.

She woke me about three days later.

'It's Mr Heller,' she said sweetly. 'He's just been telling me what a wonderful job you did in Biafra. So wonderful, apparently, he's chosen you to do another *Man of the Month*.'

'Where?' I whispered.

'They say Mexico,' she said, with very little interest.

Chapter Seven

This marked the beginning of a period in which Bob Heller set out to get full value from his investment - his gamble - in me. He started to pitch me into programmes with a speed and ferocity that reduced the arrival of the Seventies to a blur. For three years I averaged four one-hour documentaries a year, which must come close to a British record. Each of these was at a different location.

I went to Mexico for three weeks, travelling the length of that continent-sized country twice, to make a *Man of the Month* about Dr Norman Borlaug who was creating a green revolution in Asia with a new strain of short-stemmed wheat.

Dr Borlaug was another Dr Lindt, ever on the move, as active as an ant. His Mexican wheats (they grew huge heads, not stems and leaves) had doubled the crop that year in Pakistan, turning the country from a famine area to a wheat exporter.

The Pakistanis themselves were, however, reluctant to eat Borlaug's wheat because it was red and they were used to white chapattis. So I caught and filmed Dr Borlaug playing Dr Strangelove, rushing up and down Mexico - which is so big you have different seasons at the top and bottom of the country - selecting out strains for their whiteness. He had started this genetic change by subjecting red wheats to massive doses of radioactivity.

I came home and reported almost immediately to the Mansion House in the City of London, where the current Lord Mayor had agreed to be Man of the Month. We rode in the great gilded coach (almost the first sequence I ever shot for television which interested my children) and got coach-sick. This is apparently quite common and a great embarrassment for Lord Mayors who travel in the unsprung coach on the day of their investiture and are afterwards supposed to enjoy a rich celebratory meal.

Next to the coach, the meals themselves constitute the other great hazard to Lord Mayors, who have to survive something like a thousand of them during their year of office. These and a similar number of events, most of which involve a change of clothes, mean that the Lord Mayors (who are never young) run a gauntlet with heart attacks.

They do, admittedly, get an automatic knighthood. In my opinion they earn it.

Quite the nicest outing I had was the four weeks spent in Cheshire and Ireland making a film about one of England's richest aristocrats, Anne, Dowager Duchess of Westminster, and her love affair with a horse, a legendary chaser called Arkle.

At the time this seemed a rather peculiar choice for an investigative programme-maker of my ilk (for it was I who suggested it to Heller), although it did verge on natural history in which I still had a residual interest.

In fact the research revealed that the story had all the ingredients of a fairy story – poor horse makes good, the princess and the peasant, Cinderella – plus rich overtones of money, class, gambling and death. I got Heller to agree that there was something in it for everyone.

Arkle was an ugly, scarred Irish gelding who could run faster and jump higher than any horse in history, including the most legendary jumper ever, Golden Miller. In Ireland he was the national hero.

He won the top race open to him, the Cheltenham Gold Cup, three times in a row and then broke his leg. He was given the most intensive care any horse has ever received in the world, thanks to the Duchess's deep concern and bottomless purse, and now the foot was healed and Arkle was to attempt what no horse of his standing had ever done after such an accident – a comeback.

I went to see the Duchess on the great Westminster estate in Cheshire. She was living in quite a small house, lined with exquisite paintings of Westminster horses, the majority by Stubbs.

She was charming and funny and spoke in a voice as deep as a man's.

'They're going to think it's someone in drag when I first open my mouth,' she boomed. 'But I'm used to that.'

The idea of her taking part in a documentary about a horse was not something she would normally have contemplated and she was very nervous, but she loved Arkle dearly and she saw the programme as a way of recording his memory for posterity just as her ancestors had with Mr Stubbs.

We walked round the grounds through wonderful greenhouses, a huge classical covered riding school where the young Arkle had been schooled, across stone bridges where she still rode every morning, alongside the lake to a walled paddock where two little dark brown horses were running briskly around.

'If you want to film those you'll have to check with my people,' she warned. 'Being who they are, we're being pretty careful of them.'

The foals, it turned out, were the first progeny of some incredible stallion, now resident in America and worth millions. But money was something the Duchess did not talk about.

Nor, seemingly, did she think about it. Mostly she thought about horses, and one horse in particular, Arkle.

I learned the truth of this the hard way. We continued our walk with the Duchess's estate manager and I asked her how Arkle had come by his peculiar name.

'Oh, it's after our mountain in Scotland,' she said. 'Now that would make a very nice picture. There's a loch up there that we land on, under the mountain. What do you think about that?'

I was starting to agree, for it would have made a very nice opening sequence, when I picked up a tiny shake of the head from her manager. Later he explained: 'She goes up in a flying boat. It lands on the lake here and takes her on to Scotland.'

'But that would be a wonderful sight!'

'Not unless you're very rich, old boy. We can't get a flying boat any more in this country, but because the Duchess likes it so much we fly one in from Gibraltar. It's not necessary to go into the costs with her, but I don't think your budget would run to it.'

Instead we went with her to Ireland (where she happened to have yet another estate) to the little hill farm where Arkle was born. She was entirely at ease with the roughly-dressed ladies who ran the place and who sent a hairy colt or two a year to the sales at Balls Bridge in Dublin.

Arkle, then, was a nameless scruff but with an interesting pedigree. The hill ladies could not afford the best stallions so they mixed and matched on the basis of their encyclopaedic knowledge of Irish blood lines. But they did not expect to get much for the horse because he had cut his leg on a barbed wire fence, leaving a nasty scar.

The Duchess also knew her blood lines and once she had unravelled Arkle's ancestors and checked her conclusions with her trainer, Tom Draper, off they went to Balls Bridge and casually bought the scruffy colt for £1,000. The Irish thought that was a lot of money but, as they pointed out, the Duchess had more money than sense. Little did they know!

Over the next four years, until he fell and broke his leg, Arkle won more than £200,000 in prize money for the Duchess. This did not interest her a great deal – she was concerned only with the excitement of running the most famous and engaging horse in the world.

Arkle's rags-to-riches story began when the Duchess took him off to her grand horse school in Cheshire where he was gently led on a long rein and then broken to the saddle by experts.

There, in the nicest possible way, the Duchess fell in love with this elegant horse who seemed to thrive on human attention. This is not just sentimental talk, Arkle's jockey, Pat Taft, claimed that Arkle listened for the crowd on the final straight, put back his eyes, speeded up and jumped higher without any urging from his jockey. I ordered up the film of all three Cheltenham Gold Cups Arkle had won and ran them through an editing machine at a frame a time until we saw his ears go back. The sound track confirmed that that was indeed the moment when Arkle heard the crowd, and my examination of the finishes confirmed that he jumped higher over the last fences than he had previously.

The Duchess then took Arkle back to Tom Draper in Ireland where he had his own stable boy and the occasional bottle of Guinness.

'He was always a bit special,' Tom Draper told us, 'although at first, because he was not that good-looking a horse, it was hard to see why. I came to conclude that he had a good heart and liked to work.'

That, I realized, was typical racing-Irish.

Tom Draper, for example, admitted that he first tried to hold Arkle back, without explaining why. Maxie Cosgrove, Arkle's vet, would never give me a straight answer about Arkle's actual chances of winning races again even though the climax of my film depended upon it.

When we went to the little race tracks around Dublin to film young horses racing for the first time, just as Arkle had done, nobody would even hint at who they thought might win. It was always: 'Well, he's a goer,' 'He's worth an each-way bet,' when I knew damn well they knew better than that. I think it is something to do with the fact that the Irish are a nation of punters and don't talk to outsiders because it lowers the betting odds.

All this Irishness was of particular interest to me because my father had been born in County Cork. I quickly recognized some of his eccentric traits as part of ordinary daily life here, such as the way he wore his hat at an angle, his love of philosophizing, of long and often incomprehensible jokes, and the way men were openly and physically affectionate with each other as well as their women.

The Irish race-goers were a wonder for a film-maker. Every face seemingly hand-picked by Visconti, the crowds as noisy and intent as any from an Eisenstein epic, the children and the gypsies running the gambling games under the stands straight out of Fellini: the whole a Breughel canvas dropped out of time.

In his third race Arkle decided he had had enough of being held back.

'He just decided to go,' Pat grinned. 'There was nothing I could do about it without ruining his mouth. It was a bit embarrassing really, knowing that the Duchess and Mr Draper would be watching me through their glasses. But he kept going. We went out in front and we ended in front, with me having a free ride!'

And that's the way it was for three years. In Ireland he became a national hero. On his birthday, cards arrived by the sackload from all over the world, many of them simply addressed: 'Arkle, Ireland'. We found out that Arkle's local postman had composed a poem to him and we recorded it for posterity over a shot of the postman wobbling on his bicycle down an Irish lane to the Draper stables.

It was all lovely. Arkle was a wonder, the Duchess a smasher who didn't give a cuss for admitting to her deep fondness for this courageous and very personable horse, the Irish countryside was as green and misty and nostalgic as the songs sung about it; for the first time in my career I was having a thoroughly enjoyable time. I almost forgot I was in television.

But I was.

We were filming at a Hunt Ball social when my researcher came hurriedly across the room and suggested I eavesdrop on a conversation taking place between Maxie Cosgrove and Draper.

Ten minutes later I knew that Arkle would never enjoy another race-track; Cosgrove had decided that although the leg appeared to have healed well, it was too much of a risk for all of them to run Arkle, the national idol, if there was even a chance he might injure himself.

This is a rather dramatic example of the sword of Damocles that hangs over every documentary director's head. Tiny incidents over which he has no control, minor accidents, or in this case a single decision in which I had no say, can completely ruin the complex structure of a film. I took this one in very bad grace and would have exposed what I saw as arrant self-interest, but the Duchess talked me out of it.

It was a decision to be accepted gracefully, she said firmly. Cosgrove alone had the knowledge to issue Arkle with a clean bill of health and if he had doubts, for whatever reason, Arkle would stay in retirement on the Duchess's Irish estate, living out the rest of his days in luxury. She reminded me that she had always refused to allow Arkle to be entered in the Grand National in case he fell and hurt himself.

And so my most cinematic film to date ended with Arkle bouncing around a field to Elgar's *Pomp and Circumstance* overture (borrowed from Ken Russell's film of Elgar on his pony) but it was the best I could do under the circumstances and we had lots of letters from the public saying that the film had been beautiful and made them cry. It made me cry too.

I made a quick biographical film of the South African coloured cricketer Basil D'Oliveira, which established Basil so clearly as a nice, homely, cheerful, ordinary sort of bloke that he became almost invisible among all the other nice cricketing blokes. You really had to watch the film hard to keep him in mind, and frankly the film was not worth watching that hard. Basil's invisibility did demonstrate quite powerfully how stupid the South Africans were to ban him from playing against whites at home, but we all knew that anyway.

Young women in the early Seventies were desperately conscious of the shapes of their bodies because, in this hippie era of liberation and bra-burning, it was the in thing to put them on display a lot. An obsession with slimness appeared to be creating its own disease, anorexia nervosa, and Bob sent me to the Atkinson Morley Hospital to find out how you got it.

The finished film was a cracker, but hardly suitable for transmission on a popular channel like ITV. We discovered that this so-called slimming disease had little to do with slimming but was a nightmare mental condition, usually associated with a disturbed family background, which could cause teenage girls to literally delay their maturity (their periods stopped) and, in extremis, starve themselves to death.

The girls looked like the living dead and behaved as if they had been taken over by zombies. The thing within actually lied to its victims about body size; we filmed the girls accurately judging wooden blocks, then over-estimating their own bust and waist sizes but as much as 100%.

These zombies then destroyed their families, because looking after an anorexic girl was a nightmare. They would eat and then sneak off to the toilet to vomit. One distraught mother we interviewed revealed that he had only discovered her daughter was deliberately vomiting after every meal by putting a tracer dye secretly under the toilet rim.

The Atkinson Morley people were grimly pragmatic about their patients, literally only admitting them when they were at death's door, because only then would a girl believe she was desperately ill and accept treatment. The girls were rarely completely cured. Moreover, the relapse was even more bizarre than the original condition – girls would binge to excess the moment they felt they had started to lose weight, and the whole wretched cycle would start all over again.

Bob Heller liked the film for its content but rightly thought it excessively grim and it was transmitted rather late at night. The film later found a more useful role as a teaching aid. I went home and made my own children's meal-times a misery for several months, insisting they finish every last baked bean and fish-finger crumb.

Bernard Levin and I were then teamed up by Heller to make a

documentary called *The Snooper Society*. The idea was triggered by government moves to centralize information on computers and we set out to show that a huge amount of information was being routinely and gratuitously collected on every one of us.

The programme was intended to be deadly serious, but Bernard kept finding himself in very funny situations with members of the public who obviously did not feel the issue was that alarming.

'Do you know how many public officials have the right to enter your home without your permission?' he asked in a series of interviews we did in the street (known in television as 'vox-pops')

'No dear – you're Bernard Levin aren't you – are we on television?'

Bernard looked exasperatedly over his shoulder (just to check that four technicians, their lights, cameras and microphones, a production assistant and the director had not sneaked off for a cup of coffee) before listing the many officials who had these rights under British law.

If he was lucky, some surprise was expressed at the numbers, but our subjects mostly wanted to know when the programme would be shown.

Bernard decided to investigate this complacency. Were the proposed government moves based on a realization that the British public had been conditioned to accept official snooping? The next time we went out he decided to ask ever more personal questions until the interviewee refused to answer.

Except that nobody refused!

The more expansive subjects (and admittedly we mentioned no names) delighted in revealing intimate details of sexual activity, numbers of lovers, frequency of affairs, sexual preferences, proud admissions of asexuality, confessions of bisexuality – everything and anything. We could find no real limits and Bernard invariably was the first to call it off, too embarrassed to continue.

I don't know whether *The Snooper Society* had any deterrent effect on the government's plans for increased electronic surveillance of the British public – I suspect it might have had exactly the opposite effect – but it was very revealing about the public's attitude to television.

I considered it further confirmation of the fact that people don't really see television as part of the world they live in. If you found yourself in the unreal setting of a television vox-pop with the famous Bernard Levin it was alright to talk about almost anything. Other people, perhaps watching with you, would understand that it was 'on television'.

In fact we had accidentally discovered a rich vein of television material which others (most successfully Esther Rantzen) have mined for whole programmes, leading to popular long-running series. I am not very keen on this kind of television which often relies on people making fools of themselves, and I am confused by its popularity.

I suppose on your side of the screen it all looks like good fun. You would be surprised how much deadpan seriousness is applied on our side to getting the best of the laughs.

While Bob Heller was giving me lots to do, it was also evident that he did not want me going too far afield while I was acquiring this experience.

This was fine by me. Annette was better and delighted with her new baby, Victoria, and a miracle had happened at tumbledown Bettridge Road.

Like a long-neglected painting, a charming little Victorian villa had started to push its way through the disgusting pall of neglect to which the house had been subjected over the last century.

We had decided to take the house back in time to as close as we could get it to the original. So the elegant stair rods were freed of their hardboard coverings and sanded down to the original glowing wood. The ornate cornices in the ceilings were carefully repointed and picked out in white. Fine decorated cast iron fireplaces sprung from behind sheets of asbestos-mounting hideous electric fires that had been nailed into the marble surrounds. We tore up mock parquet floors and found the original boards ready to be sanded and sealed to golden perfection.

Annette discovered that Sandersons still sold Willian Morris wallpapers, and in the little alleys all around us in Fulham and over the river off the Putney embankment there were shops full of brass gas fittings, iron pub tables and restorable Victorian furniture, all looking for a home as desperately as our revitalized house was looking for them.

Nowadays to do up an old house (especially your first house) is the accepted way to start on the ladder of property ownership, but in the Fulham of the Seventies we were pioneering. Young couples who did not want to commute from the new housing estates springing up in Kent and Sussex suddenly realized what could be done with the little redbrick houses which formed a great belt of neglect round central London. Property prices reflect that situation. We paid £7,000 for a house that would now sell for £300,000, and that is just twenty years ago.

In a way we rescued residential London because the town planning rubric of the time was demolition and modernization. We got in just ahead of the architects in love with their own design skills, concrete and the high-rise block. There are still a few discolouring monuments to this near-disaster rising over the restored Victorian terraces of Fulham, but thankfully no new ones.

I was so inspired by what we had achieved I became slightly

addicted to restoration and kept my eyes and ears open for other, grander, houses. Just a few months after Bettridge Road could be regarded as finished, I saw an advertisement in a local paper for a house with a garden actually leading down to the Thames.

This was a Victorian mansion. It had a huge crack in the wall joining it to its neighbour, the roof looked dicky and there were places where the rising damp met the lowering damp. Just the job!

The Nixons came and looked at it, gasped at the great brown surge of the Thames roaring by at eight knots at the bottom of the narrow garden, and wondered whether it was quite the place to be bringing up three lively little girls. But they got quite excited when they viewed the acres of walls inside, every inch of which was in need of a new coat of paint.

'Can you actually afford it?' Brenda queried.

'No'. We still had absolutely no capital at all and it was four times the price we had paid for Betteridge Road, with a lot to be spent on so huge a restoration.

But I loved the house, or more particularly, the river. It was like living with a constantly changing world at the bottom of your garden. When the tide was low great shiny chocolate banks of mud ran down to a narrow grey-green stream in which a line of pleasure craft bobbed like ducks. When the tide was full, especially at the solstices, the water was a wide steel-grey mirror reflecting the movements of the sky. In bad weather, especially in winter, it was a wild spume-flecked inland sea.

And these day-time views were ordinary compared to the wonder of the night. For an hour or so at every high tide the river was completely still and on clear nights it rapidly filled with the reflections of stars, the lights of the tall houses of Deodar Road, and the massed illuminations of the several blocks of flats around the Hurlingham Club on the north side.

Great Thames barges surged up and down the flood, police boats slid by like water beetles, and in the summer big pleasure launches commuted between Putney Pier and Hampton Court, spilling laughter and dance music.

Moreover, Deodar Road was a well-established artistic community. Roy Plomley, presenter of *Desert Island Discs,* the most famous show on the radio, lived two doors away, the great glass windows of the Australian artist Sidney Nolan's studio shone a few houses beyond that, and it was rumoured that Edna O'Brien had written *August Is a Wicked Month* in a house down the end of the road. I bought a copy and was delighted to find the heroine sitting in the equivalent of our front garden.

The only drawback seemed to be the real chance of the children drowning. I consulted the man next door whom I had seen playing boules with a boy and girl of about my children's age.

'Well,' he said. 'There are several schools of thought. When people first move in they always put up a fence. I put up a fence until I spotted my son Stevie climbing it. Fences are a terrible temptation. And they're not really to be trusted unless you put up something that would suit Alcatraz, which rather spoils the view. The river's only there half the time because of the tides and they won't get hurt falling into the mud. But the real answer to your question is that they seem to know – we haven't had any fatalities in the road all the time we've lived here.

We put up a fence anyway. It came down when Victoria was no longer a toddler and the elder girls found a hole in the fence and played with Stevie in his unfenced garden, never going near the great surging river. I think its power impressed even them.

And it came to pass that God wanted us to have the house anyway. We put Bettridge Road on the market in the knowledge that only a 500% profit would allow us to move to the river. It sold at that outlandish price within the month to an American lady who admired the structural work but wondered how we could live with such old fashioned wall-paper.

We moved into the new house in the company of the builders. There had been a storm the previous night and when the removers carried in the first pieces of furniture we found a considerable pool of water in the sitting room. It had made its way there via four of the bedrooms and when the builder inspected he announced that the back of the roof would have to come off right away if we didn't want the ceilings falling in next time it rained.

Not many weeks later the rest of my family decided to leave Central Africa. I may even have contributed to the decision with my over-enthusiastic descriptions of our new six-bedroomed house.

The first to arrive was my indomitable mother Edith, who had just become an old-age pensioner. Edith had very reluctantly accepted that war-torn Rhodesia was perhaps not the ideal place for a single woman to be living on her own protected only by her man-eating dachshund.

In fact this suggestion of a loss of nerve is not quite fair. My mother, who took the decision that we should drive overland to Africa after the war, was of the opinion that 'her' Boys would soon come to their senses. She appeared to regard the increasingly-murderous guerilla war raging all around her as a rather dirty by-election.

But her position worried her devoted sister Ada in Brighton, and Ada put me under great pressure to bring Edith 'home', promising her a room in her house and a job as a 'Country Cousin'. Country Cousins looked after rich people's houses when they were away, or very old rich people who could not look after themselves. Several of Ada's widowed friends were Country Cousins.

With considerable doubts I agreed that Edith should be extricated from hot, violent, socially cohesive Africa where the frightened whites found that a party a night helped keep the panic at bay, and returned to the bosom of her family, chilly though she might find it.

Edith hated being a Country Cousin. And Brighton bored her to death.

'Being around those old people is so sad,' she told me gloomily, ashamed that she was letting Ada down. 'It's like visiting the future and living with your old age.'

As for the home in Brighton, she could not get over how much television she was supposed to watch.

'They watch it every night,' Edith said, shocked. 'That's what you do every night. Watch television, have supper usually in front of it, then go to bed!'

'Don't you like the television? It's probably the best in the world.'

'It's very nice,' she agreed. 'But I don't want to spend what little time I've got left inside a television set. I want to spend it with people, or outside.' My mother, who often gives the impression of being naive, is not. A life spent close to the wilderness had at least taught her the difference between television images and real life.

So she came to live with us at Deodar Road, which was always in need of cleaning, and soon forgot the horrors of being a Country Cousin when she found three little granddaughters who weren't seeing that much of their father and, in her opinion, of their mother either. At that time the only habitable room in the house was the basement which, equipped with a Baby Belling stove, was also in service as the kitchen since the crack in the party wall had necessitated closing the real kitchen.

Edith, pointing out that she had cooked on a couple of Primus stoves all the way out to Africa, took over the cooking as well.

With my mother installed, my brother Peter arrived from Africa with his wife and young daughter. I was genuinely relieved to see him because he could easily have been killed in the guerilla war. He had decided to give England a try bearing in mind how well I had made out. He was a little surprised at the condition of the house and became rather quickly depressed with both the weather and the wages he was offered. He spent a lot of time at home and started to talk wistfully about Africa. A nostalgic glow lit up round my mother like a halo and even I felt the nostalgic pull of a distant sun. Only Annette's disapproving silences kept us from becoming When-We's.

Annette spent a lot of her time in the garden, or out shopping, or just plain out. I was fine, I just went to work.

That autumn, just as the air through the crack in the party wall was turning icy, June Peacock, Heller's secretary, phoned me to say I was wanted in the office in a hurry.

'Bring your passport,' June said. 'So that I can get started on the visas.'

'Where is it this time?'

'Ghana,' she said. 'There's been a coup . . . alright?'

'Of course,' I said, delighted.

'Are there any other directors in that office who are married with young children?' Annette asked when I told her of my good fortune.

'Of course,' I said, but when I thought about it properly I realized that most of my colleagues were either single or divorced.

The point of her question was not entirely lost on me. I looked at my children, munching happily away around the breakfast table, but did not see any signs of deprivation. In fact they were living a very full family life with their grannie, auntie, uncle and cousin in residence.

Admittedly I had noticed that when I returned from a trip they greeted me in much the same way as they would, say, my best friend Brian when he occasionally dropped in to borrow a paint brush – familiar, but a little shy.

I always made a great point of bringing them lots of presents although it was not always possible to find suitable ones in some of the places I went to. The tree-bark hats, phallic-worship dolls and devil masks that, for example, were all I could find in Biafra, were not a great success.

'We wouldn't have all this if I didn't work,' I reminded Annette. She followed my gesture and smiled grimly. I was pointing at the pneumatic drill which the builders would soon be using on our new kitchen floor, the planning officer having decided that it needed to be lowered by six inches to comply with building regulations.

'I shall have to remember that,' she said seriously.

Chapter Eight

Ghana! The Gold Coast – the last great African civilization – Benin gold and brass sculpture, the inspiration of Picasso and Dali–Kwame Nkrumah, who invented the African revolution and was the first of my black heroes to throw off the yoke of colonialism and lead his country out of the British Empire to freedom and independence. Also the first victim of neo-colonialism just as he had warned in his monumental *Studies in Neo-Colonialism*, toppled by what all my liberal friends believed to be a CIA-inspired coup.

I couldn't wait to feel the heat of the place and savour those singular African smells – wood smoke, raw concrete and the tang of the open drains.

'Nkrumah?' I said enthusiastically to Bob Heller when I burst into his office. 'Now he really does deserve to be on *Man of the Month*.'

'We should be so lucky,' he grunted. 'Nkrumah's hiding somewhere in China. You're going for the man who led the coup, this Afrifa character. He's supposed to be in his twenties and it seems he's taken over the country with 600 men and a couple of armoured cars. What does he think he's doing?'

My disappointment was bitter.

'Is he worth it?'

In fact, I did not have much choice. I was a staff director and Heller's *Man of the Month* was in serious trouble. It had been a brave concept, based on Bob's confidence that his young team of directors and cameramen could travel the world fast enough to bring home a new genre of documentary that expanded on the news and presented men and women actually making history.

The problem was timing. We simply could not get to our subjects, film them, and edit the material, while they were still topical. The series started out well. My film with Dr Lindt went out while the Biafran War was still in progress (although the Red Cross supply operation had been given up) and a number of others had the feeling of real topicality that Heller was hoping for.

But as the year wound on we grew ever further behind until, around Christmas, I met a colleague, Alex Valentine, wringing his hands in the editing corridor at Elstree studios and I had no difficulty guessing the cause.

'Man of the Month, Alex?'

'Right,' he acknowledged. 'There's talk of putting out my film with Harry Wheatcroft next month because everything else is so far behind.'

'The champion rose grower – in winter!'

'Exactly'

Bob was waiting for my reaction to the Afrifa idea. 'Don't you think I should go out and recce this one.' I implored him. 'We don't know anything about Afrifa. Think of all those madmen who took over in the Congo when I was there. Did you ever hear about Albert Kalongi, the Prime Minister of Kasai Province? He was accused of eating his entire Cabinet!'

'Afrifa was educated at Sandhurst,' Heller said, shortly. 'And you didn't need to do a recce for *The Animal War* as I recall. I like you to do your thinking on your feet, that's the only way *Man of the Month* can work. I see it all the time, people losing their spontaneity, their documentary-making instincts, after making a couple of good films. The longer you wait the harder it will get.' And he reminded me that I was his Africa expert.

Ghana was just perfect. It was hot and sweaty, cheerful and disgusting. After the po-faced Hausa of Nigeria, who had provoked my first-ever racial hatred, the jolly Ghanaians were a delight and their capital city, Accra, was lively and exciting.

We checked into the best hotel in town, for these were the days when the ACCT was an all-powerful trade union and its members were entitled by the National Agreement to stay in the best accommodation available.

The hotel had a front desk staffed by smiling receptionists who handed each of us a coarse blanket, a toilet roll, half a bar of soap and a light bulb. Africa's new dawn, which would soon rise in pink penury over all the newly-independent African states, had already arrived in Ghana.

Everywhere I turned I found sad evidence of that. Shortly before Nkrumah had been deposed he had built two monuments to his new status as the father of Pan-Africanism, a great arch spanning a fine new highway and a teak-lined skyscraper complete with air-conditioning for the meetings he planned to create a United States of Africa. A jolly Ghanaian taxi driver took me out to see the Freedom Arch. It was smaller than I had expected but non the less spectacular.

My driver then did a U-turn because the highway finished at the Freedom Arch.

The Pan-African skyscraper was a vast mausoleum that the city of Accra had never dared to commission because, we were told, the air conditioning units would have overloaded the city's power supply. Moreover, it was claimed that the building had not been properly underpinned and by the time I went to see it, it was sinking back into Africa, unused.

Never mind. I had been dancing that night at one of the many 'Hi-Life' joints with a happy 'hostess'. These young ladies of the night had beats in the foyer which they probably rented from the reception staff and were quite content just to go dancing for a few pounds 'dash' and drinks. This was well before AIDS but to engage in anything more exotic in this hot armpit of Africa had been unwise for a long time.

Ghanaian 'Hi-Life' was, at that time, simply a dance, a wonderful escape from faceless, and this case fittings-less, hotel rooms.

It was quite hard to do the Hi-Life, especially the political ones extolling the virtues of the Minister of Information, but when I finally mastered steps which are danced just slightly off the beat, my partner took me out to the market and bought me a quite expensive pair of dancing slippers. They had soles made of recycled car tyres but the tops were red hand-painted leather. If I had stayed long enough to get really proficient, my dancing partner would have urged me to buy a silk koti-cloth man's dance skirt which all the hotshot Hi-Lifer's wore because of the way they swirled out, heavy and slow, in the turns. I never got that good. And it was soon time to go to work.

Jolly Ghanaian information attachés informed me that President Afrifa would ride his white stallion across the sands in front of his castle that morning, just for our cameras. He had also decided to go on a state visit to Togo for our benefit, and did we have any use for the Army?

'Castle?' I queried.

'The Danish castle,' they said. 'The President lives in the Danish castle.'

'And he rides a white stallion?'

'Every morning,' they smiled. 'He learned to ride at Sandhurst.'

'And a State visit to Togo?' I said, the feeling that this was some weird Disney fantasy receding in the face of their indefatigable niceness.

'The President has to buy soap.'

My defensive shield clamped back in place.

'And I'm to have the use of the Army,' I said sarcastically.

'They will do manoeuvres for you. The President as you know is a military man.'

'You're sure about all this.'

'Yes, sir,' they laughed, delightedly. 'We promise.'

And they did not turn into Munchkins.

Afrifa, now self-styled Brigadier, mounted his white charger and rode beneath the walls of the fort which a disorientated Danish expedition had built in a half-hearted attempt to get into the slave trade. The pictures, backlit against the tropical, coconut tree-etched surf, were stunning.

The 5th Battalion of the Ghanaian army staged a mock guerilla war for our cameras, featuring Afrifa in Fidel Castro camouflage directing an assault on thin air from the back of the armoured troop carrier he had used for his coup.

And we went to Togo by helicopter to buy soap. This ultimate farce was preceded by one of my making. On a trial run while peering out of a door kept open to allow me to evaluate the shot, I fell out of the Presidential helicopter into the sea. The drop was later calculated at about 40 feet and I stunned myself entering the water. When I surfaced I had no recollection of where I was or how I had got there. I was quickly rescued by fishermen and returned to the beach where the jolly Ghanaian crew had landed and were just managing to suppress their mirth.

The state visit made more wonderful pictures, not least Afrifa refusing to walk between the double ranks of the Togo State Guard after he had considered their raised swords. They were dressed like extras in a Beau Geste movie (Togo was a former French colony) but not one of them had a complete uniform.

He took about three hours buying his soap, which he could not buy in Ghana because of the import restrictions he had imposed, and then we went home. I warmed to Afrifa when he grinned at me in the helicopter and asked if I was recovered from my fall (as if it had been from bed) and refused to let his aides relieve him of the burden of his big plastic bag of soap.

For a day or two thereafter I was blissfully happy and I allowed the crew to spend their time on the beach while we waited for Afrifa to decide when he would do his interviews.

Three days went by.

I went to the Ministry of Information.

'I am scheduled to leave in three days time.' I began.

'Yes?'

'We have to interview Brigadier Afrifa. This a film about his life.'

'Have you not got enough film?'

'More than enough background, thank you. We just have to do the interviews. It is very simple. He can do them wherever he feels most comfortable.'

Another day went by and I started to panic.

The jolly information officers explained the problem. Afrifa did not like doing interviews.

'Why not?' I shrieked. 'There can't be a programme without interviews!'

'He believes his English is not very good. He does not want to appear uneducated before the British people. He is very happy for you to tell them about his life, sir.'

It was a perfectly reasonable explanation; a single day's proper research would have revealed it. But this was television, where the sharks drown if they stop swimming.

'Tell the President this programme will never see the light of day unless he does an interview.' I bullied. 'I'll help him with the English. We'll rehearse every word if necessary.'

And so we did. Afrifa became my first (and by no means my last) glove-puppet subject.

I would ask him a question and he would give me an answer in his mission English. We would then discuss and improve the words and some of the thoughts, and record it in short sections.

Sometimes a complete sentence took five takes, but eventually we had his life story in the can. Does it matter that the young Brigadier Afrifa who was removed by the next coup is remembered as coherent when in fact he was totally out of his depth, or (as one of my more observant friends noted) his views on Africa had a lot in common with my own?

Not to a custard shark; it's just straightforward thinking on your feet.

Bob Heller smelt something of a rat, I think, but he was still stuck with the problem of rose-growers in February. Brigadier Afrifa was quickly transmitted and shortly thereafter the entire *Man of the Month* series was dropped. Indeed Bob Heller never again committed himself to a long thematic documentary series, nor, to my knowledge, has anyone else on British television. The nearest we come to it now is series with generic titles like *Viewpoint* and *First Tuesday* which are kept as vague as possible to allow them to accommodate anything.

I came home with a very nice suntan and gave my girls three African drums. They beat them lustily at dawn the following morning, reminding me very pleasantly of the lush Ashanti country where they had been made. Annette reminded me that our neighbours might not feel the same way about the Ashanti country and I went upstairs to suggest a postponement of the concert until after breakfast.

The floor of their bedroom was dusted with fine sawdust in which large African borers were waking up and heading purposefully for the chinks in the floorboards. So I had to take the drums back from the children and burn them in the garden, an act which produced a certain coolness.

Annette's coolish mood I put down to the fact that the builders had not seen fit to put in an appearance during my absence. I decided it would be appropriate for me to work in England for a while.

Turning over films at the pace Bob Heller had been demanding, I had not had the time to develop the luxury of a theme to my work. But whenever the opportunity arose (that is, whenever I was given the chance to choose the subject rather than direct an idea of Heller's) I almost invariably reverted to the simple topic that obsessed me personally - what did it take to live happily in Britain, especially if you had been raised somewhere else.

Kangaroo Valley had sold well abroad and, apart from 'Animal War' was my most successful film to date. I persuaded Bob Heller to let me do a film along similar lines about the Chinese community in Britain, which we called *The Lion and The Dragon*.

The Lion and The Dragon taught me the cardinal rule of documentary film-making - come what may, you hold your nerve and film the actual story unfolding before you on location, rather than the story as you hoped it would be.

We hired a jovial, rotund expert of Mandarin origin, Eric Low, to bustle around London's Soho district, Limehouse in the East End, and the several squalid streets housing Liverpool's Chinese ghetto, and prepared a list of locations representative of the inscrutable oriental lifestyle.

This eventual list read something like: Peking Palace, The Good Friends Restaurant, The House of Duck, the home of Mr and Mrs Lo Fung, owner of the China Emporium, and so on - it was a restaurant guide!

'Eric' I said sternly. 'This is not to be a film about your favourite Chinese restaurants.'

'Not my favourites, Lobin, just where all the action is. You have to understand that the Chinese community in Britain is almost entirely connected with restaurants and laundries. When Mao took over in China, many people at the embassy here decided not to go back to his communist country. They started restaurants and laundries.'

'The ambassador took in washing?'

'I think he had a restaurant, but his wife would probably have had to take in washing in the early days.'

'Well that's an unusual way to start,' I agreed. 'Provided we very rapidly move on to the Tongs, opium dens, gambling and that sort of thing.'

'Fine Lobin - but it does all go in the restaurants.'

I don't know to this day whether the lovely, inscrutable Eric went back to his friends and told them that the only way they were going to get their restaurants on television was to infer they were a cover for these activities, but that's certainly how it looked.

For example, we filmed our interviews about the utter addiction the Chinese have for every form of gambling in a restaurant.

'This very restaurant changed hands over a game of cards, Lobin,' Eric justified. 'The owner is now a waiter – interview him.' The waiter refused to be interviewed.

'Too much face to be lost, Lobin,' Eric said.

'What about the new owner?'

'Bad luck to boast of your luck, Lobin.'

We were told how the labour market was still controlled by the Tongs from Hong Kong and that some Chinese workers lived in incredibly poor conditions and were all but slave labour. To substantiate this Eric told us of an address where these workers were sleeping in hammocks slung between roof rafters. It was a restaurant in Limehouse.

Deciding that if I could not beat them I might as well join them, we filmed the two best sequences of the film openly in restaurants, the Luan Fung in Gerrard Street, where deft chefs steamed piles of delicate, delicious dumplings in little round baskets. Eric explained that the Chinese do not eat lunch as such. The dumpling meal was 'small chow' – a heavy elevenses – and then there was a big meal at night.

'What about breakfast?' I asked.

'There is no breakfast, the people are too poor.'

'Just a cup of tea?'

'Tea – the infusion – is believed to have been an accident. The peasants began the day with a bowl of hot water, and someone is assumed to have thrown a few leaves in to make the steam more aromatic.'

Eric also claimed that there was a Chinese legend that cooking actually began in China when a primitive man ate a wild pig that had died in a forest fire.

We filmed them preparing suckling pig at the Richmond Rendezvous where I was genuinely intrigued to discover that these crisp-skin delicacies never see an oven, but take a whole day of basting in alternate douches of boiling oil and water.

I had become genuinely interest in the food and the delicate attention to detail. Raymond said there were three degrees of judgment – appearance, texture and taste – applied to every dish and that in old China cooking had been regarded as an art form as advanced as painting and pottery. The Forbidden City, he claimed, had once been surrounded by tiny restaurants each run by a chef who had delighted the Emperor with a single dish.

We sampled 1000-year-old eggs, fishes' eyes, snippets of offal that I would never normally have sampled, seaweed, sea slugs, soup of shark fins and bird's nests – a kaleidoscope of the inedible, and every scrap of it entirely delicious.

'They seem to be able to make everything taste marvellous,' I observed. 'Is that the secret of Chinese cooking?'

'It is the secret of Chinese,' Eric observed darkly. 'Poverty and fecundity have forced us to be able to cook and eat anything. When the rest of the human race has become extinct, we, the greatest of opportunistic feeders, will linger on.'

'This,' said Heller 'is definitely turning into a film about Chinese restaurants.'

'Don't you like the line about the world's greatest opportunistic feeders?'

But he was not to be mollified.

'He obviously hasn't worked for television much,' Bob said enigmatically. 'I think maybe you should hire a new researcher.'

I heeded Heller's warning and went to Liverpool on my own to interview a vicar who had served the Chinese community there all his long life.

'They have integrated very well,' I observed. 'It is one of the few ethnic groups that never cause a breath of trouble, in fact they could be a model for the black immigrant communities.'

'The majority of them have not integrated at all,' the vicar said gloomily. 'They have no intention of integrating, they actively prefer their children not to become integrated, and the reason they don't protest about their status is because they regard themselves as visitors.'

My mouth had fallen open.

'We've not experienced any of that!'

'That's because you are an inferior white monkey. No-one would even think of taking you into their confidence.'

'I beg your pardon!'

'You are hairy and you smell.'

'Really!'

He smiled his polite weary smile. 'It is all right, I have been here so long I am used to you. Check with our local travel agents,' he challenged. 'You will find that anyone who can afford it sends their children back to Hong Kong to be educated lest they become hairy, smelly white monkeys.'

The vicar was old and had grown rather cynical. He confessed that he had made very few lasting converts and I wondered whether this was behind the vehemence of his condemnation of a race apart. But we did actually follow through his suggestion about talking to local travel agents, and as a result were able to film Liverpool-Chinese children leaving England for schooling in Hong Kong.

The idea began to grow on me that there might even be a community-wide conspiracy directed against the film when it became clear that no-one was going to break ranks and support the vicar, even though they must have known through Eric that I had filmed the children being sent home for re-lacquering.

Film what is there.

I told Heller I was shifting my editorial line to the concept that the 'special' place the Chinese had in British society was based entirely on their own perception of themselves as culturally special. Their restaurants were like time-gates between the cultures as well as being trading posts in the new territories.

I tried this theory on Eric and, ever-obliging, he agreed, 'The food they serve reflects just what you're saying.'

'Eric, just for a moment can we get off the subject of food!'

'Truly, Lobin,' he insisted. 'The western favourites like spare ribs and chop suey do not actually exist in Chinese cuisine. They were invented for the western palate, in America probably.'

'But this is very good material, Eric. I'd like to reflect that innate alienness in the film, in fact it is what the film is now about. Can you get some of your friends to tell us why they think Chinese culture is superior?'

'I know just the person,' he smiled. 'Mr Long Ho Peng of the Butterfly Bistro in Brixton was beaten very badly by young blacks just a few weeks ago on his way to buy provisions and will speak very emphatically on the subject.'

'Pekinese?' I asked casually.

'No, Cantonese.' he responded enthusiastically. 'If we hurry we will still be time for the morning dumplings . . .'

The Lion and The Dragon was, the in end, not a bad film. No-one from the Chinese community complained at my suggestion that they seemed to regard themselves as a race, or certainly a culture, apart; indeed I was soon afterwards invited to the best meal of my life, the New Years's Feast at the Luan Fung in Gerrard Street consisting of at least twenty courses.

It sold well in America, where there is a large Chinese community, at a time when foreign sales had just started to become a consideration for the British documentary-maker. Previously the 'licence to print money' had enabled us to produce in splendid isolation. Indeed, there was a school of thought which decried co-productions with America because British and US television were so intellectually incompatible; the intellect being all on our side, of course.

For me, the film changed my rather naive views on racial mixing. Until this time I had assumed that racial superiority was an arrogance practised by whites. The Chinese in Britain had quietly, and very politely, demonstrated that ethnic pride (which I think is the same thing) exists in all races.

I quietly mourned this further fading of my idealistic dream of a homogeneous world shared by a honey-coloured race of brothers and sisters, and was very surprised to discover that it had disturbed Bob Heller as well.

'You've pin-pointed a ghetto I never knew existed,' he mused. 'How many more of them are there?'

This was not just esoteric speculation. These were the early Seventies and several prophets of doom had started to voice bloody warnings of a British race war as the price of two decades of unrestricted immigration.

It was an area in which I had some expertise and a considerable personal interest.

Some days later I slipped some notes, headed by a single name, under Heller's nose.

'My God,' he said, genuinely shocked. 'Is he still alive?'

'And quite active,' I promised.

The name was Sir Oswald Mosley.

Chapter Nine

For those under forty in whom the name 'Mosley' does not strike immediate alarm (or know of it simply as a bus-stop near Manchester), I should explain that this was the Sir Oswald who, legend has it, was ready to do Hitler's work after a Nazi conquest of Britain.

Mosley was the last living apostle of a European master race. He was, I think, rescued from the dreadful fates that overtook his peer group (Mussolini and the Hitler gang) by Winston Churchill who locked him up soon after the war started and thus prevented any excesses of which he might have been capable.

Most of the public would have shared Bob Heller's conviction that he was dead. But Mosley had maintained a very low profile since the war, living rather well in a kind of voluntary exile in France.

All this I discovered from an unlikely source.

I had been maintaining loose contacts with the When We's of Wimbledon as a potential source of African story material. For no apparent reason it became noticeable that the very right-wing When We's appeared to be acquiring a new lease of life through an organization called the League of Empire Loyalists.

The league had been around for many years and had maintained active branches in white-supremacist colonial territories. Thankfully, however, it appeared to have been dying slowly with the Empire to which it professed loyalty. Now, in the foetid atmosphere of a Britain growing worried by the number of blacks it had let in to keep its hospitals, railways and roads running, the league was rising from the dead.

There is nothing a When We likes so much as to say, 'I told you so,' and the right-wing Rhodesian When We's saw the league as the perfect platform from which to say it. Evangelical When We's distributed promotional literature for the league, some of which reached me. This literature inferred that the league was just one of a network of organizations trying to Keep Britain Great which, in this context, actually meant white.

One of the fringe organizations mentioned to me by the When We's was a mysterious outfit called The Mosley Secretariat. A call to the secretariat revealed that it did indeed promote the politics of the infamous Sir Oswald Mosley and confirmed that he was alive and well - and very welcoming to the press - at his chateau near Paris.

So as well as the name of Mosley that I slipped under Bob Heller's nose I was also able to present notes suggesting that there could be a whole right-wing scenario for the exploitation of British racial fears.

'They're the idiot fringe,' he protested. 'There can be no real racial problem in this country unless people go out and make one, the numbers are too small.'

'The opinion polls are showing real support for people like Enoch Powell,' I pointed out.

'Is Powell involved in this?'

'No.'

'Well Powell is a different number, a one-man band of peculiar potency. Anyway I think Mosley would make a good biographical piece on his own. What's exile done to a political animal like him? (obviously a subject of interest to this equally political American exile). If you find evidence, and I *mean* evidence, of anything more ominous then we can shift the focus.' I was placed under injunction to consult at every step along the way.

Mosley forced me to make that most difficult of documentary decisions; whether to fabricate the story you have sold or trust in the fascination of the actuality. In this case the decision was made easier by the fact that the truth was stranger than the fiction of a right-wing plot.

The first volte-face I had to make was also the most demanding - Mosley was very likeable, indeed almost everyone who knew him, including those who loathed his politics, liked something about him.

He was outrageous, incredibly energized for a man in his seventies, and completely larger-than-life. Most of this came from a huge superiority complex, except 'complex' is the wrong word. Oz (as he liked being called) had been raised in a heady, natural environment of superiority as the rich Baron Mosley (the family once owned the land on which Manchester now stands) and up until the time of his unfortunate affair with Adolph Hitler he had been accorded a superior status by everyone, not least his political peers.

Winston Churchill had been a close chum in his youth and almost the first story Mosley told me was about a conversation between him and 'Winnie' as they walked up a crowded beach during a holiday together in the South of France. Sir Oswald recounted this story with great glee to prove to us that everyone in politics in those days was just as superior as he was. 'Winnie said to me, looking down on those layers of people, "The world is full of worms – it's a damn good thing you and I are glow-worms."'

And glow they certainly did!

Tall and elegant, Baron Mosley went off to the First World War and volunteered to become an observer in the Royal Flying Corps, a job with an average life-span of about forty eight hours. With the luck of the devil he survived this and the dreadful trenches, although he did get trench-rot and when he went home a hero he was limping.

He stood for Parliament and was soon in training for leadership. But his conscience began to trouble him. I had difficulty believing that a devotee of Adolph Hitler had a conscience, but it was a paradox like this that made Mosley so interesting and, perhaps more intriguing still, blighted his political career. A great number of people we spoke to believed Sir Oswald would have been prime minister of a Tory government had it not been for his conscience.

He decided that the complacent Tories were betraying the men who had stood in the trenches 'up to their necks in mud and bullets', and the government had betrayed its promise to provide these men with, amongst other things, 'homes fit for heroes to live in'.

So Baron Mosley quit, dumped the glow-worms, and crossed the floor to join the Labour Party where he produced one of the most caring political plans in British history, the Mosley Manifesto. Everyone who read it, not least its most enthusiastic sponsor, Ernest Bevin, now started thinking of Oz as a future British labour prime minister!

In a very short time, however, he grew impatient with the pace of socialist change and decided that there was just one person in England with the necessary vision and drive to save the country from itself – himself. So he quit again and formed his own party, the New Party.

This was not, as most people think, just another manifestation of Mosley's arrogance. He was seduced by Benito Mussolini. Oz had been taken to Italy in the early days of Mussolini's charismatic reign and Benito took Oz out on to a balcony and showed him a massive crowd of cheering, loyal Italians. Mussolini also explained how he had got the trains of Italy to run on time by bonding the people just like a stook of wholesome corn (*fascis*), a fascist. That word – just like Oz and Benito – was innocent in those days and they had yet to come under the thrall of a person who was seemingly never innocent, Adolph Hitler.

Mosley's New Party was obliterated at the next election and he founded the National Socialist Party based on Italian-style fascism, or togetherness if you like. German fascists, however, were already hard at work turning national socialism into a pair of dirty words, and Mosley's party became the target of British Jews, many of whom, to further complicate the issue, were very aggressive Communists. They invaded halls and broke up Mosley meetings, particularly in the Jewish stronghold of London's East End.

Mosley tried to suggest to me that this was unprovoked but he was patently making excuses. His overt support of Hitler was enough to justify Jewish anger, and he was by then associating with Hitler sympathizers in the Mitford family. He also tried to suggest that the black-shirted 'stewards' who guarded his meetings were simply enthusiastic followers copying his black polo-neck fencing uniform (Mosley had fenced for Britain). The reality was that these 'black shirts' were led and trained by an expert in unarmed combat and Mosley did nothing to stop them being regimented into a para-military force, similar to Nazi Brown Shirts.

He was condemning but ambivalent about Hitler, believing that he started out as a reformer, like Mussolini, then turned psychotic. But history shows that other observers of Hitler – Churchill (instantly) and Chamberlain (reluctantly) – had little difficulty recognizing him as a psychotic from the very beginning, and Mosley was better placed to make accurate judgements than most.

I went to France for my first meeting with Mosley and in spite of the bizarre setting found he fitted it beautifully. This marks the time when I broke out of the humanitarian cocoon and became a real documentary-maker; never again was personal morality allowed to interfere with the programme.

Mosley was a big man with an imposing hooked nose. His second wife, Diana (née Mitford), was a beauty and in old age they were still, obviously deeply fond of one another. Lady Mosley followed us around like an elegant ghost, listening to make sure Oswald did not say anything he would regret. She need not have bothered. Oz never said anything he regretted.

They lived in a beautiful Palladian chateau which Sir Oswald took great pleasure in informing me was called 'The Temple of Glory.'

'You think I called it that, I suppose,' he chuckled very engagingly. 'Well, I certainly did not, it's had the name since it was built.' (That of course does not disguise the fact that had it been called Chez Moi he would almost certainly have been tempted to rename it The Temple of Glory.)

He loved playing tricky mental games, a hangover from an earlier love of practical jokes. The MP Jennie Lee, Aneurin Bevan's widow, bravely confessed to a love-hate relationship with Oz because he had been physically attractive and a wonderful dancer. Jennie told us of a terrible prank he used to play on house guests.

His London home had an old-fashioned butler's lift on the first floor, which Oz had cunningly converted into what looked like a lavatory. Guests would be sent up there, allowed a minute to settle down, then Oz would press a button and the whole tableaux would descend into the sitting room, where all the other guests were assembled.

For me he took great delight in identifying what he called 'fascist' concepts, having convinced himself that everyone had them and that really most people thought like he did. By the time we finished, my own list of fascist thoughts ran to about 10, which I considered surprisingly low given the way I had been brought up.

We took Oz back to Manchester and filmed him walking through a demolition site of back-to-back slums and great piles of burning rafters. The wind swept great clouds of smoke up into the sky between broken walls of blackened brick through which big Oz stomped grim-faced. Leni Riefenstahl would have been proud of me.

Over all this we laid closely edited versions of the sound tracks in which Oz had described his fight to get homes for his heroes, the appalling conditions faced by workers after the First World War, and the virtual collapse of European politics in the Thirties which led to economic chaos, political sterility, and the hunger marches – Oz's, Mussolini's and Hitler's *raisons d'être*.

Standing there among the dying houses I experienced an extraordinary flashback in time and could suddenly see big, handsome Oz, war hero, Olympic champion, Socialist Aristocrat, making a very convincing case that he was the man to save the country from itself.

And later, in the editing room when we ran in the sound effects – faint bomb blasts, muffled machine gun fire, and just a touch of 'Jerusalem' (the lines about black satanic mills and green and pleasant lands) it made the hair stand up on the back of my neck.

'Wow,' Bob Heller said when he saw the rough-cut. 'Just remember we still have to get this past Lew!'

It is time I said something about the way television people create their illusions in the editing rooms and sound-dubbing suites. There are absolutely no exceptions to these illusions, or pastiches, of reality. You never see documentary material on television that is pristine – exactly the same as it was shot – never. This is not entirely the choice of the director. With few exceptions we have to fit everything we do into 'slots' of either twenty five or fifty two minutes and an average 'film ratio' for a network documentary is twelve to one (one foot used from every twelve shot) and I have often shot at twice that ratio.

We also have to add completely artificial 'effects' – footsteps, wind, traffic etc. – that are often completely artificially produced as well.

I am told that the BBC has an Alice-in-Wonderland person employed full time to make the noise of horses' hooves with coconut cups and other much more sophisticated artifices.

And we use dramatic effects, sounds whose purpose is to enhance the image, particularly the emotional image. Music is the most common emotional trigger. Words and music together became very fashionable in the Sixties when directors discovered that the songs and lyrics of the Beatles made very plain shots of deprivation agonizingly poignant. 'World in Action' seemed at one point of being in danger of adopting 'Penny Lane' as its theme tune.

Add to all that an arsenal of thunder, lightening, gun shots, driving rain, howling winds etc., provided by a special sound theatre where up to sixteen different tracks can be mixed to form the final track and you have your documentary. The term means 'document (or documentation) of reality' and was coined by a Scot, John Grierson. Grierson was somewhat obsessed with fish in his early years but he did go on to found the Film Board of Canada which still makes powerful documentaries. In fact the Mosley documentary required little of this electronic craftmanship. His life had been a rich pantomime anyway and I was simply polishing the chrome.

From Manchester we returned to France and the Temple of Glory where Mosley generously introduced us to his collection of 'mers' numbering at least twenty bottles of pale, lethal, regional spirits on which we all got roaring drunk.

In the morning I decided I was finished, or at least incapable of going on and, as is my wont, I asked Oz whether there was anything he thought we had left out of his life story, or that he particularly wanted to say.

'Well,' he mused, casting a wistful glance at the front of the Temple of Glory. 'You people always pass over the fact that I have always been a great advocate of a united Europe (this was about the time when Britain was entering the EEC), perhaps I might just remind people of my stance . . .'

He had Lady Diana on his arm at the time, and she gave Oz a little restraining tug as he looked up to the front of their magnificent home.

'Why not?' I said. 'Where shall we do it?'

'Up there is rather splendid,' Oz said casually, nodding in the direction of the imposing balcony on the front of the Temple of Glory. It was not unlike the balcony he had once stood on so long ago with Mussolini.

I agreed. I few minutes later, Oz took a firm grip on the balcony rail, lifted his big head, glared straight across the top of the camera and called to what the creature inside obviously still regarded as his errant flock.

'People of Britain, it's Mosley speaking!'

And then he delivered his homily on the Common Market, most of which I threw away.

We said goodbye to Lady Mosley who was watching her husband with resigned despair and I asked her to keep it on record that Oz had chosen to stand there.

'As ever was,' she said.

The finished film looked terrific and, Bob Heller said, went beyond Mosley to consider the central paradox of politics, the reconciliation of evangelism and power. I felt personally that I had come close to understanding the complexity of Mosley because after five years in television I had much in common with him, not fascism, I hope, but certainly missionary zeal fueled by the ego.

By television standards it was a very honest film: Mosley did not achieve the propaganda coup he had been working for, but equally I did not just do the traditional hatchet-job on Britain's leading fascist. Mosley was allowed his say, and most of what he said made a lot of sense, but at the end, on the balcony, he took up a rope and hanged himself, just as he had done throughout his career.

Heller happily offered it to the rest of the network for a peak-time slot - and there were apparently, terrible rumbles out of Sidney Bernstein's office at Granada Television in Manchester.

The stories about the competitions of status which went on between Sidney Bernstein and Lew Grade, the two great Jewish pioneers of ITV, are legendary. My favourite, although almost certainly apocryphal, is of Sidney coming up behind Lew in a traffic jam, both in their Rollers, both equipped with the latest in-car phones. Sidney rings Lew to tell him of some incredible deal. Lew takes this for a while, then breaks it off with: 'Hold on a moment, Sidney, my other phone's ringing.'

In fact the best (and certainly best-authenticated) story I have of Lew Grade's approach to documentary programmes is from John Pilger and John Ingrams who were cutting one of their ascerbic reports on third world poverty at Xmas when the word went round that Lew was paying a royal visit to wish everyone a happy Noel (or its Jewish equivalent). The two committed Johns stayed glued to their awful edit but the ebullient Lew finally ran them to earth in a poorly lit editing suite.

'Hope you're having a good time tonight.' Lew sang out (or words to that effect).

'Actually, Lew' said the inexorable Pilger, 'we're fighting to finish an important report on third world poverty and starvation! (or words to that effect).

'Fantastic!' cried Lew. 'Just as long as you're enjoying yourselves.'

(Let me just stress that if you examine the morality of this encounter a little more closely, it is not an anti-Grade story, in fact most producers I know who worked with and for Lew Grade during this era of British television – and that includes John Pilger and John Ingrams – remember him fondly as a man who believed and committed himself to the television medium – and what for him was our mysterious branch of it – with great energy.)

It was said that Sidney Bernstein fancied himself as the more intellectual of the pair. Granada had a serious documentary image; Lew was the king of light entertainment, although in fact, thanks to Heller, ATV's documentary output was at least as strong.

I have already explained that the Big Five ITV companies had gained monetary control of the network via a gentlemen's (I think that is the right word) agreement to show each other's programme. So if Bob Heller made a documentary he knew that he would automatically sell it to the four other main companies. This cartel was not always very gentlemanly, but it held together because it meant that only the Big 5 could afford costly programme budgets. That in its turn meant that only the Big 5 made big shows and could afford facilities for them. Big companies like ATV and Granada got bigger and regional companies like Anglia, even though they made wonderful programmes like 'Survival', stayed small, to the chagrin of their chairmen.

When Sidney and Lew used their big, cheap British studios to undercut the American production houses with shows starring Tom Jones, Englebert Humperdinck, Julie Andrews and later The Muppets, their huge fortunes were well and truly made, and the power structures of ITV were set in stone for a decade. We compared it to the mafia for want of a better example but that was rather defamatory. Nobody ever got killed to my knowledge and it certainly worked better than the system which has replaced it.

Bob Heller was literally dumbfounded, therefore, when we received the news that Granada was reluctant to show the Oswald Mosley programme. Heller believed Bernstein was taking the whole matter personally.

'Can he do that?'

'I don't know. It's never happened before.'

'What can we do?'

'I'll see Lew!' he said without much conviction.

I reminded him of Lew Grade's boast that he did not understand documentaries and preferred to have nothing to do with them.

'This is different', Heller grunted. 'Lew is not going to like Sidney telling him what to do.'

Nor, as it happened, did the IBA like Bernstein telling them that he had a veto on ITV. They had a special viewing of the programme, decided that it was 'balanced' and ordered Granada to transmit.

Bob Heller called me in after his meeting with Lew. He gave me a thumbs-up sign.

'They have to show it?'

'No. Lew could have told me to withdraw it. That would have got Granada off the hook, and he did think about it. Fortunately our press people arrived at that moment to tell him what the IBA was saying. When I left Lew was dictating a statement about the importance of free speech – and asking me privately why we were giving up valuable documentary slots to Nazis.'

'Thank you,' I said gratefully.

He went back to his work and it was some time before he seemed to realize I was still there.

'Can we talk about the film for a moment?'

'The film is finished and has been cleared for air,' he said levelly. 'The film has some nice touches and proves to me that you have the one thing without which a director cannot manage in this business.'

I glowed.

'Luck,' said Bob. 'So we should be talking about your next production while it holds.'

'Very well,' I agreed. 'Mosley was interesting but he's not planning a right-wing revolution by fanning the flames of British rascism. He doesn't seriously plan to take over the country.'

'Thankfully no,' Heller said with relief, 'Which is how I read it if you recall.'

'Nevertheless,' I insisted, 'My informants continue to report a growing body of support for that cause.'

'Your . . . what do you call them . . . When-We's?'

'Right.'

'If I understand what When We means, could it not just be wishful thinking?'

'Certainly – but this is the first time they've also been hopeful.'

'But do they have any organization outside of the loony loyalists and the right wing of the Monday Club, any credible leaders?'

'No, but they do have a hero.'

Bob paused. I could see that after his narrow escape with Mosley he would almost prefer not to know.

'Who?'

'Enoch Powell.'

He stood up.

'You want to take on Enoch Powell? I say again, Powell is no Mosley. Powell is as bright as all hell, politically adept, experienced, driven – just look at his eyes. And I don't think Powell would be fool enough to tie himself in with the far right.'

'He's not. it's more complicated than that. He's out there on his own, the voice in the wilderness, forecasting a race war. I don't know what he's after but he's on the verge of throwing down the political gauntlet, and whichever way you look at it he must be a prime subject for a documentary. I'm surprised *Panorama's* not on to it already.'

Heller winced.

'And he's in our region.' I drove the knife home (ATV had the Midlands ITV franchise at this time), 'One of our MPs.'

Short of saying that he did not think I was experienced enough to handle Mr Powell (which I suspect he did think), Bob could see there was no way out, and again with the injunction that I kept him very closely advised it was agreed that I should approach Enoch Powell.

I sensed I might be on to something substantial after our first meeting at which he agreed to the project, confidently and without any editorial stipulations. He gave me the impression he had been waiting on my call. It was also like talking to someone encased in a thin translucent coating of ice. There was no conversation, he was like an actor patrolling a lonely stage addressing a naive audience he could sense but not see.

There was a lot to research and many surprises. I soon came to realize that everything Powell said and did had to be studied very carefully for its exact meaning. He was quite capable of creating impressions that were not the same as the words he spoke (just like I could do with clever editing and sixteen tracks of sounds.)

Mr Powell presented himself as a purist, not a racist. He did, however, believe in keeping people of different races apart, not because of their race *per se* but because bloody conflict would result. And British people had priority in all things because it was their country.

I was quite happy to accept that Enoch Powell was not a racist – that the colour of a person's skin did not matter to him – because it made the man and his cause more complex and interesting.

So what were Mr Powell's real interests? Britain for the British or a grail much larger than all these – the reform of the nation. As the months went by and Mr Powell's speeches grew more and more apocalyptic, great numbers of Britons, most of whom had never heard of the League of Empire Loyalists, started to see Mr Powell as a clear challenger to the then Prime Minister, Edward Heath.

Bob was also wrong about me not being sufficiently experienced to handle Enoch Powell. I had lived all my life with people who had tried to find justification for their racial fears and Enoch Powell had much in common with many of them. No South African prime minister had ever confessed to despising black people as such. They believed in racial purity, which Enoch Powell was not espousing, but they also believed in keeping people apart in the interests of civil order, and they also gave all the priorities to the faction that was predominantly white.

He also had quite a lot in common with Oswald Mosley. They were both evangelical, had maverick political tendencies fueled by the power of their personal convictions, and denied responsibility for the lunatic fringe of their following. Enoch Powell on the subject of groups like the Empire Loyalists and the Monday Club sounded quite similar to Mosley on the subject of the excesses of his Black Shirt followers.

As for actually 'handling' Enoch Powell, this was not an issue. Mr Powell was working to his own well-written classically researched script. The best I, or anyone else, could have done was ask him questions in the forms of cues to make sure he covered the ground. My only chance of finding anything out about Enoch Powell was to film a period of his life in fine detail. You cannot work to a teleprompter all the time, even one driven by a brain as powerful as Enoch Powell's. Things come out.

Chapter Ten

People had started to march on the streets for Enoch Powell by the time I got to meet him. I acquired the rights to the news clips of these tough docker-led demos and also Powell's fiery anti-immigrant speeches. The marches and the speeches confirmed that he was an impassioned orator touching a chord in the rough end of working-class Britain.

We also found that Powell had a reputation as an original thinker; some considered him a genius.

These days, with Enoch Powell's ship come and gone, it is easier to see him as perhaps the most stumbled politician of stature of our time. From Tory Minister of Health he slipped to the backbench, fell off that, and after a brief and bizarre sojourn as a Unionist MP for Northern Ireland, tumbled out of Parliament altogether. That Enoch might be both a prophet of doom and potentially its only victim seemed obvious to me from the start of my research, but then I had been brought up in white Africa. What confused me was that few others appeared to feel like I did about his ranting. Powell was either being regarded as a serious threat or as a Messiah; strangely, that's the way it has always been.

Today, with no constituency at all, when he should be remembered as a man who many believe did serious damage to race relations in Britain and very little else, he is still a popular pundit on radio and television. It may be, of course, that this is more a condemnation of television than of Enoch Powell.

As one of his fellow panellists recently put it: 'I don't agree with a thing you've ever said, Enoch, but you do make me think.'

I proposed to a scowling Bob Heller that if reaction to Enoch Powell could be regarded as any kind of poll a large part of the British population was covertly racist.

'That of course would make Powell right,' Bob said stonily. 'The will of the majority.'

'The Rightness of Wrongness,' I countered, 'Just like it was in Rhodesia.'

'I want proof that he is wrong,' Bob insisted. 'On-the-screen proof.'

'And if he's right?'

Bob winced again. 'That too of course.'

Fortunately it wasn't.

I don't think I gave Mr Powell the rope with which to hang himself, as was suggested by the television reviewer of the *Daily Telegraph* some months later. I simply gave Mr Powell his head.

We began at his house in Chelsea where he had agreed to talk to two post-graduate students. We filmed that conversation – understandably, given our presence, a diatribe – and then intercut it with the students' comments about Mr Powell on their walk home. That is not as sneaky as it sounds; politicians who agree to take part in television documentaries are as much concerned with their own image as the furtherance of human knowledge, and they assume any director worth his salt will be working to balance this.

Powell abandoned all the rules of subtlety and went straight for the throat. Asked to confirm his belief that nothing but repatriation could deal with Britain's immigrant problems, he said: 'I've used various expressions to describe the prospect; a rather mild expression derived from a Latin poet ("those whom the Gods wish to destroy they first make mad") and later a stronger expression – civil strife of appalling dimensions – but people are either fools or wilfully blind who think they can see a future for this country without bloodshed and internecine strife resulting from what is to come!'

As he said this his eyes glowed with great intensity (just as Heller had said) and he looked at me to check that I was satisfied. I was!

'This is the truth,' Mr Powell pressed on. 'One of the ways to get things done, or evils avoided or prevented, is to make people aware of them.'

We asked Enoch Powell what he thought of his relationship with his party leader, the Prime Minister, Edward Heath.

'I think he's afraid of me,' Mr. Powell said, and I knew then that I had a successful film that would attract a great deal of publicity. Indeed, that quote made the main headline of the *Daily Telegraph* on transmission day and ensured us a large audience. 'He exhibits the symptoms of fear, indeed this is the only thing that rationalizes his behaviour where I am concerned,' Powell added for good measure.

He then rubbed salt in with a statement that was blatantly patronizing (and I thought slightly libellous): 'We all have things which we fear, and we all fear what we don't fully understand, and forces that we apprehend which perhaps may be bigger than ourselves.'

I took 'forces bigger than ourselves' to mean Mr Powell and his cause. So did Heller and so, fortunately, did the Press. It was also the first guide he gave us to his larger ambitions.

'Stick close,' Bob said, now very interested. 'Watch those eyes. Who knows, maybe he wants to be Emperor!'

I filmed Enoch's every move for days, right down to the family having lunch, which Mr Powell used as an opportunity to project himself as a firm, kindly father, actually nagging his daughter Jennifer on camera.

'Hasn't anybody laid the table?' he moaned at Jennifer. 'Surely you've got the intelligence to lay the table without someone having to tell you every time.'

Daughter Jennifer did not obviously recognize this surrogate and sulked through the rest of lunch.

Otherwise Mr Powell was a very good actor, so much so that my two bogus interviewers who also had lunch on camera at a pub by the river (on another day of course) were convinced they had been taken for a ride.

'He's aware of his ability to perform,' commented race relations expert David Stevens. 'He gets so wound up on what he's saying that he follows his own words. They are not the words of a sane strong man, but of someone who fits into a Marlowe tragedy.'

He went on: 'I'm not worried about Enoch Powell but the effect he's had on the people of this country. I just disagree with his principles, in particular his principle that the people who are here who are not white-skinned can never fit in. He told us that, and I simply do not accept that. I do not see why we cannot live together as a happy multi-racial community.'

He also defined the method he saw behind Powell's madness, which was very useful as I was growing ever more convinced that it was plain madness and Bob would not put up with that.

'What he's done is to raise the idea of the Nation and revise ideas of invasion, ideas that have a great echo in the British people and go back to Churchill and 1940; and then he's pinned onto this the idea of skin colour. It's going to be a long time before we get that out of our political system.'

You do not have to be too observant to see that what I had set up here was a stage on which the two sets of players were doing their best to get their point across, without anyone noticing the stage or their acting. In fact there is a third player also trying to get his point across – me – and my task is to be completely invisible.

The film used the technique of the hidden interviewer and a complete absence of narration. I asked hours of questions but none was heard; nor was I, the interviewer sitting right beside the camera lens, ever seen. We cut on complete, rounded sentences and used comments from one player as questions or point-raisers for another.

Equally, everyone who appeared in the film was used as a secret interviewer, even Powell's daughter, as we slowly peeled the onion of his personality. Her reaction at lunch told us, for example, more effectively than any statement or narration, that Powell was not happy with his real father-image.

While very effective – the subject appears to be engaged in a personal conversation with the viewer with no third parties to distract or stem the flow – this technique has always embarrassed me somewhat. I have never quite understood why the public – the viewer – does not object to an obvious confidence trick.

Or am I being patronizing? Is the British television audience in fact incredibly sophisticated, having learned to recognize the tricks of our trade and accept them as our means to their end. Are they conspiring in the creation of this separate estate of television, which does not exist in the real world anymore than tele-prompters, invisible interviewers and cue-cards do?

The other possibility is, of course, much worse. Is tele-land a Metropolis-like world where tired workers come home, fix themselves in front of the box and simply don't notice that all the questions have been cut out, don't wonder where we hid the camera crew, don't question the uncanny way one person's remark promotes a reply from the next, and don't see that people like Enoch Powell stare into the void and talk to themselves: the first sign of madness accepted as a vehicle for home truths!

This paranoia is not a jaundice of recent origin. I had such a bad conscience about it at the time that I shot a special opening sequence of Mr Powell climbing a hill where he was born in the Black Country with our cameraman, Stan Evill, marching along in picture behind him (this admittedly involved bringing in a second cameraman who was of course not seen). It was noticed by a couple of reviewers, but they thought I was hinting that Mr Powell was an inveterate TV performer and gave me Brownie points for thinking up a new trick.

We travelled with Mr Powell to his house in Wolverhampton to observe him as head of the family and local MP, which produced several surprises.

His acting at the domestic level did not really improve, although the tolerant reaction of his wife and child told us quite clearly that he was not really like that, and when I suggested we film him enjoying himself he revealed this bizarre trilogy; picture-framing, graveyard-visiting and hacking.

The last I found particularly surprising as I had always thought that Powell saw himself as working-class intellectual with his roots in the Black Country rather than as a country squire; but on the appointed day there he was immaculate in riding boots, tailored jodhpurs, hacking jacket, black bowler hat and large brown horse. He sat his horse well and galloped like a cavalryman to round off the sequence.

I was fully expecting a similar round of rather posed performances when we began our coverage of his daily routine as a local MP, but suddenly the transformation was extraordinary.

Enoch Powell was a wonderful constituency MP. We filmed his clinics which he staged regularly and industriously in an awful little office in a dreary suburb. He listened with genuine concern, gave good and reasonable advice, and committed himself with vigour and great good humour to the truly mundane duties of his job. We filmed him opening a flower show and he was a star; later he proudly took us to see a piece of waste ground he had had cleared of dangerous rubbish.

But his opinions continued to be expressed from the mountain-top:

'I sometimes tell my constituents of the legend of the Greek god who lost strength every time he was lifted off the ground. One's constituents are one's contacts with reality.'

Of course this drew me ever closer to the possibility Heller and I had not wanted to believe: that Powell really was in touch with the British heartland and his warnings of an impending race war were accurate despatches from the front.

He was also remarkably open about his personal ambitions and the evangelical nature of his entry into politics.

'It's my experience that all the big decisions are ready made when you discover you've made them, or to put it another way, you open the door one morning and there it is standing on the doorstep, complete, you knew it all the time. The decision to go into politics after the war – if I survived the war – had matured slowly over the war years. Maybe it had been there before, very deeply buried (he had been a very successful young academic). It suddenly became conscious and specific in the middle of 1944, in Delhi. I can remember saying to myself, you've made a mistake, chances are now you are going to survive and the over-simplification with which you have lived, that the war ends everything, that you will have a splendid *Götterdämmerung* is not right. I realized there was going to be a life after the war, something I had denied, and almost simultaneously with that realization was the decision – it must be politics.'

We took the opportunity to snatch a quick interview with Mrs Powell about where she thought her husband's ambitions lay. Mrs Powell was attractive and although politically committed and experienced stayed much in the background. She did not beat around the bush at all. Her husband regarded his destiny as 'the top' and she did not think there was any dishonour in that.

But where was the top?

Enoch went out into the garden to deadhead his roses and reflect on this point and soon we had our second headline.

He was telling us that when the political call came in 1944 he interpreted it as a call to serve the life of the nation 'or the life of the Empire as we would have called it in those days.' Then he added quite casually: 'It had seemed to me that to be Viceroy of India was the highest and one of the greatest positions to which an Englishman could aspire.'

This set my head reeling. Had one of Britain's most concentrated Indian communities suffered the desperately rotten luck of being represented by an MP who covertly admired the British Raj and perhaps still nurtured strange dreams of Empire?

Perhaps Enoch *had* wanted to be Viceroy of India?

'Certainly I aspired to it,' he announced, whipping heads off roses with one hand.

But of course that had not come to pass. Instead the Indians had attained their freedom and, in his book, were now taking over England.

'It is literally true to say that whole areas of mostly lower middle class housing have been taken over. They are no longer part of England. They are part of somewhere else – India, Pakistan or the West Indies – that's the way to imagine it. To the extent that this Asian population is a piece of Asia encamped in Wolverhampton, then of course one cannot be of service in the same way to the members of the caravan as one can to one's own fellow countryman.'

You can see here what I mean about the need to examine Powell's words very meticulously. The first impression given is that as an MP he is disowning these coloured constituents. But on closer examination he does not quite say that. On television, however, the viewer does not have time to take sentences apart, and Powell knew that.

Heller and I ran this through a great number of times before either of us dared believe that Powell had been so emphatic and that these were the views of a man who a large part of the population thought should be Prime Minister.

'It's pure racism!'

'Far from pure, very complex,' I pointed out with my expert knowledge. 'He sees them as a passing problem or a problem to be passed on. If he'd been Viceroy of India they would have been his constituents and he would, I'm sure, have done a very good job looking after them. He's more a nationalist than a racist.'

'You try explaining that to the milkman,' Bob said. 'Those people are here by law, just like you and me. This stuff could provoke a riot, and who's to blame them?'

'Enoch is forecasting just that.'

'Is he using us?'

'Let's just say he's a goal ahead at half time.'

'I want to hear from the caravan,' Bob said. 'Pronto!'

I went about this assiduously and (to Bob Heller's growing satisfaction) a picture rapidly began to emerge of a man completely out of touch with the problem of immigrants in Britain's cities.

The 'lower middle class areas' that had been taken over by Indians were in fact slums that whites had not wanted. The hard-working, commercially-aware Indians were rapidly improving property values in these derelict parts of Enoch's constituency.

The city's Community Relations officer said diplomatically: 'He has either accepted a fatalistic view, a point of direct inevitability, and therefore sees community relations as being wasteful, or there is some measure of insincerity in the point that he attempts to make.' This was a nice way of saying that Enoch was contributing nothing to the community relations work in the city.

This officer also pointed out that Enoch never defined what was wrong with the immigrant communities. He simply made ominous references to numbers.

This was not altogether true; Powell had often repeated the claim he first made at a Tory Party Conference that the greater part of the coloured immigrants and their families did not regard Britain as a place of permanent settlement and still regarded the countries from which they came as home.

But everywhere we went we found working examples of people achieving good race relations in spite, and in contradiction, of Powell's prophecies of doom.

The Youth Volunteer Force was running completely integrated programmes, in fact the only problem expressed by the youth leaders was not whether their young people understood segregation but whether they could spell it.

'All we need in this town is schools, job opportunities, decent welfare and support for improving living conditions,' they said. (This was long before inner city problems had become fashionable) Wolverhampton has a terrible reputation because of the publicity given to one or two (Powell) speeches that were totally out of proportion to the scale of the problem.

That was true. Enoch's most famous speech in Birmingham before had warned: 'Those whom the Gods wish to destroy they first make mad. We must be mad – literally mad – as a nation to be permitting an annual inflow of 50,000 dependants.'

People actually working on the problem regarded this as pure huffing and puffing. We talked to the headmistress of a school with a majority of coloured pupils who said Enoch's speeches had deeply disturbed parents but the children – the future little Britons – had not been affected at all.

She had a problem with her assistant headmistress who had set up a special class for forty three immigrant children who could not speak any English.

'After three months half of them were fluent and all but two after twelve months. My colleague is very proud, indeed jealous, of them and really doesn't want them going off into other classes.'

She had no doubt that Mr Powell had a racist problem. 'Racialism stems from a fear of the unknown, not knowing enough about the people, lack of knowledge. I am sure that if those who do fear had a closer contact their fears would be diminished.'

In the editing room a few weeks later I spun through the miles of interviews with Enoch to see whether he had said anything about fear. We found an extraordinary passage in which his eyes glowed with conviction, but he actually said: 'Large numbers of people at my time of life and older are saying to themselves, thank God I've reached the age I have. We shan't live to see what is to come. Ten to fifteen years will see me out and perhaps it won't come in that time.'

The jigsaw was nearly complete. I was now convinced (and felt I could prove on film) that Enoch Powell, one-time academic genius, was expressing what he sincerely felt – and it was rubbish. It was a phenomenon I knew with great familiarity from my years in white Africa: fear of domination by another race/culture disguised as brave calls to the barricades. Ian Smith had even used similar images to Powell's wrath of the gods. He had called for a 'last-ditch stand' when the courageous gesture involved an olive branch and compassion.

If I was right then Powell was also a litmus test to the extent of covert British racism, and by revealing it Powell could paradoxically make an important contribution to race relations in the United Kingdom. In fact this appeared to happen. I don't think Britain would have passed laws making racial segregation illegal had Powell not brought the possibility bubbling to the surface like the released gases of a noxious volcano.

The prospect of the utter collapse of his cause obviously never crossed Powell's mind. His triumphant closing statement in the film made to a Tory women's club ended with the boast: 'You may remember that there was the usual disposition to scoff and to ridicule, and you may also have noticed that what was then, less than a year ago, thought to be so outlandish a point of view has now become orthodox, so that people have forgotten that they every held any other opinion. That shows us an important political fact, the only one indeed that I want to register here this afternoon, and that is: 'what Wolverhampton thinks today, the country thinks tomorrow.'

'Now there,' said Bob Heller, 'is a truly frightening thought.'

After we had packed up our gear for the last time in Wolverhampton I said our thanks to all who had contributed. To the Community Relations Officer who had first suggested Enoch did not know what he was talking about, I expressed the lingering doubt that I had not quite established that there was a yawning gap between Powell and the problem.

'It's like two sets of people talking on either side of the ocean,' I observed.

'Ask him where I live!'

'Where do you live?'

'You ask Mr Powell first; I'll rest my case on his answer.'

So I went back to Powell and asked.

'No, I don't know that,' Enoch smiled carefully.' But I don't know where you live either.'

I phoned our CR contact with this information.

'I'm his neighbour. We've been watching you going in and out of his house. You may even have my front window in some of your shots.'

I regard *Enoch Powell* as the best political documentary I ever made, and not just because a lot of people saw it as my transition from novice to full-blooded custard shark with proper teeth.

I am not suggesting we changed many minds by interpreting Mr Powell's statement of a national crisis as a manifestation of his personal one. Mr Powell always preached to the converted and those who were watching television that night probably enjoyed his rhetoric as much as ever. But I do believe the film helped thinking people to stop taking Mr Powell so seriously, and it was significant that he made very few speeches about racial crisis thereafter.

Mrs Thatcher, who loathed him and had no television presence at all, became Prime Minister instead of Enoch Powell, which surely proves that television has less influence on the voting public than we (and politicians) like to think.

What *Enoch Powell* did for me personally was to get me out of the rut of Africa expert into the rut of a director who could handle pretty much anything. This of course was not true, but few such reputations are.

'Edward Kennedy,' Bob Heller mused aloud a few weeks later. 'Does he still want to be President of the United States, I wonder?' (The ripples from Kennedy's Chappaquiddick troubles had recently settled.)

I was thrilled at the prospect of a first visit to the United States and meeting a famous Kennedy but I felt obliged to point out to Bob that I was almost totally ignorant of American politics.

'That's okay,' he said. 'Kennedy's agreed to do a long interview with Henry Brandon (an old friend of his from the *Washington Post*).

You just need to set it up and take care of the editing. Give you a chance to get to know the States and maybe pick up a few ideas for programmes.'

'That's three trips abroad in less than eighteen months,' Annette observed. 'And what company – Baron Mosley, Enoch Powell, and now Edward Kennedy. I'm not surprised you find it difficult talking to us mere mortals.'

I did not feel like that about her, of course, and perhaps I should have taken her with me. But she did have the babies to look after.

Chapter Eleven

America literally took my breath away.

New York where I went first was particularly breathtaking. You could literally feel and hear the city's pulse racing as the subway trains ran through steaming tunnels and the lurid yellow cabs thumped across the potholes.

I can think of no city like it on earth, nor can I conceive of how anything like it can ever be built again. It is both a monument and graveyard to the value systems of the twentieth century. Depending on your nerve, it either asserts itself as the ultimate urban disaster – the fate that awaits all cities – or is a noisy celebration of city lifestyle topped with candles the size of skyscrapers that never go out. For me it is the latter and those candles attract me like a moth. It is a city of taste, wit and the will to live, with the last unquestionably the most dominant.

I fell into the throbbing heart of New York trying to find a train. As a youth I had been imprinted on the lovely old steam trains of Africa and I have since always sought trains when there is time to spare for civilized travel. There was, I had heard, a spectral silver train, the Metroliner, which travelled from Penn Central Station to Washington, where Edward Kennedy had his offices.

At Kennedy Airport after my passport had been examined by a grannie poring through a large-paged book (was this truly the land of the computer, I wondered) I walked out into the bedlam of the taxi pick-up area, lost my nerve in the avalanche of dented yellow vehicles, and was smooth-talked into 'sharing a limo.'

Three-quarters of an hour later, bereft of other suckers, the disgruntled negro driver demanded to know how much cash I had. I told him ten dollars.

'Then you gonna have to get out,' he said. 'Coz it ain't worth my time moving for no ten dollars.'

I pointed out we had not moved for almost an hour.

'Tough shit,' he said. (It takes a little while getting used to the way Americans use obscene words quite casually. I know the British do so too, but I still wince when I hear my first 'son-of-a-bitch' which is used as commonly as 'damn' or 'mother-fucker'.)

'Then oblige me by calling that policeman over.'

'What you want wit' him?'

'Arbitration. I'm new to this country and I don't know how much I can charge you for waiting time.'

'Sheet,' he sighed, with a little grin that made me feel much better. 'Got myself a smart-arse. Okay, but I'm gonna have to pick up a fare or two on the way in, and that ain't going to be easy at this hour.'

'Be my guest,' I agreed. 'I'm here to see America.'

'You ever see the Bronx?'

'No.'

His smile widened and the big limo surged forward like a sack full of horse power.

The Bronx is hard to like; in fact the Bronx is a nightmare, a place to go when there is nowhere else to go in life. We were there looking for reasonably respectable people walking urgently between the few lit areas of street, certain in the knowledge that they would pay almost any price for a taxi.

In spite of my upbringing in troubled Africa I was scared witless after half a mile of it, convinced that I was being driven into an ambush where I would be robbed and left bleeding in the ditch. In fact the driver was every bit as nervous as I was and kept up a running condemnation.

'You ever see anything like this before, hey man, you ever see such a pile of shit, you ever think people could fall so low, so down and out? Can you imagine kids growing up in a place like this, can you conceive of the violence a person meets in these neighbourhoods? Hell man, I tell you this place is not safe.'

'Then what the hell are we doing here,' I demanded hoarsely.

'A person has to work,' he snapped. 'There's only one place worse than this and that's Harlem.'

'What's Harlem got to do with here?'

'That's where I have to goddam live, man.'

'I actually have twenty dollars,' I confessed, both ashamed and convinced he was under-estimating the dangers of stopping. 'You can have that if you'll get out of here and drive me straight to the railway station.'

'Shit man, why the fuck didn't you tell me that before?'

Why not indeed?

So we swung out of that jungle up a ramp onto the comparative safety of a freeway, and in a sense that brief detour into the Bronx was a useful education. Never since have I been troubled, as are most of my friends, by the general squalor of New York outside of the pristine golden mile round Central Park. After the Bronx, the crumbling buildings of SoHo and NoHo, the litter on Broadway, the steel-planked holes in the roads, the dark detritus under the flyovers, the grimy bridges and the disgusting cabs driven by a small cross-section of the world's refugees disturb me not. I just listen to the place throb and watch it glow, and if I am on foot, work out the risks a hundred yards ahead.

He dropped me outside Penn Central railway station. I gave him twenty-two dollars and fifty cents.

'You be careful man,' he said kindly. 'There's rough people in there too.'

Everyone has a story about a New York cabbie, but the best I ever heard was told to me by the British humorist Dave Allen, whom I was to work with a lot in the future.

On his way into New York one night Dave had to suffer an entire life story, which included the cabbie agonizing over whether he should send his daughter on a vacation to England as a reward for graduating high school as his wife wanted, or insist she go directly to nursing school which he wanted.

'Who knows who she might meet in the Yoo Kay,' the cabbie said. 'She might catch the British Disease.' (This was in the days when we were having a strike a minute as the Heath government died.)

It was late and Dave let the cabbie talk on to himself, paid his fare and the cabbie drove away without ever really looking at him. Two weeks later — an extraordinary coincidence — the same cabbie came to collect him from his hotel but obviously did not recognize him.

'Waddya do then?' the cabbie demanded after a few seconds of oppressive silence.

'I'm a mind reader,' Dave said.

'Come-awn!'

'That's right,' Dave insisted, turning up his brogue. 'I'll trade you the fare to the airport for a reading.'

'Come-awn!'

So Dave told him in some detail where he lived, and recounted the problem he was having with his daughter.

'Which daughter?'

'The one who just graduated and you want to go to nursing school. I can also see into the future,' Dave said, gambling that the two women would get their way. 'The girl will go to England.'

'Shee-it!' the cabbie cried, almost too distraught to drive. 'She leaves Monday. You're really good, you know that! Just nobody's ever going to believe this!'

'On the contrary,' said Dave. 'At least ten million people will.' And he promised the cabbie he would use the story on his television show, which more than secured his free ride.

There were a lot of funny people in the station, tramps, drunks, pick-pockets and straightforwardly mad people, but they were easily avoided and the station was liberally patrolled by policemen carrying a formidable array of armaments strapped on incredible belts around their bulbous waistlines. I soon learnt that New Yorkers have a vicarious love of the dangers of their city. In all the years I have been going there I have never come close to being mugged, robbed or otherwise molested, and neither have the vast majority of New Yorkers.

My best friends in New York, Nancy and Bernard le Gette, vividly demonstrated the ingrained nature of this love-hate relationship with the city the first time I stayed with them in their apartment in Greenwich village. They are typical New Yorkers: Nancy an ambitious, super-energized, garrulous publisher working all hours, and Bernie a writer with a great love of music and New York bookshops who is at the same time a tough business manager.

The first time I went to their apartment, Nancy fixed dinner. I volunteered to take the garbage to the waste-chute in the hall. Coming back into the kitchen, Nancy called out: 'You didn't lock the door right.'

On the contrary, I had carefully re-set the three massive devices on this steel-faced portal.

'No, you didn't do the bottom bolt. Turn it twice.'

'How did you know?' I asked her in the kitchen.

'I know the sound. In New York you pay attention to that kind of thing.'

Bernie had driven a taxi in their impoverished days and his stories of murder and mayhem in places like the Bronx were positively lurid. The steel cages through which a cabbie would accept nothing bigger than a five-dollar note via a little metal latch were basic to survival in the New York concrete jungle, and the city had a number of no-go areas for cabs, Harlem in particular.

It has to be said I have always listened to these legends and never attempted to take a cab to Harlem. Cabs are hard enough to find without wasting them on no-go areas. One day, however, I'm determined to take one out there and expect to find it no more dangerous and at least as interesting as, say, Brixton.

Having run the gauntlet of Penn Central I took my seat on the marvellous Metroliner. Its seats outclassed the best first class accommodation on any aeroplane, and it had a saloon and a glossy buffet where jolly black stewards dispensed first class American fast food in little cardboard trays.

The American train system is one of the country's few great cultural failures. It started out magnificently, opened up the country, graced most of the large population centres with buildings of genuine architectural importance (rather than the neo-classical monuments which Americans have started to revere) and was then allowed to collapse when the aeroplane took over. I will return to the topic in more detail in a little while because fortunately the vital core of the US national railway was rescued in the nick of time, is now being modernized and, as I learnt on the best holiday of my life, is much the best way of seeing, touching and smelling mighty America. So in great style and with all of eastern America unfolding like a movie outside the window I was eventually deposited in the heart of Washington.

Washington was, in its way, even more extraordinary than New York. I knew that it had much the same social problems as New York – a large, poverty-stricken, socially-deprived community of blacks making heavy demands on social services. But compared to New York where you have to run the gauntlet of this to reach Manhattan, Washington looked as if it had been made the night before and polished that morning. Admittedly New York is older and more concentrated than Washington, but the differences I was seeing could only be explained by attitude, not population density.

New York is New York. Washington is America, squeaky-clean America where most things, particularly the toilets, run on time. The fact that it has more in common with Disneyland than with New York and is much less exciting than either is a price Washington is happy to pay.

In a clean taxi, with no assault screen between me and the driver, I drove past immaculate mansions set in large gardens, one of which was called the White House, until we reached the low-slung granite skyscrapers that house the splendid beaurocracy that makes this vast disparate union of states work.

Bureaucracies are not often applauded; this American machine deserves it because it provides the only answer to the great American paradox.

If you stand back and take a serious look at the American political system it seems utterly impossible that it can work as well as it does.

Firstly there are the strange presidential incumbents of recent decades: the charismatic boy-President John Kennedy who many think died at exactly the right moment to establish his political reputation for posterity; the adept but seriously amoral Nixon; the likeable but unlikely Carter; and that star of the silver screen, Ronald Reagan. Better political brains than mine have already pegged Reagan as the best of the bunch, not for what he did but for the way he identified what an American President in the age of television must be. In spite of them all, America thrived.

Similarly with the people who make up these united states. There are Irishmen more fiercely patriotic to Ireland than the Irish, vast ghettoes of affluent Yuppies, sullen Latinos, fiery Jews, clannish Italians, Greeks (who have already provided one Vice President (Spiro Agnew) and a Presidential contender (George Dukakis)), Poles, Germans and assorted middle Europeans from states that no longer exist, not to mention a whole fiercely independent nation of black people.

These are all somehow folded like rich egg yolk into the 50 states, most as large or larger than the nations of Europe, each fiercely proud of its singular identity: Texas and California are as chalk to cheese, likewise the East Coast and the West, or tropical Florida and arctic Alaska. In spite of them all it works better than any political union the world has created thus far. It is politically and economically stable and its people join together on the important issues of nationhood. The bureaucracy (which the Americans call 'government' and not, as in Britain the Civil Service) rises above it all.

Edward Kennedy's offices were a surprise and added to my liking of America. It looked like he lived there and his huge staff, half of them women, all acted as if they were members of his family.

His personal office was more like his den with casual furniture and jolly primitive pictures by his children pasted all over the walls. Her greeted me in his shirt sleeves and proved able to carry on a smiling, relaxed conversation with me, two telephones and as many aides as chose to come in, all at the same time.

I found him open and, by British political standards, humorous and self-effacing. It was not at all what I had expected and, feeling the effects of this new country I had discovered, I found myself disarmed.

Would he be prepared to talk about the Chappaquiddick incident, I asked with great caution.

He beamed that big Kennedy smile.

'I don't suppose I've been talking about much else these past few months.'

'And about your Presidential ambitions?'

'Don't you know about these Kennedy men?' a ravishing black girl aide sang out as she stalked by the big desk to empty the in-tray. 'There's two things they can't get off their minds – and you just touched on the other one!'

Kennedy laughed joyfully.

'Is there anything you would particularly like Mr Brandon to bring up?' I asked.

'Sure. I'd like to explain my position on Irish independence,' he said.

In those days our IRA troubles were already a highly sensitive topic. We also tended to avoid the fact (and perhaps still do) that the American Irish and the Libyans rate about equal as supporters of IRA terrorism – or, as they see it, the freedom struggle.

'You mean the IRA?' I queried carefully.

'Them too,' he said. 'Unless it's taboo.'

'I'll tell Brandon,' I promised cautiously. 'I don't think anything's taboo.'

'Well, I'm happy to talk about anything you like.'

And that was about it. He said I could leave all the arrangements to him as they did interviews in his office about twice a day and he knew exactly where to put the camera and lights.

I had expected the process to take at least a couple of days and had allowed three before meeting Brandon.

The Washington monuments took up the rest of that first day. I could not escape the feeling that they were copies of older monuments and that the real dirty and chipped versions were tucked away somewhere else. The White House looked like a mausoleum at close quarters and it was hard to think of anyone, even an American President, actually living there. My hotel was also mausoleum-esque, but the designer had obviously not been able to decide on the era.

The front was Greek classical with Doric columns, the foyer art deco with Venetian glass mirrors, and the dining room Shakespearean.

The head waiter noted I was English and pointed out that the ceiling of the dining room was an exact copy of the one in Anne Hathaway's cottage. I pointed out that Anne Hathaway's cottage was half the size of the dining room.

'Exactly,' he smiled proudly. 'An identical copy twice the size of the original. That's how we do it in America. You might also be interested to know that it's made of plastic.'

'You'd probably be interested to know that Anne Hathaway's cottage probably did not have a ceiling when Shakespeare was a visitor,' I said. But he wasn't. That was sacrilegious talk.

'I have some time to kill,' I told him. 'I'd like to stay at an original American hotel in New York.'

'Kill it here,' he said bluntly.

I pretended to a work commitment in New York.

'This is a traditional-style hotel,' he explained. 'If you want a traditional American hotel I suggest you go to a Holiday Inn.'

It was a language problem, which can easily happen in America. Americans do not speak English (there is no reason why they should); they speak American.

'I want to stay at a hotel that was built by Americans, for Americans, when New York was in its heyday.'

'Gotya,' he said. 'Something like the Grammarcy Park only she's falling down. I suppose there's the Wyndham but that's pretty much taken up by long-stayers. There's the Chelsea, but I hear that's just plain weird.'

I went to the Chelsea, which was indeed weird, but had a reputation as a writers' haunt from way back and was especially beloved by Dylan Thomas. But in the early Seventies read Dylan, Bob, for Dylan Thomas, and there he was (Bob, that is) in the foyer ahead of me.

The foyer, a delicate faded mess of inlaid woods, marble and wrought iron was dominated by a huge safe with its door wide open and its interior painted bright red.

I waited patiently for Dylan and his entourage to check out, fascinated by the huge empty safe.

'Was that Bob Dylan?' I inquired of the reception clerk.

'It might have been.'

'It looked like him. Isn't he pretty famous over here?'

'Mega-famous!' the receptionist grinned. 'But around here a lot of people look like Dylan and this is a pretty jokey sort of place. I had three Mickey Mouses check in already this week.'

'Hence the safe,' I suggested.

'No the safe is for real empty. The safe is open and painted in that way to tell any bad person who thinks we might be storing valuables that we most certainly are not. That way, unlike two of my unfortunate predecessors, I may see the year out and still have my life.'

'You're serious,' I said.

'Deadly serious, sir. This is New York. Would you like a suite?'

'I would like a room.'

'This is the Chelsea. We don't have rooms.'

'I can't afford a suite.'

'Fifty years ago you couldn't afford a suite. Now you can. Look around you and you will see why. It is a tragedy. It is a disgrace. A powerful committee has been asking the city to preserve this wonderful ancient building for ten years. Nothing happens. I have a small suite on the 18th floor. That is high up given the state of our elevators, but you asked for cheap.'

I did not really need my suite, which comprised two huge rooms and a kitchen built into a cupboard with a large decrepit bathroom. I could have happily have lived in the big elevators which groaned between the floors.

I rode up to the suite with a little old lady dressed in black, who clasped a huge bag of groceries. As soon as the doors closed she said: 'We're alone!'

I nodded.

'Would you care for one?'

My mouth fell open again – that day it was open most of the time.

'Ten dollars, the stick!'

'No thank you.'

'Genuine Thai stick, I don't touch Columbian. You know they split it with cocaine to destabilize the American administration?'

Fascinated, I bought the Thai stick from her. She watched me sniff it. It was good quality cannabis, of which I had considerable experience as it was a cheap commodity where I had grown up in Africa.

'Good shit,' she smiled.

'Do you live here?'

'Sure. I ride this elevator every midday at this time. I reckon to give service.'

As we rose between the floors the elevator filled slowly with another Visconti cast. Florid Central Americans in black hats with wide jazzy headbands and sharp striped suits, an extremely fat woman in a bright red flapper dress with her red hair bound in a bandana, two huge negroes in sweat-soaked grey training suits with the hoods up who ran on the spot, several more Bob Dylans in blue denim on which someone had drawn psychedelic pictures, and a businessman in a black suit, Ivy-League shirt with button-down collar, homburg hat, black shoes. He looked genuinely frightened.

I sat on the cleaner of my two beds, turned on a television with iridescent colours that could not be tuned and was running eternal game shows, ordered beer, crisps and a club sandwich, which arrived in a very short time (the orders were sub-contracted to an efficient nearby deli) and, without really thinking, lit my Thai stick.

I surfaced twenty eight hours later after what seemed like ten years of wandering on Mars and a number of other even more exotic planets.

It was essential I got some air so, ignoring the legendary dangers, I set out at what seemed like crack of dawn to walk to the Battery and visit the Statue of Liberty. I managed about five blocks before being placed under temporary arrest. The cop waited for me as I crossed the street and his injunction to stop came as no great surprise as I was sure that the buzzing kaleidoscope that had replaced my brain must be showing on the outside.

I weaved on the spot resignedly wondering how this was going to go down with Mr Heller and what the girls would think of a father gaoled in a foreign land for drug abuse.

'Sir,' he said. 'I think you should get off the street.'

I nodded as best I could.

'I'll come quietly,' I said.

'Your ears looks kinda red.'

I nodded, remembering from episodes of *The Naked City* how important it was to say nothing in America until you had called your lawyer. Any moment now he would be reading me my rights and I would be bundled off to a place called The Tombs.

'I guess you didn't hear the frostbite warning they just broadcast. It's 12 below. Get inside and grab a cup of coffee. You an Australian person?'

'No, I'm an English person actually. But thank you for the warning, I will do as you suggest.'

'One thing,' he said, and now I really was convinced he had spotted my near-hallucinatory state. 'Over here jay-walking is a serious misdemeanour, right?'

'Jay-walking?'

'Crossing the street against the light. You're not the first Britisher I've had to warn. I wonder, don't you have law officers on the streets of Olde Englande?'

'We do,' I said a little frostily. 'And we have zebra crossings and belisha beacons to take care of people wishing to cross the street.'

He looked at me suspiciously.

'Zebras – is that right? Anyway just get off the street before your nose falls off.'

Two or three cups of good American coffee in the warm haze of the companionable breakfast joints which hold the American street blocks together like bookends soon put me right, and I discovered I was ravenously hungry; a combination of my long fast and a post-dope condition known as the munchies.

With utter fascination I watched a short order cook preparing an endless stream of orders for what is rightly called fast food. I consumed great quantities of strange delights with names like Hash Browns, Eggs Easy Over, Pastrami Rye, Toasted Bagel Lox, and Jello and Whole Wheat.

Every time I heard a new name I ordered it. The flying waitress took my never-ending order without concern and yelled it at the cook who worked in a blur over a large smoking hotplate, which frequently had to be lashed into submission and cleared of fat with huge flashing spatulas.

Finally when my call for a malted shake produced a foot-high glass of whipped milk so thickly laced with malt the spoon stood upright in it, I realized I had had enough.

'Is it still frosty out there?' I inquired of the waitress during one of her rare pauses.

'Too right, it's down to 12 below they say.'

'How are my ears?'

'They're nice ears,' she said. 'Do all you Britishers eat so much?'

'I was told by a police officer that my ears might have got frostbite,' I explained.

She peered a little closer.

'They are kinda red. Here,' she said, rushing over to a coat stand and returning with a pair of bright red furry testicles on a springy clip. The sides of the balls were Mickey Mouse faces. 'You can take these.'

'How kind, but I can't take your . . .'

'They're not mine,' she laughed. 'You think I'd wear something like that?' Some kid left them but it's been weeks. You take them until you can get to a store for a beanie.'

I rather liked the Mickey Mouse ear muffs. They were very warm and kept out a lot of the New York traffic noise like police car sirens and drivers leaning on their horns at street intersections. Indeed I forgot I was wearing them.

'D'ya think . . .' said Henry Brandon when, smartly dressed in my best suit and tie, I met him for the first time, 'that those would fit over headphones – they'd be great for outside broadcasts.' A nice man, Henry, though I have to confess I was amazed at how rough he got with the nice Mr Kennedy. It confirmed an opinion I still hold that American journalism stands out like a landmark of excellence in the US television swamp.

My embarrassment with the Chappaquiddick issue was thrown to the winds.

'You're doing well in the polls – especially with women,' Henry pointed out right at the start of the interview. 'Maybe the Chappaquiddick tragedy is not any more a political liability?'

'It'll always remain a personal tragedy,' Kennedy replied adeptly.

'But you don't think any more that it's a hindrance?' Henry did not mention the Presidency but Kennedy knew very well what he was getting at. Kennedy played the ball back along the same line.

'I'm continuing my political career and I'm going to continue to be active in public service.'

By tradition (one which I frankly don't understand) American Presidential hopefuls spend the early part of their campaign vehemently denying that they are going to stand. Kennedy duly made his denial, but when Henry pursued him he followed with a statement which left us in no doubt of his long term ambitions. 'I'm not going to be a candidate this time, but I'm ambitious in terms of my state and my party and my country. Where that is going to bring me over the course of a career I'm not prepared at this time to say.'

Henry decided that that was as good as he was going to get and went on to the next most controversial topic, Kennedy's apparent support for the IRA which had surfaced in a resolution he had put to the US Congress proposing peace solutions for Ireland.

'You didn't denounce the violence.' Henry said.

'I hold no brief for violence and that I believe is clear. If that hasn't been understood then I welcome the opportunity to say it again on this programme.'

'Well say it in exact words,' Henry said. I can remember wincing at his venom, but he knew exactly what he was doing.

Kennedy essentially refused to condemn IRA violence and even under Henry's dogged assault would go no further than condemn 'either the violence of the IRA or the violence of the (British) troops.' The power of the Irish vote was almost palpable.

The power of the British vote (or the Special Relationship) was nothing like as powerful even for a man who we suspected might one day have to deal at the highest level with the British.

'The present policy is bankrupt,' he said unequivocally. 'It's not unlike the continuing United States involvement in Vietnam which thinks it can only be resolved by the presence of soldiers. I don't believe the presence of British troops in Northern Ireland is going to bring peace to that part of the country.'

He then listed a series of 'considerations' for the British Government which I am told caused the Cabinet to all but choke on its Brown Windsor soup the day after the programme was shown.

'Within that falls the idea of ending internment,' Kennedy said with lethal casualness. 'The withdrawal of British troops, perhaps the establishment of some sort of constabulary force which would be agreeable to both sides and might well be some kind of UN presence – and steps towards the unification of Ireland.' He could not have selected a more powerful list of anathemas!

'And you would be prepared to act as a mediator, I understand,' said Henry, all sweetness and light.

'I'm interested at any time to help and assist,' Teddy said with that big Kennedy smile.

Henry laughed. Being present at an interview running as subtly yet as powerfully as this is a little like being a referee (for I would have to edit it) at a world chess tournament. Henry was certainly not laughing at Kennedy, in fact the opposite. He was acknowledging the end of a game played perfectly to stalemate. For more than an hour he (Henry) had asked personal and, frankly, offensive questions without giving any offence at all. Kennedy had essentially ducked straight answers to anything while clearly conveying his message.

They parted, as they had started, friends.

I called Bob Heller that night to report the successful conclusion of our mission.

'And how are you liking America?' Even at such a great distance he could not hide the longing in his voice.

'I am agog,' I assured him.

'Well eat a bagel for me,' he said wistfully.

Chapter Twelve

I brought the film back to London in my personal baggage and quickly ran it through an editing machine. In the flesh, Kennedy had left me in no doubt that he still had Presidential ambitions but on the television screen his heavy hints and loaded nuances were not very satisfactory.

It is my conviction that the television interview is never a satisfactory source of hard information. Generally speaking, interview subjects (other, perhaps, than ordinary people on the street) tread carefully on television because it has so huge and so general an audience. There is bound to be someone out there taking offence if you deliver anything more than generalizations.

Thus the most interesting insights to come from interviews are usually accidental. Our interview with Kennedy attracted a large audience and press because it offered one of the first real indicators of the degree and power of American support for Irish independence (and for the IRA, if not quite spelt out). If Kennedy, unofficial spokesman for the hugely rich and politically powerful Irish community in America, was publicly expressing his support for an end to British colonialism in Ireland, what were the more fiery members of that emotional community up to?

Yet I do not think Kennedy realized the reaction he would provoke. He simply did not know that only a tiny percentage of the British public saw our presence in Ireland as anything but a peace-keeping operation, or the IRA as murderers.

The interview was edited in a few days and transmitted in a very good slot. Bob Heller was so pleased with its topicality he toyed with the idea of long interviews conducted by acerbic journalists as a possible successor to the *Man of the Month* series.

Bernard Levin and I went to the States to do a similar job with Vice-President Spiro Agnew, but this turned into a farce unmatched in my career and steered Heller away from the tricky waters of the generic documentary series for ever.

I again travelled to Washington via New York, this time staying for the first of many times at the lovely old Algonquin where America's '*Bloomsbury*' set had held their intellectual (and rather bitchy) luncheons at a large round table. The Algonquin has lots of muses, a foyer that is the most interesting rendezvous in New York, and perhaps the cosiest bar in town.

I thought I had by this time experienced the worst conjuring tricks employed in the television business, but seeing some American variations caused me to conclude that we British sharks were mere tadpoles in the custard.

Because Mr Agnew was a Vice-President his interview had to be arranged through a special press division run by a strange mock-Englishman. Cleared and tagged by a heavy security inspectorate, I was escorted through a maze of traditional American offices (grey-green metal desks with silver edges, grey upholstered chairs on large castors, buff-coloured rotary file indexes and banks of filing cabinets) and eventually ushered into a room posing as an English office.

In fact it was a hotch-potch of English furniture, a Victorian desk, an Edwardian roll-top cabinet and a litter of English memorabilia, silver spoons, snuff boxes and paper weights. The man behind the desk wore English tweeds and there was a deer-stalker hat on the sideboard. Smiling conspiratorially he put on the hat, enjoyed my amazement, took it off, then shook my hand with great enthusiasm.

'I'm Joe, Robin, and as you can see this is a special pleasure because I love everything English. I happen to think the European culture is unquestionably the finest in the world.'

'I was just coming to the conclusion that yours might be the freshest,' I said. 'But then I'm an African.'

'You don't loo . . ., er, sound African,' he said. 'And don't think I'm denigrating Uncle Sam. Greatest place on earth for most things, and I think raw is maybe a little kinder than fresh.'

Language problems again. Fresh obviously did not mean new and lively as I had intended it. 'Is Mr Agnew ready for us?'

'Ready when you are, old chap,' he said with a mock English accent. 'Did you bring the questions?'

We had been warned of this condition. It is not one we would have accepted in Britain but Heller acknowledged it was common practice in America with a politician of the rank of Vice-President and had agreed to supply what he called 'a general area of questioning.'

Joe glanced quickly through this document and returned it.

'That's okay, he can handle those.'

'Doesn't he see it?'

'Vice-Presidents are pretty busy people, Robin. He'll be briefed, but I can tell you now there won't be any problems.'

I should have smelled a rat then.

'Shall we go clear the set?' he asked.

'The set? We understood the interview would be done in the Vice-President's office. That adds a lot from our point of view.'

He laughed and waved me to the door.

'No problem,' he assured me as we walked to a large studio. 'Hell, you can have the Oval Office or a view of the Rose Garden if you'd prefer, but we're set for the Vice-Presidents's office.'

As indeed they had – an exact replica of the office and its furniture with simulated views through the windows on back-projector screens.

'Are all the official interviews shot on fake sets?'

He looked pained and with some justification. Reproductions are not fakes in America, a lesson I perhaps should have learned from his office.

'Mostly – someone like Walter Cronkite might be invited to sit down for real. But interviews play havoc with official business and the security people don't like them at all.'

'Has the public ever suspected, do you think?'

'Suspect what?' he asked, this time genuinely bewildered. 'I promise you there's not a detail out of place.'

'Instant reality,' I said.

'Right,' he enthused, taking it as a compliment. 'So if you'll okay this – they need to reset for the Secretary of Defence's Pentagon piece.'

'Can we do anything about the armchairs?' I asked, conscious that I was about to ruin his day.

'We can't change a thing, Robin. It defeats the point!'

'Well Bernard Levin is not a very big chap and we might not be able to see him at all over those armrests.'

'The Vice-President is a substantial person. I think we may assume he will insist on the chair that suits him – not to mention the integrity of his office setting. I could possibly arrange a cushion for your Mr Levin.'

I could sense I was in real danger of destroying the Special Relationship, so we compromised on that.

At the appointed time a few days later the Vice-Presidential entourage marched in. They were all substantial people and, apart from the fact that they did not wear straw hats, were obviously all graduates of the Elliot Ness G-man school. For a minute or two they stood around glaring at me, the technicians and the studio equipment with equal suspicion. Bernard had obviously been cleared officially, or perhaps they just couldn't see him in that huge chair. Then, as one, they faded into the grey paintwork.

Bernard began his interview.

Mr Agnew (who has not gone down in history as America's cleverest Vice-President) stared woodenly across the set and delivered deadpan stock answers. I watched poor Bernard slump down ever lower in his cushion, hoping I think to become completely invisible as this performance went on.

For one paranoid moment it crossed my mind that this Vice-President might be no more real than the set, an android kept for interviews with a programmed response to any question within his brief. But we were never able to prove it.

Bob Heller sighed and sucked his fingers a lot when we watched and listened to Agnew's faultless monologue of clichés, official positions, considered views and other buzz-phrases – and scheduled the piece to a transmission slot so obscure I cannot now remember when it was.

Bernard and I did our best to forget it altogether, a process in which Bob Heller assisted in my case by calling me in to meet an adventurer with the unlikely name of Sid – Sidney Wignall.

This meeting led directly to a programme title which leaps uncharacteristically out of my otherwise staid portfolio – *The Search for Revenge* – and, more importantly, revived my interest in wild places and returned me to an avenue of television which has served me well, natural history.

There was unfortunately a terrible personal price to be paid, but that was all still eighteen months in the future.

Sidney Wignall, tanned russet-red and with a fringe of a beard, looked like a pirate and admitted that most of his values were better suited to the age of the Elizabethan privateers than to the present.

He had excited Bob with a totally outlandish idea – a marine search for the wreck of *The Revenge,* Drake's flagship which sank near the Azores after a battle of such epic bravery that Alfred Lord Tennyson was moved to compose a long poem about it.

There was also excited talk at this first meeting about other historic wrecks and artefacts around the Azores. These Portuguese offshore islands (once thought to be the remains of sunken Atlantis) had been the favourite hunting ground of the Elizabethan pirate/privateers, their prey the overloaded treasure ships from South America. Sidney said his research indicated that the present-day value of this sunken treasure could equal the world debt. This was such a vivid image for a commercial television company that none of us thought to ask him how he had calculated it.

I thought that to start with such outrageously high hopes could well mean the the expedition ending in tears – but what an adventure!

Nevertheless I felt obliged to ask Bob Heller why he had chosen me.

'I heard you were a good swimmer.'

'That's it?'

'Well, I don't know how you direct this one,' Bob said. 'The action's all a hundred feet under water.'

'I don't even know how to dive!'

'I guess Mr Wignall can teach you that.'

But it turned out that Sid Wignall, marine archaeologist extraordinaire, could not even swim.

Even I had the foresight to recognize that a two-month junket to the Azores coming hard on the heels of my second trip to the States was not going to go down well with Annette. In fact she took it remarkably well and when I mentioned a consolation prize she was obviously quite taken aback.

'We're hiring a huge villa on Terceira island, which is beautiful. If I keep the villa on you could all come out for a holiday afterwards. Plenty of room for the girls, house-guests even.'

She reminded me that my mother was still in residence, although Peter, after discovering that his wife Aurora was expecting another baby, had decided to go back to Africa, to Cape Town.

I countered with the observation that my mother ran the house as if we weren't there anyway, and secretly wanted to follow Peter to the Cape, but Annette still said she would have to think about it.

ATV paid for a special instructor to teach me the rigorous British Sub Aqua Club disciplines at Guildford public swimming pool. I would drive down after work and was so drained of energy after we finished that I ate several chocolate bars on the way home.

The cameraman on *Search for Revenge* was a young Czech, Ernest Vince, who is now a famous cameraman-director. Ernie was imaginative and progressive from the beginning of his career and he talked Bob Heller into letting him shoot the film on Super-16 stock which had a slightly larger negative and could be blown up for showing on cinema screens. We all thought the film would be exciting enough for this wider audience.

'You can dive, Ernie?' I checked.

'Sure, Robin. I did some on *The Association*.' This was a famous East Indiaman wreck stuffed with a cargo of silver coins which had been found off the Scillies.

That was all right then. As soon as I had my class 3 Diver certificate we went off to test the massive Super-16 underwater camera built especially for the film. At the same time I would do my open-water drills that had not been possible in Guildford.

We chose the Scillies and the harbour of St Mary's because the skilled British naval salvage diver who had been with Ernie on his *Association* dives had a boat there.

It was grey, raining and freezing when we baptized our new wet suits in sea water. Compared to the deep end at Guildford it was a weed-infested, claustrophobic nightmare. I would never have gone near the project had I had any idea what sea diving in British coastal waters is really like and I have never bothered to repeat the experience, although diving on tropical reefs and corals has become my favourite sport.

I noticed that Ernie was also less than happy as he wrestled with his huge camera in shallow water so I suggested we put it all aside and go for a short shallow dive to sort ourselves out.

We managed quite well on the outward swim across the harbour considering that the bottom appeared to be composed of a forest of brown strands of oily kelp which I swear reached up for us. None of our new equipment really fitted so we flapped along in a mild state of disarray, clearing leaking masks, adjusting unfamiliar weight belts, losing our snorkels and generally having a most unpleasant time until we hit the opposite wall.

There we just hung around together at about thirty feet trying to get our breathing under some sort of control. Breath control is vital. Take too many big breaths too quickly and you bob up and down like a ballcock as your lungs fill and empty. If this goes on too long you bring on anoxia which can lead to unconsciousness and death.

But not as quickly as being run over by a cross-Channel ferry.

When we were breathing only about twice as fast as we should we started the return journey. Abruptly the liquid sky above us filled with noise and fury, and glancing up I saw a massive rust- and barnacle-encrusted hulk coming straight at us.

Ernie was already on his way down, signalling frantically. I put my head between my legs and thrashed down into the kelp forest until I hit a rock. Even then, looking up, I was still able to see the ferry's huge propeller turning quite slowly in a vortex of bubbles.

Ernie popped up out of the kelp like a small Polaris missile and, seeing me safe nearby, began to fin rapidly for the surface. This was rather difficult as we were at the centre of a maelstrom of strange currents produced by the ship's docking manoeuvres, and anyway a warning bell learned at Guildford was sounding loudly in my subconscious.

'He's going up faster than his bubbles,' I thought. 'That's lethal, his lungs will burst!'

With a spurt I was able to catch one of Ernie's legs while waving up frantically at his bubbles and shoving my pressure gauge in front of his face. None of this made any sense of course, and Ernie started up once more. Again I grabbed him and I think he concluded that

I needed his help (or his company) during the ascent. Anyway we went up at my speed with our expelled bubbles rising safely above us, breaking surface a long way offshore with very little air left in our tanks. Fortunately we were both wearing the new adjustable-buoyancy life jackets. We inflated them and, exhausted beyond description, kicked our way to the shore.

It is the first time I have ever looked death properly in the eye (the other times have been in retrospect) and I did not like what I saw.

That evening I asked Ernie who had taught him to dive.

'Jock,' he said. Jock was the salvage diver who had taken him down on the *Association*.'

'You didn't take a course?'

'There wasn't time,' Ernie admitted. 'I wouldn't have got the job.' (Evidently there are big sharks in the freelance camera custard as well.) 'Jock told me what to do, clearing pressure and all that.'

'And coming up?'

'He was with me all the way.'

I gave him my copy of the BSAC manual. Ernie is a very serious person and he read it from cover to cover, grinning at me now and then when he came across something he didn't know that could have killed him. When we reached the Azores he had the expedition's Dive Leader, Peter, a Class 1 BSAC instructor, teach him all the disciplines properly.

Admittedly he very nearly killed himself again the following day.

We were still having major difficulties with the big camera. We could not get it to sink!

'It does not wish to be an underwater camera,' Ernie spat. Under duress his faint middle-European accent hardened. 'I vill kill it!'

But we couldn't kill it either. We called in Jock, who explained that the camera had been weighted to be neutrally buoyant at depth, not on the surface.

'You just need to kick it down a few fathoms,' he said, wiggling his huge shredded Jet Fins. 'You two aren't fit enough to do it yet. Why don't I take it down on a line and, Ernie, you swim down the line and practise with it.'

The camera was tied to a thin rope fitted with a plastic marker buoy. Jock thrashed briefly on the surface but eventually disappeared below the waves with the camera. Five minutes later Ernie swam to the buoy and hauled himself down the line. That was the last I saw of either of them for nearly half an hour and I was contemplating summoning the coastguard when Ernie bobbed to the surface, bleeding from the nose and ears.

Jock appeared beside him followed by the camera. Jock grabbed Ernie and appeared to be trying to drown him. They were under water for at least another ten minutes and I assumed all was lost.

Then suddenly they appeared beside the boat and we hauled the blue, bloodied Ernie aboard while Jock swam off to rescue the camera which was now going rapidly out to sea, fortunately still secured to the orange buoy.

Their saga unfolded as follows.

The camera was grossly underweighted. Jock discovered this by swimming ever deeper until at about 130 feet he decided it needed technical alterations. Meantime, Ernie was going down the line looking for him. Ernie had never been that deep before. He was, I suspect, so anxious about finding them that he did not clear pressure properly as he pulled himself ever deeper into that black hole.

Seeing him coming down the last ten feet (which was about the extent of the visibility) Jock realized Ernie was too deep for his own good and waved him up. Ernie came up a bit too fast and because this was what is known as a 'bounce dive,' with no real time spent at depth, did not see the need for a decompression stop. Jock disagreed. He had been down there a while. He grabbed Ernie on the surface and took them both back down a way to dispel any nitrogen bubbles in their blood. As a result neither of them was affected by that crippling, agonizing condition known as the bends. Ernie's bleeding was superficial and he recovered rapidly in the warm cabin on Jock's boat.

'I really cannot believe that anyone would choose to do this for a living,' I said to Jock. He was diving every day on *The Association* in very poor visibility against a strong bottom current. 'Other than to make one's fortune, I suppose.'

He laughed and drew our attention to a rusty steel drum in which chunks of grey scrap metal were sloshing around in an acidic solution.

'There's my fortune – crud!'

'Crud' was the word they had given to silver bullion welded into lumps by centuries of immersion in salt water. It was very cruddy staff indeed and there was a lot of heavy, dirty work involved in reducing it down to the shining coins collectors will buy.

I am very pleased to report that nothing daft like this ever happened again. The camera was fitted with new weights and we flew to the Azores to join Sid Wignall and his team of divers from universities in England and Sweden, all of whom, especially the Swedes (who were led by a woman, Siggy Klep), were very experienced and took us immediately under their wing. I was never allowed thereafter to dive alone, and it was a long time before they regarded me as sufficiently experienced to 'buddy' Ernie.

I shall never forget my first real dive in the clear ocean. In place of the single bottles we had hired for the St Helens fiasco, Sid's team was using huge twin-sets with enough air for almost three hours under water.

I descended like a bird into a crystal bath of champagne-clear water onto a bottom of fine white sand about 60 feet down. Fish large and small of every conceivable shape and colour swam past. To my right a pair of divers were surrounded by shifting cones of large and very inquisitive barracuda. As they descended the fish went down with them, maintaining exactly the same distance from the divers.

Ernie came down with Peter our dive leader. Peter had the most incredible control under water of any diver I have ever met. In fact he had become semi-aquatic, like a seal. He never bothered to dive or even swim very much (it wasted energy) but would descend rapidly simply by completely evacuating his lungs and not breathing again until he had reached his chosen depth.

The visibility was least 100 feet and the pictures Ernie was getting were very glamorous – the blue void lit by rays of white lights, divers descending apparently under waterfalls of iridescent bubbles, the whale-like shape of our big grey inflatable hanging like a dirigible in the 'sky', and the shining bottom which gave off twinkling puffs of fairy-dust as a diver came to rest.

I realized I had passed through the magic threshold that Peter had promised us, when you forget you are under water breathing air from a steel bottle and start to fly like a bird.

The team formed 'swim-lines.' Wignall had mapped to a grid pattern the search area where he thought the wrecks might be. Ten divers then descended onto that hypothetical grid and took up positions about 15 feet apart along a light rope. They swam forward together, searching, and each afternoon Wignall marked off sections of his map in the certain knowledge that somebody had been over every inch of the ground.

In fact we found our first wreck on the very first day. It was not the *Revenge* but it soon became obvious that Sid had used the *Revenge* as a romantic lure to attract interest in his expedition. He really wanted to see what there was around the ancient harbour of Angra where almost every galleon making the journey from South America to Europe, many loaded with treasure, had been obliged to take shelter while they stocked up with fresh provisions and water.

Fierce storms were frequent in the area and the islands had claimed many of the ships.

The *Revenge,* if anything was left of her, could be anywhere. She had been pulverized in her fight with the squadron of Portuguese men 'o war and had sunk while being towed towards Angra harbour. The realists on our crew thought it most likely she would have sunk in the immensely deep waters just off land (for the Azores are the tips of steep submerged mountains). Sid continued to believe that we might find her on the coastal shelf, and when we came upon that first wreck on our first day there was great excitement.

I had expected to see something like the *Mary Celeste;* gaunt masts trailing shreds of sails rising from a half-buried hull with, hopefully, treasure chests lying on their sides in the sand.

What we found was a mound in the sand with two drainage pipes sticking out of one end. At first sight I thought it was an outfall from Angra's raw sewage disposal system but Sid, who used a clown-like sky-blue wetsuit, was anoxicizing himself with excitement and I concluded that the mound was an important find.

I said earlier that Sid Wignall could not swim, which is true, although he could dive after a fashion. No-one had ever taught him how to swim and when he became interested in marine archaeology in the early days of scuba equipment he had taught himself how to use it in a basic way. The adjustable buoyancy life-jacket was a great boon to him because he just hung around in it on the surface waiting to be picked up.

Sid tied a buoyed line to one of the pipes and waved us all up. In the dive boat there was a long discussion which concluded that the mound was of the right length for an Elizabethan wreck and the pipes were undoubtedly badly weathered cannon. Sid explained to me that the mound was the ship's ballast, granite blocks if she were a lowly merchantman or iron cannon balls in a man 'o war. Underneath the mound some of the hull timbers would have survived, in which there could well be treasure and valuable artefacts.

Excavating it would be a big job and Sid first had to assess whether it was worth it. The cannons would probably tell us. Ordinary ships, he explained, had mostly iron cannon and would at this stage be ignored in favour of more promising finds. Basically we were looking for bronze cannon because they were costly to manufacture and were usually installed only on interesting men 'o war or galleons with treasure to protect.

As Sid had suspected, the cannon on that first wreck turned out to be iron, parts of them as soft as cheese, and we moved on. But for my uninitiated viewers I knew this would make very exciting pictures and I found I was enjoying myself immensely. Was this really the television business – and if so why on earth had I wasted so much time in a sleazy Wolverhampton, Manchester and the dangerous slums of Africa?

Hardly a day went by when we did not make a find of archaeological importance. Angra harbour was positively littered with ancient anchors, iron cannon and ballast. But bronze cannon continued to elude us.

You can only film so much swimming, so Ernie and I would leave them to it while we filmed the lovely flora and fauna. The clear waters of the Azores teemed with a mixture of coastal and deep-water fish and marine mammals. The huge barracuda, who some said were as a dangerous as sharks, swam in schools of thousands. We found rock outcrops literally covered with crayfish and other crustacea (and gathered enough to feed a huge farewell party in one dive). We saw whales regularly, including the giant Sperms who came to these waters to feed on squid including the giant squid which can reach a hundred feet in length. None have ever been filmed.

The dolphins took my fancy most of all as I became aware of their absolute mastery of their marine world. They would gather around our boats as soon as we left Angra harbour, surfing with obvious enjoyment on our bow wave. If you jumped in the sea with them they would play around you as if they liked company. These are not quite the anthropomorphic images they may seem because later on, still intrigued by these encounters, I researched everything known about dolphins for a book (*Lure of the Dolphin,* Avon) and met a great number of people who on the basis of personal experience believed that dolphins keep a watchful eye on humans in the sea and will rescue them if necessary.

In the stillness below the waves, surrounded by creatures infinitely more competent than myself, I also became aware of a singular truth: our planet is not entirely dominated by an increasingly aberrant naked ape. Here in the oceans, a domain covering almost four fifths of the earth's surface, we were just tourists. Nor could anyone who has watched whales and dolphins for any length of time believe in the arrogant human claim that we are the greatest sentient intelligence on earth. As my friend Dr Roger Payne (who made the discovery that humpback whales compose songs together) has said: 'I don't want to live in a world denuded of whales – it would be the final proof that I was a member of a criminally insane and murderous species.'

Each day's dive was an idyll, a perfect symbiosis of ourselves and the marine eco-system. It fell apart just once but that, typically, was the result of an act of human aggression in which I am ashamed to have been involved.

Sid Wignall had been given a 'humanitarian' shark-gun to test. It was a hideous device comprising a large hollow needle attached to a high-pressure air bottle. We were supposed to stick it into attacking sharks and trigger a shot of compressed air which would temporarily destroy the shark's delicate buoyancy controls. We all considered the shot might so unbalance the shark (which must swim on an even plane at some speed for the gills to work properly) that it could cause them to drown.

And to test such a device you have to find sharks and annoy them.

There were plenty around, particularly hammerheads, but like all the other marine creatures of the Azores they had been politely keeping their distance. Finally we set out to molest a small school of sharks we knew frequented a particular rock outcrop. I did not particularly want to film the gun test but thrilling underwater shots of attacking hammerheads were too good to miss. All my nice new values went out the window as I reverted to shark pursuing shark for the sake of a gung ho television sequence, so I no more than deserved what happened.

Sid and his 'buddy', each with a gun, fell backwards into the water from the boat as we sighted the several fins of the school. Ernie and I and the camera went in a little later so we could see Sid with the sharks in the foreground.

Hammerheads are biters, so Peter and a couple of support divers stayed above in the boat, ready to haul us out fast if the hammerheads grew too agitated.

Sid kept bearing down on them and the gap between us narrowed. The sharks, not used to this kind of behaviour, continued to swim away from him in a leisurely fashion until Sid, thrashing as he always did, finally spooked them.

Instead of attacking him, however, the sharks fled straight towards us!

A hammerhead is not a pretty sight, and I like sharks. The hammer blades seem to stretch their eyes and mouth into a wide, toothy 'I'm comin' for you' smile of anticipation.

The lead animal made a definite attacking pass, and turned. Ernie, who you will recall has a penchant for fast ascents, filled his lifejacket and shot up at sixty feet a second, well out of shark range. Now better trained, he neatly deflated just below the surface, doing himself no harm.

I, conditioned by the BSAC against these dodgy crash lifts, did the exact opposite. I made an emergency dump of the little bit of air we kept in our lifejackets to aid buoyancy, breathed out hard and let my weightbelt pull me down like a stone.

I stopped this descent when I could just see the sharks in the twilight zone above me. But that meant I was very deep and I did not have a lot of air for lengthy decompression stops if the sharks kept me down for a long time. They continued to swim lazy circles in the sky, and if anything seemed to be coming down themselves.

I sank even deeper until I could actually see the bottom, or I thought it was the bottom until it moved. It was actually an enormous manta ray, at least thirty feet across, hanging like a fireman's blanket to catch me with its great stinging barbs raised and waiting (or that's how it felt).

I did what Ernie had done at the other end of the void; slightly reinflated my lifejacket until my descent stopped and I was just hanging in the water between the devil and the deep blue sea.

This enforced manoeuvre proved rather fortunate because on checking my depth gauge I found I was almost at 140 feet, far deeper than I had ever been before and close to the dangerous threshold where you can get nitrogen gas poisoning known as 'raptures of the deep.' In that condition I would quite likely try to ride the giant ray into battle with the hammerheads. And to add to my problems my air gauge was now confirming that I had at best half an hour's air left - and I would need at least that for a safe decompression stop if I spent any more time at that depth.

My only chance was to ignore the sharks and get near the surface fast. There is a bizarre drill for such emergency ascents - you breath out as hard as you can all the way up to dispel the air compressed into your lungs, even though your brain is screaming at you to breath in. But if you do that, or even hold your breath, you can burst.

I cracked the bottle on my lifejacket wide open, the jacket filled like a balloon and I went up as if in a rocket lift, straight through the school of sharks before they even knew I was among them, blowing out a great stream of air until the sky above me lightened to a milky blue. Then I jerked the ripcord which dumped jacket air and hung there, deaf from the ringing in my ears, trying not to be sick into my mouthpiece.

I was already dropping back down into the domain of the hammerheads when a hand caught my harness straps and Peter, wearing two huge tanks of air fitted with a spare demand valve, shoved a rescue mouthpiece between my teeth and gave me an 'O' signal, indicating 'You're okay now.' You could have fooled me!

He kept us there, decompressing, for a full half hour. Peter read a paperback, tearing off the sheets as he finished them. They floated down as food for the still-circling sharks. Halfway through our dangerous sojourn he took a banana from under his jacket and ate it!

He offered me the stub but having observed that the trick involved holding your breath, removing your mouthpiece and not taking in water, I waved it away, certain I would drown on it. It seemed altogether too ridiculous to drown on a banana after all I had survived.

Ernie personally hauled me into the boat obviously very relieved that I was all right.

'I have been sitting here, Robin, thinking how I can tell Mr Heller that I caused you to be eaten by a shark.'

'He would have put it down to my own tardiness,' I consoled him. 'He thinks he's trained me to outswim them.'

The sun was shining on the sea, there were silver dolphins all around the boat behaving as if they were pleased to see me too, I could see the Villa Carlotta on the hillside where our cook would be baking a big fish with onions and tomatoes and the girls would be playing in a few short weeks. I was very pleased to be alive.

'And perhaps he has,' I smiled at Ernie.

By the time we finished swimming Sid's grid we had found four major wreck sites, discounting those in Angra harbour. This was well beyond expectation and he began making the arrangements with the local authorities for full-scale excavations the following summer.

We did not find any bronze cannon but two of the wrecks were in quite shallow water and Sid speculated that their cannon could have been salvaged. The Angra fishermen dived to considerable depths for crayfish equipped only with a large rock, a net and a noseclip. He also speculated rather wistfully but with no great conviction that one of them might be the *Revenge,* but we, who had now read the accounts of that savage last battle in detail, felt she was more likely matchwood in the purple abyss just a few hundred yards offshore.

More detailed examination of these two shallow wrecks was also brought to an abrupt halt by the arrival of the pirates, a quite extraordinary episode which gave our film all the drama of a fictional thriller.

We were returning to harbour one lovely evening when Sid was suddenly transfixed and all but fell into the water. The source of this consternation was a grubby, battered motor cruiser with an English registration tying up for the night.

That evening Sid called us all together and explained, almost gibbering, that the boat was owned by two treasure hunters with whom he had been involved on the wreck of a Dutch East Indiaman in the Irish sea immediately before he came to the Azores.

He was convinced the new English arrivals had followed him to share in any spoils, and indeed there seemed no other probable explanation. They were, Sid said, very tough characters who would stop at nothing where treasure was concerned but had no interest in marine archaeology and conservation. He ordered us to keep well away from them and banned any further work on 'our' sites. I filmed the pirates through our longest lens, and they were indeed a motley crew, although there was no evidence of eye-patches or peg-legs.

We heard from our island friends that the pirates had been making inquiries of the harbour master about our activities. They took their cruiser out once or twice and one of these outings hovered very close to one of our wrecks, but they did not dive.

Meanwhile we made diversionary dives under the cliffs of Angra fort where the flora and fauna was prolific and on one of these recreational swims spotted a huge bronze cannon lodged in a cleft of rocks. Ms Klep from Sweden was an expert on the preservation of cannon and after a quick inspection (for it was rather deep) she pronounced with great excitement that it was the best she had ever seen.

It was the perfect culmination to a marvellous adventure but its discovery pitched poor Sid into a paroxysm of anxiety. The cannon was worth thousands of pounds and was exactly the kind of loot the 'pirates' were after; easy to transport and in such excellent condition they could sell it anywhere.

He was so outraged by this possibility that he decided to go to the authorities and inform them that 'the pirates' were British treasure hunters. To convince them he would have to reveal his previous association and he knew this would almost certainly start an inquiry that would use up the little diving time we had left.

Which is exactly what happened. All marine exploration was stopped while the local officials asked Lisbon what they should do. Fortunately this forced inactivity proved more costly for the pirates than ourselves and one fine morning their ship was gone, never to return.

Sid went immediately to the authorities and told them about the cannon, offering to raise it and present it as a memento of our expedition to the local museum. He waived his finder's share of its value. This was agreed and *The Search for Revenge* climaxed with that magnificent cannon, twelve feet long and still gleaming green, being slowly raised from 120 feet while it was held level by a school of our divers, frantically directed by Sid in his silly blue wetsuit.

Only when we had it resting safely on the quay did we see, in bas relief, the face of King John of Portugal, indicating that it was the work of the royal foundry and a very fine find indeed.

But what was totally incredible was that the bearded King John was the spitting image of Sidney Wignall!

Annette arrived a few days later looking rather wan, which I put down to the fact that Victoria had chickenpox. Sid and several of our divers had also stayed on for a bit of a holiday and we took Annette and the girls out in our fast boat until they were pink and breathless. They were fitted out with our spare masks and snorkels and the girls soon became adept snorkel divers. Every morning was spent on the little black beach below the villa where we started a collection of marine life. The girls even caught stinging Portuguese Man 'o War jellyfish in their little plastic bags.

One morning a group of fishing boats manned by men who had helped the expedition came ashore and invited us to join them at a bullfight of a very unusual kind. The bulls were chased through the streets of a nearby seaside town out on to the quay, from which they would leap, followed by their white-clothed pursuers.

We sat in a great gathering of boats, eating a picnic of sardines grilled on tiny barbecues, octopus stew, great hunks of bread and a huge quantities of rough red wine while this extraordinary spectacle went on directly in front of us. The bulls came crashing down into the sea and for an hour my daughters' mouths only closed when some jolly fisherman's wife popped something delicious in for them to chew. The bulls just swam ashore, coming to no harm.

It was unquestionably the best time we ever had together as a family. And it was the last time, because a few weeks after we got home Annette explained that she had been seeing someone else and intended, with the girls, to go and live with him.

End of a chapter.

Chapter Thirteen

Divorce seems to have a lot in common with most terminal illnesses – by the time its extreme symptoms are revealed it is usually too late to cure it. Parts of me simply died of it.

Some of those parts concerned with the ego, which at the time seemed the most important, I can do without but there are parts of my emotional fabric which I need but no longer have.

The only other worthwhile observation I can make about divorce is that a large part of the pain is self-inflicted. Instead of facing the facts and building a new life, we moon around hoping the clock will somehow run backwards. As a third or more of marriages break up, it must be a tremendous drain on the vitality of humankind. At any one time at least a third of the adult population is walking around in a state of deep despair, recrimination and loss. Moreover, half of that number will remarry and then divorce again. No wonder the rest of nature does its best to avoid us.

For most of the next twelve months I lived like a monastic celibate in the unfinished emptiness of my riverside house, pickled in gloom. Then there were a tacky few months of over-compensating resulting in a maze of double dates and items of female underwear around the house I was unable to exactly identify. Fortunately, all the women who helped me through that time knew what was going on and none of them allowed themselves to take me very seriously.

There was however, no replacing the children, even though my job over the last few years had meant that I had seen very little of them. I resolved that somehow or other I would stay in close contact with them, and see whether it was possible to be a father one step removed, which was at least better than a father *in absentis.*

Just before this all happened I had rented a little farm cottage in the fields of the Upton Estate near Banbury. Annette and I had already agreed that there would not be any limitations on my access to the children. I could take them alternate weekends, and as often as I could manage in the week. The cottage soon became a gift from God, providing me and the children with a place that was ours alone, well away from homes tainted with old memories.

It was there that Annette and I chose to tell the children that we were splitting up. Tiffany, who was eleven, took it very badly indeed, Lisa, nine, began a thoughtful silence on the subject which continues to this day, and Victoria, five, fortunately did not really understand what it meant.

After the children had been told, Annette left and we went fishing. Well, the children went fishing in Upton's little lake while I untangled lines and loaded worms on their hooks, which is the fate of fathers on fishing trips.

'Do you mean you are not going to live with mummy ever again?' Lisa asked.

'No, I'm not. She's moving out now and when we go home tomorrow night I will drop you at the flat.'

'So who will look after you?' Tiffany demanded.

Eeek! who would look after me? The self-pity poured through me like warm syrup and this time I had to turn away from them.

'Mrs White will still be coming in to clean and I'm perfectly capable of looking after myself. Anyway, you lot are going to be coming over twice a week and every other weekend, plus holidays. We'll all have to learn to cook.'

'You'll never be able to learn how to cook,' Lisa said darkly. 'Think of those pancakes. Maybe we could get mummy to do us lunch packs.'

'You could come and have school dinners with me,' Victoria suggested. 'Except they're horrid.'

'So are his pancakes,' Lisa reminded her.

'I don't want to move anyway,' Tiffany snapped. 'I'll stay with you, they can go if they want.'

Lisa and Victoria cast her alarmed looks.

'Mummy and I have thought of that too. It isn't possible. I have to go to work. And anyway it will be better if you're together.' Actually, Annette had not given me the option of looking after the children, which I would have actively contemplated, and my lawyer had told me that no court would separate girl children from their mother unless the mother was awful, which Annette patently wasn't.

Fortunately the day remained very pretty and the instant tea I had bought from Marks and Spencer – tinned rice pudding with real cream, angel delight layer cake, and a meat loaf in tin foil which I 'cooked' by doing no more than insert it in a hot oven, was a great success mainly because it was the kind of expensive stodge Annette would never have dreamed of giving them.

It taught me a very fast lesson about feeding children, which stood me in very good stead over the next few years. They are creatures of extreme habit and much prefer 'favourite' foodstuffs to innovative foodstuffs. I proved this by taking a French Provincial cookery course. They taught me to undercook everything and cover it with various roux-based sauces, the secret of pancake making (let the mix stand), a few very smart supper dishes for impressing girlfriends (my favourite was a sole Véronique served with a food-buff homily about the importance of seedless Muscat grapes) and, when the chef-teacher learned of my situation, a baked alaska to impress my daughters.

On their first visit after my passing out parade I served them a wonderfully rich cassoulet containing delicious spiced pork sausage and French haricot beans covered with a rich gravy.

Victoria pushed her sausage to the side of the plate and fiddled with the beans.

'Actually they're the same as baked beans.' I told her. 'The gravy is just rather better.'

'I'd like ordinary baked beans,' she said belligerently, adding as an obvious afterthought, 'please daddy.'

'Does anybody like it?'

'Well I like sausages and beans, but not like this,' Tiffany compromised. 'The sausages and beans we had last time were fine.'

'Those were Mr Walls and Mr Heinz. These are mine. Why don't you just munch for a bit? I promise you the flavour's spot on.' They did so dutifully, but not much went down and eventually I succumbed and allowed them my fall-back fare, cheese and pickle sandwiches. I would have done better not to force food down them, but I had this feeling that Annette weighed them when she got them home.

I hoped the baked alaska would restore my reputation. It looked incredible as I strode with it to the table, but I had not quite got the meringue mixture stiff enough and as it cooled, the crisp, black-tipped caramel outer coating settled rapidly on to the big block of ice cream in the centre. This then melted more rapidly than any baked alaska on my course and by the time I could get a knife to it we were all looking at a dish with a flat disc of burnt egg white floating on a lake of yellow vanilla cream.

'Is that custard?' Victoria demanded hungrily. She loved my Bird's Eye Devon Cream Custard, especially direct from the tin.

'No, it's rather good ice cream actually.'

'Oh daddy,' Lisa laughed. 'You're not supposed to cook ice cream. Wait till we tell mummy that!'

'I would rather you didn't pass my failures on to your mother.'

'She won't,' Tiffany promised. 'If you do, Lisa, I'll have my whole class put a voodoo curse on you.'

'She will anyway,' Victoria confided, sticking her finger into the gunk. 'This is all right, it tastes just like custard.'

And so there evolved two distinct feeding patterns in my house, patterns which bemused and sometimes amused those girl friends who attended meals without, and very occasionally with, my daughters.

'Do you like meatloaf, Heather?' Tiffany asked the one I finally fell in love with. Heather was a very striking English blonde who was retraining as a journalist after a successful, international modelling career. Her normal culinary venues were the Aratusa and Annabelles and she had seemed rather impressed with my sole Véronique and crêpes suzettes the week before, hence her return visit at the weekend.

The meatloaf from Sainsbury's, still in its tinfoil, was standing smoking in the middle of the table on a baking dish. It looked like a large turd. In a bowl beside it were Sainsbury's new potatoes, machine-peeled to look like billiard balls, and another bowl of frozen peas. Afterwards we would have chocolate or strawberry tinned sponge pudding, Mr Bird's florid custard or, as a special treat, a rich dessert called Ambrosia Creamed Rice.

'I don't know, I never tried one,' Heather said.

'It's great,' Victoria assured her. 'We have one every Sunday.'

'Daddy can't cook,' Lisa explained. 'Don't ever let him try his pancakes on you:'

'I think we've had enough of the pancake joke.' I suggested. 'In any case Heather knows that's not true. I cooked her crêpes suzettes in the week.'

That caused three sets of eyebrows to go straight up, as there was great interest in who spent time in their abandoned nest.

'He can cook funny things all right,' Victoria said. 'But we only like him to cook our favourites. If you stay for tea you'll get moon bread.'

Walking along the Putney Embankment that Sunday afternoon, Heather, who had very bravely eaten her portions of stodge, asked rather nervously what moon bread was.

'Well, it's really only French toast,' I assured her. 'Bread dipped in egg and fried. But that's their favourite too which basically means they would rather not eat anything else, and they have a million ways of not eating anything they don't like. I got so fed up making it, I made some with vegetable dye that was bright green, hoping it would put them off. But they loved it and now I'm stuck with it.'

'Why moon bread?'

'It's what Martians eat.'

'Of course,' she said, watching me and the children carefully.

Down the many years that Heather and I have spent together,

she has assiduously tried to improve the children's eating habits and has never conceded failure even when now, as young women, they poke around her kitchen suspiciously demanding to know what they are about to be given, because I am pleased to say the once-a-week 'tea' still happens.

'Dead dog stew!' Heather says almost ritualistically these days, because we have not eaten instant food for years and all of them, particularly Lisa who has followed in Heather's modelling footsteps, are much too concerned about their figures to even think of eating moon bread.

So as can be seen from all that, we all survived the trauma of the divorce, thanks in no small part to Bob Heller being very understanding.

I went and told him about Annette's decision to leave and indicated I thought it best that I should resign.

'What are you planning to do?'

'Freelance writing.'

'It doesn't pay as well as this.'

'No, but I can work irregular hours. I'm going to try picking the children up from school twice a week. They get out at four o'clock. Then there's the weekends. So I don't want to work out of England for a while either.'

'So don't,' Heller said. 'How long is this going to go on?'

'For as long as it's necessary. I feel the children have to have some continuity.'

'You and them both, I think,' he observed. 'Okay, we'll see how we go. I don't care how you put in the hours and there's plenty of good subjects in this country. Find me another popular one, you seem to have got the hang of those.'

At this time the divorce settlements were gobbling up money and I used public transport a lot. The awkward journey from the ATV studios at Elstree north of London to Putney in the south exposed me to the worst that British Rail and London Transport had to offer.

'Why do we let them treat us like cattle?' I swore to one of the several faces against which my own was crushed.

'You just have to grin and bear it,' its owner said in a cheerful voice, giving me a huge mock grin. 'It's the test of being British.'

I came up with a nice title: *The Great Train Race.*

Heller frowned at my treatment.

'People travelling to work on crowded trains? That's going to be entertaining?'

'You wouldn't believe what they get up to on the trains – gambling, affairs, sports, arts. It touches everybody and everybody touches everybody else; there you are, it's funny.'

'It's going to have to be funnier than that.'

'We found a man who commutes from Swanage to London every day. He spends at least eight hours on the round trip.'

'That's not funny, it's insane. Why?'

'He moved to rescue his daughters from the evils of a university town.'

A faint trace of a smile had started at the corners of Heller's mouth.

'He sees Oxford as sin city?'

'Not Oxford, Reading.'

Bob snickered.

The idea was still quite hard going for both of us because without quite realizing it we were formulating a new genre of documentary programming, now called popular documentary, at which I was to become something of a specialist.

Bob knew that the pioneering days of television when documentaries could be fiercely didactic no matter how few people watched them were already on the wane. To keep our product in the prime time slots we needed to leaven it with some factual programmes that could appeal to mass audiences who would not normally watch 'serious' programmes. Admittedly, this pandering to commercialism was the start of a process that will almost certain kill the serious documentary within my lifetime.

We all went hunting for such topics. Charles Denton, who had joined Bob's team from the BBC, explored what was then 'swinging London' with a film about the rag trade called *See Through Fashion*, Francis Maghee did the Soho music business featuring a bunch of young hopefuls who were putting a huge amount of effort into an obviously hopeless musical about Jesus! (It was *Jesus Christ, Superstar*). David Bailey made an outrageous film about Andy Warhol in which a naked lady did an interview seated on a lavatory, Chris Menzies made his directing debut with a film about the circus, and Tony Snowdon teamed up with Derek Hart to film dwarfs with great style and compassion.

We have a slight excuse – this was the Seventies!

The *Great Train Race* was a significant film for me because it introduced me to the English eccentric, and that discovery made living in England more bearable. The film also convinced me, and particularly my cameraman Louis Wolfers, (from *Arkle and the Duchess*) that the British really will, with a great deal of quiet humour, make the best of everything and it could well be a national characteristic. Was I becoming one of them?

We started at five a.m. one freezing morning in January in a storage shed at Brighton station, with little Louis lying with his camera in the luggage rack of the train as we trundled off to pick up our first commuter. This man wore a shiny black mac and carried a large official-looking book – and he was in my pay.

By the time we reached London the train was, as usual, packed. Louis filmed the amazing dexterity with which the seasoned commuters managed to unfold and read newspapers cheek by jowl with their neighbours while each pretended he was the only person on the train. There was no need to record sound because nobody said anything. My man in the mac slowly vanished into this morass of humanity. Only the English find no companionship in adversity.

At Victoria my man-in-the mac waited for the entire train to disgorge and then, standing alone on that bleak station, opened his book, waited until we were zoomed in to a close-up and announced that he was a Government Veterinary Inspector and it would be illegal to carry cattle under the conditions he had just experienced.

That was about all the documentary content I allowed the film, because from here on the passengers simply refused to support so gloomy an editorial line.

The eight-hour commuter, for example, had the most extraordinary routine of which he was rather proud and was quite happy for us to film.

He was woken at dawn by two alarm clocks. As if clockwork-driven themselves, he and his wife rose from either side of their bed and made off in different directions, he to shave, she to cook. They met to the second at the breakfast table and consumed eggs and bacon in silence while listening intently to the radio. As it grew light a taxi drew up and he climbed in for the half-hour drive to the station.

There he took up an exact position on the station which would align him with his chosen seat. This selection was something of a trade secret, having to do with draughts, wheel noise, crowdedness, distance from the barrier etc. Once on the train, he read his paper for exactly twenty minutes before falling asleep for exactly an hour.

'It is an extraordinarily long journey,' I pointed out.

'I find it quite relaxing.'

'It must be costing you a fortune.'

'I retire in five years, no point in jeopardizing that.'

I could not bring myself to film the return journey, especially as I now knew he was doing all this for nothing. At the little hotel where we had spent the night prior to our predawn start there had been two mini-skirted ravers boozing at the bar. His daughters!

Instead we joined the jolly Littlehampton train and filmed the annual general meeting of the Littlehampton Golf Club which took place in the same carriage every year because that's where the club had been conceived and founded.

A week or so later we were ready to travel down to Littlehampton and film them playing, but my researcher kept avoiding the subject.

'I want to intercut their carriage-bound AGM with the freedom of the great outdoors,' I pointed out rather irritably.

'I know that!' (all researchers are directors in embryo) 'There just doesn't seem to be a golf course in Littlehampton.'

'Look harder,' I said.

'You're going to like this,' She said gleefully a few days later. 'There isn't a proper golf course in Littlehampton. They play on the pitch and putt course.'

Bob Heller liked it even more.

'I guess they feel more at home all cramped together!'

We did a wonderful interview with an immaculate middle-aged secretary who always sat on a neatly folded plastic bag in the corridor outside the guard's van on one of the Kent commuter trains. We filmed her sitting there as further proof of our thesis that conditions on the trains were intolerable. She ruined the shot by smiling sweetly at us, quite obviously content, throughout the journey.

A day or so later I found her in exactly the same position. We had filmed our way down the train and there were a number of empty seats. I told her about them.

'I'm quite all right here,' she said. 'I'm used to it.'

'You like sitting on the floor?'

'Well, I don't exactly like it,' she admitted. 'But it's better than standing up. You can't be sure of getting a proper seat on this train so I've taken to coming straight here where I can always sit down.'

No wonder Hitler lost the war!

On these same Kent trains there were poker, gin-rummy and pontoon games that had been running for years. Members of these card schools had a roster whereby one of their number always got to the train early enough to claim their regular table. British Rail had accepted their tenure and even put up narrow tables between the seats for their use. We were told that the games had years-long waiting lists and places had been known to be bought for considerable sums of money.

To be a successful commuter you needed to know certain things, most important of which was where to stand on the platform.

On several occasions we arrived early to film them boarding and I noted with fascination how they all formed neat little queues at certain set points. These points were not marked in any way.

'How do you know where to stand?' I asked one of them.

'What?' It was obviously an idiotic question.

I explained that we were making a programme for television (which immediately explained the idiotic questioning) and repeated myself, pointing out that there were no marks on the platform.

'The door's there,' the commuter explained, pointing at the air directly in front of him.

'How do they know so exactly where to stand?' I demanded of the station master.

'It's what you might call acquired knowledge,' he smiled. 'They just know.'

'That means you have to keep the trains the same length all the time?'

'On these busy commuter lines, of course,' he said in a hushed voice. 'My God I think we'd have a riot if we messed them up, certainly in the rush hour.'

By this stage of filming, my hard-hitting exposé of intolerable travel conditions was in shreds. It was quite obvious that a great number of commuters were enriching their lives by travelling on the trains. The real victims of commuting were the wives.

'We moved out here for the country air,' one disgruntled housewife observed. She was trapped in her bungalow in the Kent Weald, which was a pretty unexciting place even before they built large housing estates all over it. Her estate was seven miles from the station which meant she either had to get up at dawn and drive her husband in or let him drive himself, which meant she was marooned car-less on the estate.

'All those things you read about in the *News of the World* about what goes on out there in the home counties: white witchcraft, flower arranging, wife-swapping – it's all true. What else have we got to swap? None of our husbands get home until eight and they've just enough energy left to digest their dinner and watch the tele. I'd give anything to go back to the Smoke.'

Unfortunately, we were never able to film the best story I found. I learnt about it from Our Lady of the Plastic Bag when I explained that we would be coming back to film her if she was willing.

She agreed, but couldn't quite see my interest in someone who had spent probably a quarter of her adult life sitting on a plastic bag.

'There's something much more interesting than that,' she confided, nodding in the direction of the closed door to the guard's van. 'The ghost of Hamlet prowls through there twice a year!'

I gingerly sat down beside her.

'I never heard of a guard's van being haunted before,' I confessed. 'Have you seen the ghost?'

'No, but I hear him quite regularly. Just before Christmas and then again round about May.'

'It's May now – is he in there?'

'He's not a regular commuter,' she confided. 'He seems to favour Fridays. Will I really be on television?'

'If there's a ghost in there, you certainly will be,' I promised.

'Then I must be careful in what I say, mustn't I,' she whispered. 'Last December he was Nanki-Poo.'

As everyone who does not work in television knows, there is a fine line between eccentricity and madness and I began to suspect that my film's prize eccentric was on the wrong side of the line. She appeared to detect my unease.

'From the *Mikado,*' she insisted. 'He sings, in a muffled sort of way, but quite clearly Nanki-Poo.'

'Tomorrow's Friday – I'm going to be on the train talking to the weekenders!'

My lady looked askance. Weekenders were regarded by the daily commuters as a depraved group. They had dumped their wives in the very deepest corners of the countryside, so deeply in fact they could only afford to travel home at weekends, and it was inferred by the regulars that to catch up on their sex lives their weekends had to be orgies. The regulars pointed out, with lots of nudges and winks, how tired the weekenders all looked on Mondays.

'Is it all right if I join you tomorrow night for Nanki-Poo?' I asked my plastic bag lady. She agreed, a little suspiciously.

The weekenders were a dead loss. Mostly they were worried about how they would get through all the jobs that would need doing when they got home.

'Sexual orgies,' one of them roared with laughter. 'I should be so lucky. I've got to weed the garden, mow the lawn, mend a puncture or two, walk the dog properly, drive my wife in for the Saturday shopping, play football with my boy, have a dinner party. My wife's lucky to get kissed goodnight!'

So I hurried on to find my bag lady, with no great hopes there either.

'Didn't come tonight I suppose?'

'Oh yes – he's in there now.'

I swear the hair stood up on the back of my neck.

'Listen!'

And listen I did, huddled down beside her on the floor, and heard through the guard's van door, muffled but as clear as a bell, that famous stanza:

> 'A wandering minstrel I, a thing of threads and patches . . .

I poised myself, stepped quickly forward, swung the door open and charged in, freezing Nanki-Poo in mid-gesture. He was wearing a bowler hat, pin-striped trousers and black coat of a City gent.

For a long minute we stared at each other.

'Er . . . I have had a word with the guard,' he said. 'It's the quietest place, you see.'

'It's coming to me – but there is a lady out there who thinks you're a ghost.'

'Really,' he smiled. 'Of whom, pray?'

'Of Hamlet – and someone called Nanki-Poo.'

'Oh, I see!' he laughed. 'Good Lord, I hope I haven't frightened her.'

'I don't think so. I suspect she's going to be very disappointed you're flesh and blood.'

'Is she the one who sits on the plastic bag?' he inquired conspiratorially. 'I always thought she was a bit . . . well, you know!'

'When she finds out you're not a ghost she's going to be thinking much the same about you. What actually are you doing?'

'Rehearsing, old chap. Breaks the tedium. Amateur dramatics. Very keen on it myself. Have you ever done any?'

'Two shows a year,' I suggested. 'Christmas and summer?'

'Exactly, how do you know?'

'It's when the ghost walks,' I nodded back into the corridor. I explained my interest and asked for his permission to reconstruct the encounter for the programme.

'Out of the question, old chap. I work for the Bank of England and the old lady of Threadneedle Street would not take kindly to that at all.'

He smiled again.

'You say she's all right?'

'Perfectly.'

'Then I'll buy her a drink,' he promised. 'And perhaps she might like a couple of complimentaries. We do a rather good *Mikado* if she finds Shakespeare a bit heavy. But she knows that already, doesn't she?'

I do hope they lived happily ever after.

According to the ratings *The Great Train Race* was watched by almost every commuter in Britain. Bob Heller was mightily pleased and I acquired a new label. The Africa Expert cum Political Exposist was hereafter his conduit to the proletariat; I had acquired that most valuable of all television production attributes, the Common Touch.

Admittedly I was still a beginner. To complete my education Bob apprenticed me to a master, the British humorist Dave Allen.

Chapter Fourteen

Whenever I was working late on an edit at the Elstree studios of a Saturday night I would go and watch the recording of the *Dave Allen Show*.

This fantasia operated like a rogue planet on the outer edges of Bob Heller's empire and being in charge of it was a little like being obliged to keep a firm hold of a shorting electric fence. Heller knew that every week there would be a crisis of some kind. I think Bob found the shocks stimulating.

If the material itself did not provide the required degree of shock, Dave would get in on the act. The Pope was already a prime target and Dave had started to refine his ability for spotting the pretentious and projecting it as the preposterous.

Rehearsals, which Bob Heller often attended (an act of masochism unrivalled in the history of television production) were usually a riot. My favourite rehearsal featured a very merry Patrick Wymark, star of *The Power Game* which was also in production at Elstree, storming onto the set to have a screaming row with his illicit girl friend. Dave pretended it was all part of the show.

Another time I arrived just in time to see him climb on top of one of the sturdy studio cameras and do an introduction with one foot resting casually on about £20,000-worth of lens.

The show was a huge success. People watched, I'm sure, to see whether God would strike Dave dead in the middle of one of his religious jokes, or because they realized that beneath the air of anarchy was a sturdy social message, hence Heller's fascination.

Dave Allen is, in my professional opinion, the best satirical comedian television has produced, rivalled only by Stanley Baxter and Al Read. Indeed it is rather unfair lodging Dave with the comedians (and I love comedians!) but I can't find a more accurate classification for him.

My golden age of television produced a host of fantastic comedians, in fact it may say something about television that its very best creative product was laughter produced by Morecambe and Wise, the Two Ronnies, Benny Hill, Tommy Cooper, Monty Python and so many others.

But while these stars were very funny and their jokes often relevant, they lacked Dave's inexorable and original social message delivered on a blank set from a high stool.

Following up Bob Heller's injunction, Dave and I met in his dressing room at the Coliseum where he was playing Captain Hook in *Peter Pan*.

It's hard to discuss documentaries, even of the popular genre, with a man wearing an eye patch and an iron hook in place of a hand. What would the subject be, I wondered, humour, fantasy, satire, Wendy's relationship with the Lost Boys, Peter Pan's transvestism?

Over the next few weeks we talked our way through a great number of very serious topics and actually made a recce to a black ghetto in Liverpool called District 8 where Dave thought we could find hopeful evidence of integration. In fact we were confronted with the rawest black power movement I have ever come across outside of America and (wrongly, in retrospect) we backed off.

Sadly we got back on the train.

'Why is the world so full of that sort of thing?' Dave mused.

'Human nature. Even the sweetest custards are shark infested.'

'I still think it's to do with living like rats.'

'It's the fat cats not the rats that end up with the power,' I pointed out. 'And humans get very eccentric if they live alone too much. The trick seems to be to find the balance.'

'That would make a nice piece for Mr Heller.'

'Finding the balance? I'd defy anyone to fit that into the documentary hour.'

'Eccentrics,' he grinned. 'Finding the balance!'

And thus began a five-year partnership which produced fourteen hours of very popular television; in fact it is not too large a claim to say that these programmes pioneered the early evening popular documentary. We transmitted in the seven o'clock slot between two soaps, *Crossroads* and *Coronation Street*, and to the delight of Bob Heller and the other ITV controllers (who had not shared his confidence that you could show anything factual at that hour, even with Dave Allen presenting it) the audience of many millions stayed with us. In fact we regularly handed *Coronation Street* a bigger audience than we had inherited from *Crossroads*.

This pleased everybody; the IBA because they could boast of an extension of factual programming on ITV, and the moguls because it allowed them to run two soaps virtually back to back. We were the salty savoury in a very lucrative white-bread sandwich and the scheduling formula for this hour has stayed much the same ever since.

For Dave and me the show was a double delight. We met some incredible people as it slowly and joyously dawned on us that true eccentricity was a formula for great fulfilment – these people had, in their funny way, found happiness in the balance!

The first programme we did together was a single one-hour documentary called *In Search of the Great English Eccentric*. It was so well-watched it spawned two popular half hour 13-part series. Of these 26 programmes, thirteen were shot in England with an average of five eccentrics per show, and 13 in America, some of which had just one or two subjects in each half-hour. Altogether we researched several hundred people who had chosen to live off the beaten track of life.

That meant I was also off the beaten track most of the time, and if you stay off for five years, I'm not sure you ever come back. Fortunately I came to believe in 'the balance' too, particularly the importance eccentrics give to life's values, and I never really wanted to come back all the way anyway. Dave? – well, if I had spent more time studying his performances I should have realized that 'the balance' was to him what the Golden Fleece was to Jason and the Argonauts.

It also meant that for the first time I was doing something in television that did not seem in any way morally suspect. I felt I had discovered something of a vocation (or as everyone else was soon suggesting, a vacation). The custard sharks couldn't understand the world of the eccentrics at all: there was no money in it and therefore nothing there for them to eat. Significantly, the most engaging eccentrics rarely had the time to watch television.

Finding our subject material was both difficult and time-consuming. Contrary to general opinion not all eccentrics court publicity, indeed many of them are so jealous of the very special lives they live they become reclusive.

I started out, with the help of researchers Christine Fox and Guy Nevill, by calling every local newspaper in the UK, slowly evolving questions which bracketed our target.

'We're looking for unusual local characters.'

'This is Edinburgh, chummie, the town of floppy wrists and the petit bourgeoisie! Fifty per cent of the town works hard to be unusual, the other half works on invisibility.'

'Not groups – characters, odd collectors, the kind of person you'd expect to take a soap box to Speaker's Corner.'

'You mean nutters!'

'Not quite. Sane but different.'

There was then a long puzzled silence followed almost invariably by a flash of inspiration.

'Well there's old Charlie Varley, I suppose, he's got this collection of tram lines. You wouldn't believe it but he actually goes abroad with his little hacksaw and shopping cart and come sneaking back with hunks of old iron. He claims he sticks to abandoned lines but I wouldn't put it past him to bring about a derailment if he wanted the piece bad enough.'

Very soon I became adept at guiding local journalists and regional stringers down the right track. Everywhere had at least one person fitting our requirement and it soon became apparent that Britain was squirming with eccentrics. There were pockets of them in some areas, from cowboys engaging in fast-draw competitions in Yorkshire to Cavaliers and Roundheads refighting the Civil War, to Devonians who were well on their way to re-forming a 2nd World War armoured cavalry company.

When we extended our horizons to include eccentrics from the past whose legacy was still with us, our files positively bulged. Staid Edinburgh produced its folly, the fake Greek amphitheatre on a hill overlooking the city, a line of massive columns erected at huge expense before the cost cooled the mood of municipal eccentricity. It has never been rekindled.

There is even an Eccentrics Club in which the spirit of English eccentricity is maintained by a clock which runs ever backwards, and the continuing presence of Mr Jeremy Bentham at the club's annual general meeting, even though Mr Bentham died more than 200 years ago. A famous surgeon, he had ordered himself to be stuffed so that he could continue to attend the meetings of the club he helped found.

Clubs and follies found their way into the series as our tastes matured and we saw ourselves as mapping a rare feature of the British character which had remained with us down the centuries. I shall never forget Guy Nevill, whose own family is almost as long as English history and who was typecast in the role of researcher of the eccentric, reporting on the skull he had found in an ancient house in Devon which was said still to be possessed of the powers of its original fourteenth century owner who had been famous for his practical jokes.

'Perfect,' I said. Dave agreed. 'If we can get a 600-year-old ghost to play a practical joke on me, we're made.'

Guy was still looking uneasy.

'Well', he confessed, 'I actually handled the skull myself. And on the way back up the motorway I have to tell you that my trousers mysteriously caught fire. This is absolutely true.' We found the story so compelling I insisted Guy actually come on camera and tell it.

More and more Dave and I became intrigued by the possibility that these weird but fulfilled people had somehow stumbled upon the secret of a happy life.

In Search Of The Great English Eccentric opened traditionally enough to the sound of the Dam Buster's March, a howling aircraft engine, machine gun fire and a close-up of a Battle of Britain pilot at the controls of a Spitfire in a power dive. It was the kind of audience-grabbing opening Bob Heller really liked.

Indeed Bob was contentedly transfixed all through the opening sequence – until the half-smiling face of Dave Allen appeared in the void outside the cockpit and he tapped loudly on the perspex, calling to the pilot: 'Mr Lacey, Mr Lacey – can I come in for a moment?'

The lovely Bruce Lacey held the illusion for a precious second or two before switching off his sound-effects, swinging up his cockpit-cover and making room for Dave to climb in beside him.

'I was just re-fighting the Second World War,' Bruce said. 'You can have a go if you like.'

'Oh come on!' said Bob Heller in despair. 'Is this documentary?'

I'm not at all sure he ever accepted that it was through all the years we went on in a similar zany vein, but he did grow to like it.

We cut to a wide shot, revealing that the 'Spitfire' was two chairs inside a scrap cockpit and that the dog-fights and the bomb runs were videos on a television monitor strapped behind the joy-sticks; the whole mad contraption hand-build by the eccentric Mr Lacey from the myriad bits and pieces crowding out his even more eccentric workshop.

We went back to the bombing with Dave crammed alongside Bruce in the cockpit. In a moment the illusion and Lacey's fierce concentration had taken over, making it almost impossible to remember that this was really a garage in London's East End.

'Have a go, you fly.' Bruce insisted. 'You move the stick forward to dive – be careful, be careful, we don't want to go into a stall!'

Dave said, 'Can I fire at that aircraft?'

'Yes, it's one of ours but fire at it anyway, you're not going to hurt anyone. Press the button there, press the button quick.'

There was a burst of gunfire.

'There's a certain amount of pretence involved' Bruce apologized.

'True,' said Dave politely. 'Do you do this often?'

Bruce nodded enthusiastically: 'In fact I really don't know where I am actually. I live in a strange world of illusion somewhere between fantasy and reality.'

Dave nodded.

'Marvellous world to be in,' Bruce enthused, as if it were as simple as taking a trip to the Costa Brava.

We leave him in mid-air. His fantasy aeroplane becomes our magic carpet to other regions of fantasy. In his chair in the viewing theatre, Bob Heller sucks his teeth with approval at this artifice.

The music of Edward Elgar pours from the speakers and the picture dissolves to a perfect English churchyard, the interior of the church, to a vicar in High Church vestments, preaching. Dave is seated in the pews, listening.

'It is written: "Man shall not live by bread alone." Adventure,' the Vicar acclaims, 'Adventure, whether spiritual, physical or mental, is surely an essential in the life of anyone who is to be truly alive. Life can be oh so dull and oh so mediocre and so inward looking in this day and age ... So dead! Some people, it would seem, will never be more dead than they are at the moment. Yet what is faith but the greatest adventure of all, the greatest gamble with the highest stakes a man can possible lay – his immortal soul.'

The observant listener will have noticed that I have started to introduce a cowboy tune behind this stirring invocation and the picture slowly dissolves to the back door of the Rectory through which the vicar, now dressed in blue jeans, leather chaps with silver trimmings, stetson, leather waistcoat and coiled rope, emerges in slow motion to live the theme of his sermon.

Bob Heller, who is watching all this in the rushes theatre shifts uneasily in his seat.

The vicar neatly lassoos a log horse and jerks it across the vicarage yard. He looks wonderful, the perfect incumbent of the grand tradition of eccentric English clerics. Indeed, our research has thrown up so much eccentricity among the clergy (not all of it as healthy and outdoors as this) that we have wondered whether it might not be what others call divine inspiration.

As the cowboy vicar mounts his horse (a black and white pinto) we re-introduce his sermon as a voice-over: 'The important thing in life is the far horizon; the urge to see always round the next bend and over the next ridge. (The eyes of the children watching in the congregation visibly enlarge. Bob Heller sucks his teeth) ... or at least seem to be.' Slow mix out to rejoin the cowboy vicar riding in silhouette across the headland ... his message resumes: 'Or that is how it must seem to the comfortable, orthodox, in-the-rut, inward-looking, dead, self-satisfied sort of person.'

'He said dead twice,' Bob says from his chair. 'I think that calls for a cut.'

'Down with the comfortable, orthodox, inward-looking, self-satisfied, dead people,' I remind him fiercely.

'You think people are going to take him seriously!'

'I certainly hope not,' I avow. 'But they are certainly going to listen.'

'Does Dave ever tell a joke?'

'Certainly not,' I snap, and he never did.

'Kipling wrote in *The Explorer*', the vicar said,

'''There's no sense in going further, it's the edge of cultivation

[*Cut to* vicar galloping on horseback down an English arroya]

... Till a voice as bad as conscience rang interminable changes on one ever-lasting whisper, day and night, repeating so:

Something hidden, go and find it, go and look behind the ranges,

Something lost behind the ranges, lost and waiting for you ... Go!'''

Dave and I sit in silence waiting to hear our fate, for this is the first rough cut Heller has seen.

'I like ''a voice as bad as conscience'',' Bob says. 'Do you have more of that kind of thought-provoking stuff?'

'Oodles,' I assured him as Part Two flickered onto the screen to the beat of an Indian drum.

Hard on the heels of the cowboy vicar (or so the impression was given) rode a Sioux Indian chief, magnificent in eagle feather head-dress, deerskin clothing, feathered spear and seated bare-back.

Slow mix to the back streets of Eastbourne, zoom in over the bloomers airing on the lines, the cucumber cold frames and last winter's spiky Brussels sprouts to a huge black and white teepee. Dissolve inside to a figure draped in skins and pelts, making fire with a hardwood stick and a bow. Smoke puffs up slowly. In the corner his squaw sits smiling at Dave, resplendent in soft doe-skin, bright with bead-work. Dave wears his old blue raincoat and a smile reflecting mild disbelief. The chief lights a pipe of peace and hands it ceremoniously to Dave.

'Don't the women get a smoke?' Dave asks politely.

'No,' says Mr Blackmore, one-time postman and life-long surrogate Sioux, while his wife looks embarrassed. Dave apologizes.

'And what's more,' says the chief, 'You must never pass the pipe beyond the doorway. If it goes beyond the doorway it must be passed round again.'

Dave observes the rule we made for the whole programme and the two series which followed it: he took it in. No snide grins, no deprecating side-long looks, no making mock, no cheap wisecracks. These are real people who have something important to tell us if we can just have the good manners to listen with an open mind.

In any case we discovered that among eccentrics disbelief is soon suspended. These were true Sioux, be they ever so far from their historical hunting ground and the only members of the Eastbourne branch of the tribe.

'Mr Blackmore,' Dave suggests to help our audience make the

transition, 'This is not exactly what one would expect to find in a place like Eastbourne.'

'No,' Mr Blackmore (who the close-up reveals has a black ring drawn round his eye) agrees. 'I suppose I'm rather a misfit in a civilized society like this,' he adds without a trace of sarcasm.

Mr Blackmore picks up his deerskin rawhide drum and his snakeskin rattle and begins to drum and rattle and soon to sing in a strange monotone. It is the leader's song, he announces, of the Omaha Indians.

'It was sung when the Omaha Indians were going on a friendly visit to their old enemy the Sioux to patch up some sort of peace between the tribes, hoping that they would be received as friends.'

The alien words of the song rang out across those small back yards and had evidently worked well on the English natives who, our research revealed, had no animosity at all towards the Blackmores. They loved their surrogate Sioux dearly and spoke of the good work they did at Rotary fetes and children's Christmas parties.

'The words actually mean,' said Mr Blackmore, 'We are advancing, we are moving towards you, the almighty father decides the destinies of men.'

By my side at the rushes viewing, Bob Heller sighed contentedly at 'more of that thoughtful stuff,' adding: 'And it's good to have the racial balance. In the States, you know, the Indian gets a pretty bad press.'

Dave winked at me.

Disbelief, as I say, suspends itself in the right company.

Back on screen, Dave, who felt the documentary nature of our programme obliged him to pose such questions, asked Mr Blackmore how long he had been interested in Indians.

'All my life.'

'And you, Mrs Blackmore?'

'Well,' she said shyly, 'When I first met my husband.' She produced their wedding photos: black and white snaps taken back in 1926 on their honeymoon in a teepee. The teepee was exactly like the one in which we were filming.

'It was pretty cold and miserable at Easter,' said Mr Blackmore. 'But we kept a fire in the teepee day and night and that kept the ground nice and dry.'

I can remember thinking, 'could the secret of a long and happy married life be to spend your honeymoon in a teepee? ' Sadly no. To tread that simple road requires extreme innocence. The joy of being with the Blackmores was that their individual innocence was still a shining light.

It was a powerful innocence, because a few years later they went to America (a rare expedition from those back streets) and were formally adopted into the Sioux tribe. Curly (as Mr Blackmore called Mrs Blackmore even though she was wearing a wig of long black Indian tresses) was adopted by the actual grandson of Sitting Bull and given the name of Red Leaf Woman.

Mr Blackmore had a more formal initiation a week later into Sitting Bull's family and was given the name of Hon-kesh-nee, which we were not surprised to learn meant 'Slow, deliberate or thoughtful.'

'They are a very serious and honest people,' Mr Blackmore said. 'Lying and stealing were two things absolutely unknown to them. When the Indians met the white men in the first instance they always greeted them as friends and did all they could to help them. But the Spaniards burned the Indians to death to convert them to Christianity. Thousands of them were burned to death, and that's how they learned to torture prisoners. They never did before the white men came.

'The scalping of enemies was another thing that the white men started. We always blame the Indian for scalping enemies but there is not the slightest doubt that far more Indians were scalped by white people in the old days than there ever were white people scalped by Indians!'

By now I had entirely forgotten that we were still sitting on wet English soil among the Monday washing. Only later did we come to realize that our subjects could tell before we could when this happened – and we were ready for a little gentle indoctrination, for all eccentrics are evangelical given half a chance.

Dave worked hard to keep one foot in the real (*sic*) world of his television documentary. Often, if we had travelled a long way through the looking glass, these questions from another dimension brought us sharply back to earth.

'Would you have liked to have been born a Red Indian?'

'I would in the old days,' said Hon-Kesh-Nee. 'But of course since the coming of the white man they've had a pretty miserable existence.'

So he and Mrs Blackmore had decided to stay in Eastbourne, turning Indian only for charity and television. We left him in full warpaint and cut back to our lovable lunatic linkman, Bruce Lacey.

Bruce had the advantage of not being trapped in one fantasy, and this time we joined him in his 'mad professor' workshop with Dave in tow.

'What are you yourself,' Dave asked, 'Something of an overgrown child?'

'Well yes,' Bruce agreed. 'More a child that never grew into an adult. I believe children are what adults are meant to be. When you see primitive families like Red Indians or Eskimos, the children and the adults all play, together. In this country we only play on the beach with our children or at Epping Forest on August Bank Holiday. Adults are too embarrassed to play any more.'

When Bruce Lacey made that observation I had never heard of the term 'neoteinia' nor, I am sure, had he. It is the ability of creatures to play as they become more mature. Psychologists have used it as a measure of intelligence in the animal world because the more intelligent animals like dolphins, chimps and humans play into adulthood much longer than smaller brained animals like chickens or cattle. Bruce had realized instinctively the link between playfulness and intelligence, or if you like, play, art and sensitivity.

Some of this rubbed off on us and increasingly we began to look for adults engaged in forms of play, behind the play, and what play was giving them. Soon we also began to see that Bruce was right, the only thing that was making them appear peculiar was that they were adults.

Our next cut was to another idyllic English scene, a thatched stone cottage, in front of which a tall bearded man was brushing leaves into a road-sweeper's tricycle cart.

The shot dissolves to the same man riding a similar conveyance converted to a vision of splendour. The cart is festooned to a height of ten feet with gaily-coloured balloons, bulls horns, bells, statues of animals and the stuffed head of a small deer. The cart itself supports shelves filled with rabbits wearing pink ribbons and small white mice.

Dave, drab in his mac, stands waiting for Mr Snowy White, eccentric road-sweeper who is now resplendent in red fez, crimson guards' tunic and white riding breeches, and watches with open wonder as Snowy cycles his extraordinary conveyance dangerously down a hill to the village green.

We join him there for his Saturday morning performance. The tinkling noises made by Snowy's bells have attracted the local children like the Pied Piper once did to the children of Hamelin. Snowy now dons a top hat covered with white mice and lifts an umbrella on which are perched three fan-tailed pigeons. He pops mice in his mouth, chews dramatically until the children grow pop-eyed, then retrieves the rodent (which he has palmed) from someone's ear, smacking his lips. The pigeons fly round his head and perch on his shoulders.

He is a travelling player who has turned his cleaner's cart (for all this started when he was made redundant by the Road Cleaning Department) into a tiny circus.

'So how do you live now?' Dave asks, ever the determined documentary-maker.

'I live off the land,' Snowy smiles. 'Mostly on potatoes, brussels and greens. I live like my rabbits.'

We flashback to Snowy working his allotment. He has changed

to a bowler hat. The cart, stripped of its finery, now does service shipping sturdy cabbages and spuds back to his thatched cottage.

'If you could change the world, Snowy, how would you do it?'

Snowy, who like most of his kind does not recognize the enormity of the changes he has made to his own small world, says: 'Ooooh, I don't know about that! I wouldn't have so many cars,' he says eventually. Then he gains confidence.

'People don't see anything any more,' he affirms. 'They just hop in a car, press a pedal or something, and go. They don't see the lovely countryside or the trees same as I do. And if they were to see them they wouldn't know what they were there for. My life's much different, you see, I look at the grass to see how it's growing for the rabbits. And I see which trees have blossomed and which haven't. I talk to my brussels sprouts and tell them "You keep growing so as I'll be all right next winter."'

'So man is going wrong somewhere,' Dave insists.

'Wrong?' queries Snowy, apparently confused by the question. 'Aren't we all going wrong?'

Dave decides rightly that Snowy's world is his decorated carts and all joy resides there, and accepts an invitation to pedal one of them home. We film the guardsman-roadsweeper and the man in the mac, each on a ludicrous cart, riding off into a more colourful world where even the brussels sprouts respond to care and conversation.

'There,' Snowy says, 'Isn't this wonderful.'

Dave, pedalling hard, is working at it.

Bruce Lacey has now quit World War Two and is explaining to Dave the mechanics of suspending reality. It is not, apparently, all in the mind but can actually be constructed from the detritus of the throwaway society. Bruce has a vast, rambling shambles of a workshop in London's East End littered with old sewing machine motors, valves, bits of metal and discarded electronic junk.

Bruce, who at first glance is difficult to take seriously in this new role of genius inventor because he is still wearing his flying helmet, goggles and sheepskin jacket, takes Dave over to a formidable array of tape recorders and explains that the flying and battle noises they have been using to re-bomb Germany he created himself, mostly using his own voice.

He throws back his head and sings aircraft engine noises while jiggling the levers of an electronic drum kit to evoke machine gun fire.

'You've got plenty of the stuff of dreams here,' Dave observes. 'What are you working on at the moment?'

'Well, this year I'm going to be a pop star. It's getting more difficult to be a pop star the older I get so I've got to get on with it. I've made lots of wigs and I shall use a lot of make-up. Nobody will be able to tell how old I am.'

He has built a very primitive synthesizer as a backup for his weak voice. Bruce yodels away and the synthesizer follows behind, a key or two off.

'Nice, isn't it?' Bruce grins, knowing exactly how awful it is. That was another lesson we learnt. Eccentrics obviously have to be careful never to let their alternative realities become too real, as that would obviously defeat the purpose.

'What would be even better would be a robot Me that could sing with the synthesizer,' Bruce says. 'I've made a start on a Me, actually.'

Dave looks warily around. Eccentric humans, he has learnt, are gentle souls, but a mad robot built by Bruce Lacey out of washing-machine parts might need to be watched! And there it was in the corner, grinning at him.

'I used to build robots for television,' Bruce confessed, loath to remember the days when he worked nine-to-five. 'But they were just cardboard boxes painted silver with men inside them. I dreamed of making real robots and this is the first – she's called Rosa Bosom.'

'She – it's – a girl?'

'Well, sort of. It's actually a Radio Operated Simulated Actress, Battery or Standby Operated Mains: R-O-S-A B-O-S-O-M.' (Never take eccentrics anything less than seriously.)

'How do you mean actress?'

'I'm doing a play with her called the *Three Musketeers*.'

Dave kept silent. Bruce really didn't need him to ask questions anyway.

'I'll bring her over,' said Bruce, pressing knobs.

Rosa Bosom had much in common with Snowy White's carts. Her head was a road works lamp and her torso a stack of shelves on wheels, each shelf mounting electrical bits and pieces for which we of the real world could find no further use. Mounted on an arm in front of the lamp head were a pair of huge red foam rubber lips which swung out and gave Dave a kiss, complete with loud sucking noise. On Shelf Two a huge red heart flashed on and off as the lips pulsated across Dave's face.

'And she can talk,' Bruce said proudly. The robot started to speak French in the Queen's voice.

'Why French?' Dave asked carelessly.

'The Three Musketeers!' Bruce reminded him patiently.

'She plays the Queen,' Dave proudly deduced after only a moment's pause.

Bruce stared fondly at his robot.

'She must be improving,' he observed.

The robot suddenly swung away and careered across the workshop. Bruce hurriedly cut the power.

'I'm going to have to adjust her.'

'To what!' Dave hooted.

'No, seriously,' Bruce said. 'I've discovered that she's on the same frequency as the cheap Japanese walkie-talkies the kids buy round here, and if you whistle the right note she'll come for you. Can you imagine what the papers would make of that?'

They wander on.

'This is my memory room,' says Bruce in a vast cavern of junk. 'All the things from my childhood hats, dressing-up clothes, toys, books. 'There is also a full set of Japanese armour and a life-size medical skeleton.

'What advice would you give to me about fulfilling dreams? 'Dave probes. 'I think I represent the fairly standard average normal sort of person.'

Bruce does not have to think very long.

'Give up any job that brings you a regular income. Take a year off from all the pressures, think very carefully and ask yourself what would you like to do most in all the world and then do it – it might just be blowing bubbles.'

Cut to a limpid soap bubble floating slowly past the camera. From the balcony of a rather seedy London house they are being blown though a ring by a little man in pebble glasses wearing a deerstalker hat, the poet Ivor Cutler.

We find Dave down below in the street, trying to catch them. On the background music-track (I am rather ashamed to record) someone is singing 'I'm forever blowing bubbles.'

Ivor Cutler is another breed of eccentric entirely. He does not dress up, he builds no artefacts, and he still lives in our world. But those little pebble glasses evidently have peculiar lenses. What he sees is not what we see.

'I play games all the time,' he tells Dave. 'Life is to play games, to have a good time. I learned that from Rebecca West. She said something like "If it gives pleasure that's your touchstone."'

'I'll sing you a song' he offers and, dropping his voice into his boots, intones:

> I think very deeply
> I'm a very good thinker
> People don't bother me much
> They can see I'm using my mind.
> What's my conclusions
> Mmmm . . . hmmm.. hmmm . . . hmmmmm

Dave decides he's losing his grip on this one. 'Ivor,' he says, 'How would you describe yourself?'

'Well,' says Ivor, 'It depends how I'm feeling. I could be described as a humorist I suppose but that's too like a job and not what I am. I'm a child, yes, I think that's better. Let me sing you another song. It may help.'

It doesn't.

> The grass springs up to meet the air coming down
> And that's a good idea
> For if the grass lied low
> The air would have to come down
> The extra amount – 'Cos there has to be something there,
> 'Cos there's got to be something there all the time,
> 'Cos there's got to be something there.

Nothing rhymes, nothing scans, there is no harmony, but it all makes a weird kind of sense. Look at it more closely and you can see a breath of quantum theory, indeed I had now begun to wonder whether the discordant nature of the eccentric life was not somehow in tune with the laws of chaos that have been shown to govern the universe: a symmetry of the asymmetrical.

We cut to Ivor and his girlfriend drawing in front of the flamingo pool at the zoo.

'What are you doing?' Ivor asks.

'Drawing.'

'What are you drawing?'

'A hexagonal nut.'

Ivor's eyes lift to the beautiful flamingoes, then fall to the waste bin on the rail in front of them which is secured to a post by a hexagonal nut.

Ivor, who hates linear thinking, smiles appreciatively.

Dave also smiles, recognizing a kindred spirit. 'There's a touch of the anarchist in you Ivor.'

'Oh, I'm a non-joiner,' Ivor concedes. 'And in the sense that a child is an anarchist because he hasn't known any bosses or discovered that there are people you have to obey – or ideas that you've got to obey. I must say I like pushing the boat a little – it's my pleasure.'

Ivor gives us an example of this. 'They have tape recordings at the zoo and they are very full of good information, but not completely to my taste. I thought, not that I could do it better, but differently. I made a recording, took it to the zoo and hid a tape-player close to the giraffe house. It went something like this.

'This is an animal. It has four legs, one at each corner to keep it up off the ground. It helps it also to see the people who are looking at it over the barrier. The animals stay here until six o'clock when the people go home, then they retire to the cafeteria where they have a slap-up feast and a dance and form some very interesting relationships.'

Ivor's eyes twinkled. 'The people listening were absolutely frozen. They were immediately aware, as though they had been touched up or something, but nobody did anything. They just kept very very still but did not even turn round to see where it was coming from.

'It wasn't a silly schoolboy prank, I made sure it was well-enough done. The people were faced with something they couldn't deal with. And perhaps that, in a way, is what I'm at – creating loopholes for people who have got themselves so surrounded by rules and regulations they can't understand life itself. I come along and push this all aside, simply making a statement and leaving them to deal with it so that they are actually forced to think – and that's my pleasure.'

Back in his Aladdin's cave Bruce Lacey is also singing and playing Dave a selection of his favourite records.

'The sun has got his hat on, hip hip hip hooray' and 'Oh in eleven more months and ten more days I'll be out of the kalabaloo' and 'Roses round the door, kiddies on the floor, who could ask for any more . . . in slee..pee valley.'

We told him we had been with Ivor Cutler.

'He knows how to suspend disbelief' said Bruce reverently. 'You can get vertigo listening to Ivor.'

But perhaps the most fascinating feature of eccentricity is the ability of some people to sanely suspend both disbelief and time. One or two very lucky people we found had stopped and thought about what they most wanted to do in all the world, as Bruce Lacey has posited, and then chosen the perfect time frame for it as well.

Our next scene was of Dave on a railway station platform studying a sign which directed him to the main station. He enters and meets the station master, Mr Martin who is wearing a pre-war railway worker's uniform of cap, black waistcoat and tie.

'You're just in time to see the 1.10 from St Pancras,' says the Station Master. 'It will be through here in just a minute.'

And in exactly a minute it comes through, complete with passenger cars, coal wagons and guard's van, none more than a few inches high.

'Mr Martin, where am I?' Dave is genuinely bemused.

'Five miles from St Pancras on the Midland line.' (In fact we were on the Isle of Sheppey.)

'And when is this?'

'1938 – before nationalization of the railways. We're in the steam age and we've decided to live in the era of steam.'

But don't be fooled into thinking that this is a model railway, even though it looks like one. Three thousand feet of track stream out from the main station in little tin tunnels all over the garden, complete with platforms, signal boxes, sidings and model passengers. And, of course, dozens of beautiful old A gauge electric trains and the rolling stock necessary to run a complete service. Mrs Lu Martin, who also wears a proper 1938 railway worker's cap, operates the signal box. The walls are painted with accurate views of the old Midland line; a *trompe l'oeil* transition to pre-war England.

Dave contently watches a few trains stream by before deciding to go back to work.

'Have you always loved railways?'

'Yes, from boyhood.' says Mr Martin. 'My mother used to take me to see the Great Western at Oxford.'

'So you worked for the railways?'

'Oh no,' Mr Martin sighed. 'I would like to have done that but my father had other ideas.'

So he started to build his model railway until there was enough track and rolling stock to run an actual service. Eventually they were able to run to a real 1938 timetable which they had rigorously observed for fifteen years.

Again we found that once we had forgotten what was actually going on outside these walls, the Martins were startlingly normal – in fact their insistance on keeping to that timetable from the distant past was positively pedantic. Mountains of mail came in after the programme was transmitted and the Martins were the universal favourites because, I am sure, they were a bridge between the mild eccentricity most people think they might practise and enjoy, and the reformist style of full-time eccentrics like Ivor Cutler.

All the time we were talking, trains came and went their busy way. Mr Martin had to pause to signal point changes to his wife on proper telegraph equipment bought at railway salvage sales.

'If you want to see that first train again – which is the down train to Carlisle – you'll need to be here until 4.03 this afternoon,' said Mr Martin consulting his train board. 'There's nine trains on the main line in front of it.'

This surely had to be the ultimate manifestation of the joys of the eccentric life, I thought. Take early retirement, find yourself a little house with a large garden and vanish in a puff of smoke into the golden age of steam.

It is however, a commitment not to be taken on lightly; indeed the illusion cannot be sustained unless one's commitment is absolute, as Mr Martin demonstrated.

'Excuse me, I have some horse boxes to put on. These are just the usual bookings but it can get very busy during the Derby and Ascot weeks. We send trains down via Acton to Newbury and if those horse boxes have horses in them we have to be sure nothing gets messed up.'

Dave wondered what they did at weekends.

Mr Martin looked pained. Dave obviously hadn't got the message that this was a lifestyle, not a pastime.

'Weekends are especially busy. We have to run excursions and before Easter, Lu and I get together and plan the holiday timetable because a lot more people will be travelling. We're going to be running twenty or thirty special trains.

'On Sundays we have to run scenery vans because the Reps (drama companies) change venues on Saturday. That one there, that's *Pirates of Penzance* which went up to Leeds in the week and has just come back.

'We really have to run every day to keep it all going,' said Mr Martin, lapsing practical for a moment. 'With all this wiring the more you use it the better it is. My wife gets relief for two or three hours a day to cook our dinner but in the winter we sometimes spend all our time in here.'

'Do you go on strike?' Dave probed.

'Yes,' said Mr Martin reluctantly. 'We do. There was a go slow very recently and we worked to rule in sympathy.'

'Apart from industrial disputes are there any other problems that can stop the trains?'

'Mice,' said Mr Martin. 'We've got central heating in here – we don't have it in the house but we have it in here – and the mice all move in when the weather gets cold. Quite often when the first train goes out a couple of mice leap out of the tunnel in front of it. And they steal the passengers.'

Dave did allow himself a ghost of a smile at this.

'But we're very fond of animals and we wouldn't put poison down or anything like that. So we told the mice that they were welcome to the corn that we put out for the chickens but they had to leave the wiring alone and so far they've done so.'

'Do you ever get bored with it?'

'Never,' said Mr Martin emphatically. 'They say life begins at forty, but it began at sixty for me when we came here. I've now had thirteen-and-a-half years of great joy and happiness. We always say tomorrow will be even nicer than today.'

And it showed in their faces. There were no sharks in the Martins' custard and they had ended up owning and running a whole railway!

And suddenly we had run out of time. No television hour I had ever filled had gone by so quickly. We played the programme out to Bruce Lacey's favourite song over a reprise of Cowboys and Indians, Game Players and Fighter Pilots and a Station Master and his wife eating their lunch at the approved hour on a bench in the sun.

Just a cosy nest
Sweet and heaven blessed
Like a bluebirds nest
In sleepy valley . . .
Love is everywhere
Happiness is there
Love beyond compare
In sleepy valley.

For the first time in years I was not just pleased, but in a sense triumphant, to see my credit rise over the last frame of that film, for in its funny way it was an almost perfect television documentary – a powerful message for life, sugar-coated for easy swallowing, colourfully wrapped, serious but in no danger of being taken too seriously.

I have some public justification for so boastful a claim – it rated No 4 in that week's Top Twenty, the highest rating for an ITV documentary then or, so far as I can establish from the IBA, since.

Chapter Fifteen

Bob Heller's reaction to *In Search Of The Great English Eccentric* was frightening – he proposed a series.

'How many?'

My children had adjusted very well to our new lifestyle, in fact my divorce had had the paradoxical effect of allowing me to get to know them. My relationship with Heather had held up. I felt instinctively that too deep a dive back into the career custard could wreck everything. 'And where?'

'There seems to be an abundance of material in Britain,' Bob said, and he outlined his concept for a new early-evening series of popular half-hour factual programmes. 'How about thirteen by this time next year – but you don't have to direct them all?'

This meant I was being promoted to Executive Producer, but it did not quite disguise the fact that I would be responsible for seven hours of television in a little over a year, effectively doubling my already heavy workload.

I discussed it with Heather.

'How do you think it will affect my relationship with the children?'

'The children are much less vulnerable than they allow you to believe; indeed having a guilt-stricken father has observable advantages. They'll manage perfectly well provided you keep in proper touch, and you could certainly use the extra money. What about us?'

Such questions always threw me into some confusion as I had yet to come to terms with the idea that Heather could be that serious about me.

She was, and is, an outstanding beauty – though this is not a description she likes – a perfect example of the blonde, radiant look which has been termed 'English Rose.' She was much sought-after for commercials by England's famous photographers of the swinging

Sixties and Seventies and she had started to appear in films and on television.

Heather was also the first person I had met who was knowledgeable musically (where I had been raised there was not even a professional orchestra) and she had surrounded herself with friends and acquaintances who were a new breed of classically-trained funky musicians. Moreover she had travelled widely as an international model, could pick and choose her rich dates, and literally did spend her spare leisure time in smart places like the Aretusa and Annabelles which I could not have afforded. I thought, frankly, that she deserved better than an emotionally-damaged nuclear gypsy on the breadline (indeed I still do).

But Heather, who had had more to do with the swinging Sixties than I, was already tiring of the life and seeing the need for a more substantial career for herself. And part of that exercise involved acquiring a permanent home and (it seemed) someone in it to look after. I could see nothing wrong with the idea but, given the suspicions I had of anything emotional, I was content to go on as we were, leaving her to propose any further initiatives.

'Do you think it will affect us?' I therefore prevaricated.

'Probably. On the other hand it will be a very good test. Can I have a promise that we can spend a decent stretch of time together after you've done it, to decide about us.'

'Yes of course.'

'And one other thing,' she added. 'This Mr Heller of yours whom you revere so much. Are you absolutely sure he's not just obsessed with work and is not one of those – what do call them – custard things?'

'Shark? Certainly not. He's in a pool of his own with not a shred of personal ambition. He doesn't even take a credit like everyone else. And money only concerns him when we overspend.'

'Is he married?'

'Absolutely.'

'You surprise me,' she said, and never mentioned the subject again until Bob Heller ended up the loneliest man I ever knew.

There is neither the room nor much editorial point in going into the thirteen programmes that made up *Dave Allen And Friends*. They were a simple extension of *In Search Of The Great English Eccentric* and proved quite positively that if you desire to live a happy, fulfilled life you simply have to do your own thing and not worry what other people think about it.

The series steadily increased its audience during the run and Bob Heller commissioned me to produce a second 13-part series exploring the eccentricities of America. I plotted a schedule and realized that the collection of that quantity of material would take a nightmarish nine weeks on the road, with the unit (numbering seven) filming a different subject in a new state either daily or every other day!

I finally had become a nuclear gypsy.

At which point Heather called in my promise of our trip together.

She had spent her own year at least as successfully as mine, even though the first part of it was devoted to a bizarre row with her local authority over something called a TOPS course. My sympathies were soon with the TOPS lot as it appeared she was nagging them to subscribe to a scheme which would reduce her weekly earnings from about £1,000 a week to less than £50, a proposal they were understandably viewing with extreme suspicion!

The TOPS courses had been introduced to soften the impact of rising unemployment which was starting to soar away from the million or so of the Sixties. Unemployed miners could take a TOPS course free, on a pittance of a grant, hopefully to emerge as useful plumbers or bricklayers.

No one in the TOPS beaurocracy had ever had a gorgeous blonde try to use the course to reduce her income so dramatically, nor could they understand the desire of a habituée of Annabelle's to sit with 30 teenagers at an ILEA College for a year.

But this is what Heather had determined to do. She was resolved to retrain, using her considerable experience of the fashion business, as a fashion journalist and she had discovered there was a course tailor-made for this at the ILEA's London College of Fashion in Oxford Street. Hence, she argued, she was entitled to a TOPS programme and grant.

The college had accepted her vocational qualifications in place of the necessary third A-Level, she had sat a difficult entry exam (for someone fifteen years out of school) and gained a place on the course against massive competition. The course was well-regarded all over the world and some twenty entrants were chosen from several hundred.

'I'm just about old enough to be mother to most of them,' Heather told me grittily.

'You don't look it.'

'I'm going to! Anyway it's all irrelevant because the bloody TOPS people are blocking it. They keep saying I'm not what it's intended for.'

Heather had just completed *Spiral Staircase* with her friend Peter Colinson directing (another Bob Heller protégé as it happened) and it is quite likely that the TOPS people might also have seen her about that time at their local cinema as one of Orson Welles' glamorous body-guards in *Casino Royale*.

'Well you're not exactly an unemployed miner,' I pointed out. 'Your situation is, well, different.'

'The course starts in October and I've got a lot to organize,' she said firmly. 'I don't even know whether a person can actually live on £25 a week.'

'They can't,' I confirmed. 'Look at me. But the TOPS people aren't concerned with that.'

'Right! They keep asking me stupid questions like 'Aren't you the the Cadbury's Moonlight girl' – honestly, what has that got to to do with anything?'

This sexist sweetie commercial, which was transmitting almost nightly, involved Heather at her most glamorous, swathed in mink, vamping Patrick Cargill.

She caught me smiling.

'I'm getting out while I'm ahead,' she said firmly. 'You can teach me how to lobby, especially if you want dinner.'

'I'll happily skip dinner.'

'First the bedroom.'

'Exactly.'

'The typewriter's in there, let's see how good a writer you really are.'

We wrote letters to every local politico there was and finally hit paydirt with Heather's local MP, the redoubtable Kenneth Baker who soon became a minister in the Thatcher Government. Baker obviously shared Heather's view that his smart constituents of Regents Park were as entitled to be Topped as anyone else and he wrote a stern letter. All resistance to her application collapsed and Heather went back to school.

I have never seen anyone happier! The 'babies' as she referred to them on her course absolutely adored her and made her their private agony auntie. They in their turn realized that Heather's brain was not school-tuned like theirs, and they helped her with her homework.

She repaid their favours with stories from the big wide world of the movies, her adventures in Haight Ashbury in the days when it was America's hippie heartland, commercials in the Bahamas, modelling in Morocco, and innocently widened their eyes with casual references to the famous musicians, film stars, producers and directors who had been her friends in her other life. Needless to say a lowly documentary-maker did not feature very large in all of this, although I was allowed to drop the odd name when I joined them for their sandwich lunches at a coffee bar in Oxford Street.

The college also had design and modelling courses and when the aspiring designers heard that the famous Heather Lowe was slumming it on the journalism course, they queued up in long begging lines to get Heather to model their extravagant creations in the end of the year show. When the 'baby' models got to hear of this, the atmosphere surrounding the show became as as electric as a tropical storm.

All the baby designers had decided, rightly I suppose, that if they wanted to make a name for themselves in Swinging London their creations would need to be outrageous.

'How do you propose to get me into it, darling?' Heather demanded when she went for her first fitting of a garment that had not yet decided whether to be a parachute or a set of curtains for a stately home. Moreover it was orange, not the colour (I was told) blondes are often seen dead in.

Darling shrunk to about half her normal height at the prospect of losing this celebrity model who would have cost her her year's grant in the real world, and nearly ate the pins gripped in her tight-set lips.

'I hadn't thought about that, Heather!'

All around the dressing room baby models began having tantrums about their impossible dresses, and how they were going to get into them.

'You're only going to wear it once at the show,' Darling said, desperately. 'Couldn't I sew you into it?'

'Not if you then want me to walk in it, 'Heather said ominously. The baby models immediately began to stalk about and complain about their restrictive garments.

'They don't need to move!' Heather swore at me when we went out after the rehearsal for large whiskies, she not being too keen on how much I had been enjoying the rehearsal. 'Lovely little wraiths just out of school, with their glowing skins and . . .'

'Competitive as hell,' I suggested. 'It's just like television. I felt quite at home.'

'You looked pretty contented,' she snapped. 'If I need anything to convince me it's time to go, that rehearsal has done it. Darling is genuinely going to have to sew that bloody frock on me, and she's not going to be at all concerned where she puts the stitches so long as it looks right.'

'They can't take their eyes off you,' I observed. 'They're studying your every move.'

'I've decided not to move,' Heather said flatly. 'I'll stand there like the Statue of Liberty and let the babies flow round me. That should bring your eyes out on stalks.'

On the night the show was a huge success (if I had had the sense I should have written it up as a television series and called it *Fame*). Heather threw caution to the winds and strode about with great energy and confidence while the babies minced up and down doing newly-learnt turns. One missed her footing and fell off the ramp but Heather struck a pose in front of her which more than covered the retreat. Afterwards there was a noisy party at which everyone drowned Heather in effusive thanks, rum and cokes, laughter and a few sentimental tears.

'We both need a holiday anyway,' Heather said. 'It's a pity we're so hard up.'

I had rather forgotten my promise but the idea of taking a trip with Heather was very attractive and it was just possible I could kill two birds with one stone.

'We could afford a couple of Amtrak tickets,' I suggested somewhat nervously. I knew she was tough underneath all that peaches and cream because I knew the hours she worked in the studios and the sweat shops behind the scenes at model shows, but I doubted she was Amtrak-tough.

'What's Amtrak?'

'It's a special pass you can buy to travel on the American rail system. It costs about £70 and you can go anywhere you like for three weeks.'

'That sounds perfect.' She paused. 'Wait a minute! Is this a cover for you to do research?'

'Absolutely not.' It was only a little white lie, after all there would be bags of time on a trip like that to watch and think. Also I had another inducement. The English series had been bought enthusiastically by an Australian network who had since offered me a free flight to the Antipodes against the prospect of yet another series based on Australia.

'If we can get as far as California on Amtrak, the Australian money should be good for two cheap air tickets home via the Far East.'

'Today Amtrak – tomorrow the world!' she said suspiciously, aware that she was being manipulated. 'And at a price not to exceed you doing programmes abroad with weird people for the rest of time.'

'They're not weird people,' I reproved gently. 'I could do a lot worse.'

'It's possible you can't tell any more,' she said, but the following day we went to Thomas Cook in Piccadilly for our Amtrak passes.

Train travel, as I have said, is my great passion because at a very early age I was imprinted on a Garret steam locomotive chugging slowly down the length of South-Central Africa.

I can still vividly remember that first evening and the hot, acid smell of the panting engine, the sharp-tasting smuts that stung the eyes as you watched the gun-metal black locomotive rounding the bends, the smell of the starched sheets and the dark brown blankets with the insignia of the railway stretched drum tight across what had once been the seat.

First night, first day, still within the boundaries of civilization. Farms, vineyards, sheep and cows, slowly wasting away but at a pace somehow adjusted to one's capacity to absorb so that by the time the first bush came into view, the first strange beast or wide-eyed, spear-carrying native, you were ready for it.

So mention a train to me and I ache with the desire to time-travel again, neither back nor forward, just into other people's lives without them resenting it, because, to be an observer from a train is somehow acceptable even when you are all but sitting in their back gardens.

Unfortunately train travel like most forms of exotic travel is dying fast, killed by our obsession with speed. This is a tragedy because as anyone who has done any serious travelling knows to see anything of a country you need to travel slowly across its surface.

Admittedly most people have limited holiday time and prefer to get to their destinations as quickly as possible but I still think Leonard Woolf got it right when he called his autobiography 'It's the journey, not the arrival that matters.'

It came as no great surprise that Heather had famous New York friends, the actors Hume and Jessica Cronyn, who had virtually adopted her after Heather and their daughter Tandy had set up a flat together in London while Tandy was training for the theatre. Tandy and her brother Chris nervously took us right to the door of our silver Amtrak coach in Penn Central Station as if we were descending into the underworld. They hung around protectively as the train grunted and groaned a few feet back and forth gathering the energy it need to break away from the station.

'Nobody goes by train,' they had insisted, quietly and firmly. 'Just nobody. Fly!'

'We want to see America,'

'There are many Americas, darlings. Amtrak is kind of old-fashioned. In the poor states where they don't look after the track you can get out and walk faster than the train. And it's kind of, well . . .'

'Kind of well . . .' was a euphemism for the unsavoury. New Yorkers are strenuously liberal and dislike outright condemnation of anything. So the New York Police Department was 'kind of, well . . .,' the Mayor who was then running a city on the edge of bankruptcy was 'kind of, well . . .' and anything to do with New York's social problems and divisions was very definitely, 'kind of, well . . .'

Amtrak's 'kind of, well . . .' was that the passengers were mostly old, poor or black, which did not bother us at all. None of this would have bothered Tandy and Chris in any other context, but they thought the train could be dangerous for us.

We were destined for New Orleans and as we walked down our car, friendly faces, mostly dusky or wrinkly, beamed at our travelling uniforms of beige Burberrys and Irish tweed hats. Outside, Chris and Tandy peered in anxiously, agonizing over the fate they had allowed to overtake these innocents from England.

I did not sleep a wink through the first part of the night even though the deep seats on Amtrak are better than any first-class aeroplane seat. By midnight I was entirely New York street-wise simply by eavesdropping on Mrs Kennedy and Mrs Pridhoe from Harlem. Mrs Pridhoe was aged sixty, married twice, five grandchildren (two of them illegitimate), husband on welfare, two sons in the can, another on heroin (failed cold turkey), Macey's sales were only good in the spring when you should buy winter stuff, Mavis was having trouble with her monthlies (I never quite pin-pointed Mavis) which was almost certainly hormonal because Mavis had always suffered from post-natal depression. Elroy was being taken up by Father MacGilroy from the Saved Souls Mission on the knife charge. Didn't they know that a little knife was the least you needed to carry going out at night in Harlem.

Mrs Pridhoe talked to Mrs Kennedy who was married to a cop of Irish extraction and was altogether more prosaic. She was essentially critical of Mrs Pridhoe's delinquent family, not least her estranged husbands, considered the problems of the streets of New York the product of a lack of parental discipline (she obviously had no children of her own), and was most worried of all about her husband's feet. She mentioned it at least a half a dozen times during the night.

Did Mrs Pridhoe every try disciplining her grandchildren, Mrs Kennedy asked. No. Why not, had discipline become a thing of the past, how had that happened? Any case it didn't really matter because bad feet was becoming an occupational hazard for the New York police department and soon if things went on the way they were there wouldn't be any of them left on the beat.

'I hear what you say,' Mrs Pridhoe said, 'My second husband wouldn't walk anywhere with his fallen arches. They should give them golf carts.'

'They should,' said Mrs Kennedy. 'But they won't.' At this point, squirming with suppressed mirth at the thought of Officer Kennedy racing to the scene of the crime on a golf cart, I woke Heather. I shrugged over my shoulder and held a finger to my lips.

'Discipline, you say!' cried Mrs. Pridhoe, who had the ability to pick up the conversation wherever it suited her. 'You can end up on your ass. Like happened to me when I tried to keep Leroy in off the streets, when I knew there was a man out there aiming to use him to push a little stuff because this same man had lost his regular coverage, that person being my other son, sadly arrested the night before. Not, mind, for pushing, I should hasten to say but for loitering with intent – intent to do what I ask – what is there to do in Harlem but loiter? Anyway, Tha-wap from Leroy when I attempted to stop him exiting the door. There I was lady, sitting, my head ringing, not arguing mind, just not arguing, not in that situation. (Slight pause for change of subject). How come you married an Irish cop?'

'I always had good taste in men,' said Mrs Kennedy, 'apart from their feet.'

Heather nudged me. 'You're eavesdropping!' she whispered.

'Feel free,' said Mrs Pridhoe promptly and loudly through the seat. 'Are you two English, dears?'

'We are,' I responded, just as promptly.

'Kennedy was in England during the war. Apart from the wet he liked it. Where you folks from?'

'London,' I called. The seats were thick.

'Go to sleep,' Heather insisted, and – rather wastefully – I did. In the morning, Mrs Pridhoe and Mrs Kennedy had gone, bustled off the train into some tiny southern town where they probably still did not allow them to use the buses.

But any sense of loss was more than made up for the next day by our being invited to a wedding.

The big Amtrak trains are really travelling communities and as it takes at least a day to travel through the average state, anyone making a decent journey could expect to be a part of that community long enough to make friends.

We went on a tour of the train early the following morning, pausing on the way to exchange pleasantries with three diminutive coloured guards who bustled about the community continuously, lowering the steps when we came into a station (some of which had no platforms) allocating seats, checking tickets, answering inquiries of extraordinary complexity ('Sir, can you give me the changes that'll get me to San Antone?' took an hour of study and pencil sucking) and generally administering law and order with great good humour.

Every evening one of these shiny little men had to clear the bar of its heavy drinkers, and some of these were very heavy indeed, infact we seemed to have a resident convention of beer-drinking lumberjacks on that particular train.

In the guard would bustle and take up a position by the bar, nodding to the barman to lower his security screen an inch or two.

'Now hear this,' he would say with a wide water-melon grin. 'Ten minutes from now this here bar's gonna close. I don't mean fifteen minutes, I don't mean eight minutes and I don't mean two minutes – I mean tee-aan minutes DEAD.' Everyone cheered and we all went meekly back to our cars exactly ten minutes later.

In the double-decker restaurant car we had the most wonderful breakfast I have ever eaten. This carriage was about twice the length and the same height as a London bus. The tables were set on the top deck and the food cooked in a steaming hell below, coming up in little dumb-waiter lifts.

Another bunch of hard-working comedians ran the restaurant. Again mostly coloured, they turned the taking of your order into an individual routine. As soon as they realized we were English and would be on the train for several meals, a lot of work went into their performances to us, much to the delight of the American travellers.

Best of all was the waitress who fell in love with Heather's big blue eyes.

'Here they are,' she would say loudly as we took our table by the great curved windows which had been offering a view of a never-ending swamp for all of our second day (the headwaters of the Swanee River) 'The girl with the beautiful eyes and her luckee fellah. Bat 'em for me darling, bat 'em!'

And Heather, who was of course expert at this kind of thing, would slowly lower her lids over what are indeed beautiful blue eyes, causing all the waitresses in the car to shriek with delight.

'May-an,' the waitress would then say to me. 'I don't know how you live with those eyes, I just don't know!'

Or, if the dining car had new members, we would be enjoined, in ordering the meal, to 'lay a little of that English of yours on me!'

Dutifully we played our part by ordering as we had in all innocence at our first breakfast, griddle-scones (not flapjacks), chips (not fries) and jam (not jello).

'Cute hah?' the waitress would say to our nearest neighbours. 'Did you hear that 'jaaam' – and you know what, they don't know the difference between eggs easy-over and sunny-side up. You wanna hear them say 'Teeeh' – go on, blue eyes, say tea for our new arrivals here!'

It was all done in absolute innocence and niceness and confirmed the view I have held all my life that the great charm of America, especially when you escape the pressures of the cities, is that it is a continent of innocents, practising a kind of inquisitive naïveté which you either find desperately irritating or very charming. Most aloof British folk find it irritating, but then can you imagine a scene like this in a British Rail dining car?

We could not stop meeting people. The train also had a Club Car where the bar was located which sold very filling snacks for next to nothing. Packets of crisps were given away free with a beer and we very often lunched on them.

Then there was the dome car, a double-decker observation car with huge curved plexiglass windows from which we spent hours watching the tropical countryside, laced with wide chocolate brown rivers, miles and miles of dark reedy swamp and forest of frondy, black-stemmed swamp oak growing up out of triangular root systems.

Here we were seated when the train stopped in Atlanta, Georgia, and about fifty very jolly people in extraordinary clothes climbed onto the train, accompanied by several large wicker hampers. Some minutes later one of the little guards approached us politely and explained that they would be closing the dome car in a few minutes to have a wedding.

We were gathering up our books when the groom, who was dressed in a bright blue dress suit edged with white piping, a lace shirt and a huge velvet bow tie, came in with the vicar who was also in formal fancy dress, finished in his case at the neck with a pink dog collar.

'The guard tells me you folks are here all the way from England,' the groom said politely. 'Would you do us the honour of attending our wedding?'

'Oh no,' said Heather. 'There's all your friends!'

'We would be most honoured, mam. In these parts it's considered right good luck to have a tall stranger attend the ceremony.'

'We'd love to,' I said quickly before Heather's English reserve lost us the chance.

It turned out that the groom and his fiancée worked for Amtrak. It was not exactly a High Church affair, although the music-hall vicar had an evangelical style and the congregation, which remained seated out of respect for the train's motion, said 'Amen' loudly and frequently, throwing in the odd 'Hallelujah!'

The bride's maid of honour was her teenage daughter from another marriage and the couple also had an infant of their own, which was passed around during the service for every one to admire. So, rather more surreptitiously, was a bottle of bourbon.

The bride wore a dress of hectic pink like a blown rose all the way to her ankles, from which peeped a pair of incredibly high heeled shoes covered with flashing red sequins.

Everyone was more than a little drunk when the ceremony started. By the time it finished, hugs and kisses and the bourbon bottle were exchanged. All the men tried to eat the bride (and all the excited women, the baby), everyone cried, and I realized we were all drunk as newts.

We tried to sneak off to our carriage, but no-one would have any of it. We had, the bride and groom pointed out, known them all their married life and that made us one of the family. We were left in no doubt that that they would be deeply offended if we did not stay for the reception, or as they called it the wedding feast.

This lasted for almost three days, beginning right away with food from the big hampers and some serious drinking. There was Californian champagne which in those days varied in taste and colour from bottle to bottle, mostly honey to rust. Every bottle had to open with a loud pop of the cork and a gush of bubbling liquid into a glass, or down the front of a convenient dress. There was an endless passing of bourbon ('sippin' likker') which the bourbon-drinkers sipped with a funny left-handed motion into the side of the mouth. The only soft drink was Coke which most hardened a bit with rum. Women with children drank this spiked Coke, and at first they attempted to keep the children to drinking pure Coke. Heather tried very hard to drink just Coke after sampling the Californian champagne, but every time she brought her glass down someone poured bourbon into it. I drank everything in sight including an incredibly revolting substance called 'Sippin Yogurt' which I think had been brought for the baby.

We ate lurid foods directly from the supermarket: packets of bright orange cheese which tasted like decayed rubber; a vast range of sliced cooked meats very few of which were original to one beast; ice-box lettuce tasting only of ice, huge tomatoes tasting of nothing at all, cold cooked hamburgers in buns with livid yellow mustard that was bland and vinegary, hot dog sausages squirted with blood-red ketchup, thin sausages called 'splits', big red apples, 'English' muffins that were more foreign than anything, bran muffins made of sawdust, white bread so flaccid I wondered whether they had forgotten to bake it, and an incredible range of snacks, cheesy sticks, bacon wheels, round, curly and waffled chips, little balls filled with hot or spicy goos, twigs armour – plated with a Marmite-substance, heart-shaped pretzels as big as real hearts, and bagel buns. The bagel buns were the main course and came out of big card boxes. They had been carefully overstuffed with thick yellow cream cheese and oily slices of salmon lox. I found them absolutely delicious, perfectly complimenting the sweet bourbon which I had by now learned how to sip in the approved Southern fashion.

A wedding feast indeed!

Heather finally intervened.

'You should start planning where you intend to throw up,' she warned coolly. 'Unlike English trains these windows don't seem to open.'

In fact we all somehow fell asleep in little piles all over the dome car to be woken by the guard as we pulled into New Orleans. When the wedding party discovered we had no accommodation reserved they swept us along with them to their hotel where, we were advised, the wedding breakfast would commence 'as soon as the happy couple have done a little consummatin'.'

We of the wedding party were, it seemed, supposed to keep the party going until that requirement had been fulfilled, but Heather insisted we go off to our room for a little consummating of our own and our first proper bath in two days.

Some time later, standing at our window listening to New Orleans where there is jazz music in the air day and night, I was suddenly aware that the ground was shaking slightly.

'Do they have earthquakes here?' I asked Heather.

'No.'

Heather was feeling it too, but it was nothing to do with seismic trauma. We had Amtrak-itis, as we came to call it. If you spent any longer than twelve hours on the train, its motion stayed with you for at least another twenty four.

Bobbedy-bop, bobbedy-pop, bobbedy-bop our bodies went as we walked beside the mighty, muddy Mississippi and around the elegant old streets of New Orleans, sampling the various julep drinks and the delicious Creole food. So in a sense we never really got off the train and although New Orleans was beautiful and we were pleased to see the carefully preserved old houses trimmed with wonderful wrought-iron, we could not wait to get back on again.

You can get addicted to boppedy-pop, boppedy-bop, boppedy-pop . . .

Chapter Sixteen

There were three main trains heading out from the Eastern seaboard into the vastness of America and they all took about five days to cross the continent. This is probably still the longest recreational rail journey on earth. Unlike other intrepid continental rail crossings like the trans-Siberia where you can die of starvation, or the trans-Australia where terminal boredom is the risk, the rail journey across America really is open to anyone with a little determination.

Not that many people actually do it non-stop, and we also discovered that we could not afford to sleep in a proper bed on the train because the couchettes, little curtained bunks either side of the corridor of the sleeping car, were let by the hour to passengers wishing to catch a nap between stations. Initially we thought they might be being used for more vicarious short-times, but we never saw any evidence of that. To hire a couchette for a full night's sleep worked out at about $50, twice the cost of a cheap motel room.

We decided to take the Sunset Limited across the southern part of the United States, mainly because of its exotic name and its promise of famous trainy places like Topeka, Santa Fé and San Antonio.

'Gotta see the Alamo,' our newlyweds had insisted. 'If you want to understand what makes America great.'

But the need to get off the train, normally in the middle of a dark, strange, empty American outback night, turned into an adventure all on its own. Several adventures in fact.

The best was at the little town of Flagstaff, Arizona. By the time we were in Arizona (which those with any knowledge of American geography will realize involved a massive change of trains) we were well versed in the business of quitting the train before Amtrak-itis became terminal.

Unlike British trains, where one is utterly anonymous, on the long-distance Amtrak 'Limiteds' the guard takes time and makes a point of getting to know all his passengers. Round about midday we would seek out our friend the guard and give him a rough time for our departure, and he, after much poring over the timetable, would come up with a name. It did not matter at all to us that we had never heard of it, indeed it was important that these places should be obscure as they had the cheapest motels.

Thumping Board was one, Old Hickory another, and they were quite big places. Many had unpronouncable and enigmatic names like Natchitoches and Fort Deposit but as I say their names mattered not.

'That's a good little place,' the guard would say. 'I'll call ahead and see how they're fixed.'

Then that huge machine, gleaming silver in the night, resounded with happy shouts from departing friends through the club car windows as it stopped just for us. Stewards waved cheerfully from the tower of the dome car and we would climb down the guard's little set of steps onto a gritty track to stand, desolate and very alone, in middle America.

Seconds, at best minutes, later a friendly Amtrak agent would say: 'Hi there, you must be the English folks we've been expecting.' They appeared out of the night like the spirit of the good Samaritan, caring, cheerful, attentive and invariably efficient, even when it was four o'clock in the morning.

We were usually put to bed under their direct supervision in some little motel which looked as if it had been constructed of ceiling board, where the beds were always clean, the air smelt slightly acrid after passing through old air-conditioners, and in the morning there was always some smiling soul at the reception desk to direct us into town for breakfast at the diner.

What America has that no other country I know has is a concept of order even at its lowest levels. Admittedly, it also has a violent streak you do not find in Europe and a gun-law which massages that streak. But order does not break down the further you move off the beaten track as it does in other wild places, particularly my beloved Africa. In fact, order seems more entrenched the deeper you progress into the backwoods. Thus no matter how small the town, (many we called in on seemed to have acquired that status when they progressed from one horse to two), they were little nuggets of order.

The motels always worked, the diners always provided cheap, basic American food in quantities sufficient to see us through until dinner. The service was always efficient, if robotic – 'Y'all have a nice day now' – and there was always evidence of some law and order, albeit in the form of tin-pot sheriffs and their deputies who liked to give the impression that they owned the town.

In some cases they probably did, but given the size of these places that was no great thing, and we had to be careful to hide our amusement when the swaggering sheriff, usually carrying enough firepower to wipe out the entire town, strolled into the diner to do a big and utterly pointless number on the tired but ever-smiling waitresses.

I loved walking round those little outposts of rural America. It was like being in a James Dean movie. There was usually a church, very insubstantially built by English standards but (again by English standards) with very substantial congregations. We had stuck to our travel uniforms of long Burberrys and Irish tweed hats (proof against America's ubiquitous winds, abrupt storms even in the very hot spots and a perfect cover for our often unwashed state beneath).

The pastors in these churches always liked meeting us, as if we were the bizarrely-robed representatives of old world Protestantism. A great number of them were gentle, intellectual blacks who were very keen to hear about Westminster Abbey and St Paul's Cathedral. Most of them, of course had not, nor would they ever, see a cathedral and God alone knows what they would have made of our sepulchric services.

Every town had at least one old Chevy truck, a Studebaker Golden Hawk (my father gave me one of these dream machines when I passed my driving test in Rhodesia), a Harley Davidson motorcycle, kids in jeans and bobby sox outside an ice-cream parlour or a drive-in diner, a five-and-dime and a police car, usually blue, with a bar of flashing lights and siren horns on its roof.

'I think,' Heather said, 'that if I wasn't here, you'd just stick around and become a figure in one of these little landscapes, wouldn't you?'

She was right in a sense. Rhodesian culture had been very close to that of small-town America and I was obviously imprinted on its totems.

On our first continental leg the Amtrak wedding party was replaced in the club car by a party of six psychiatrists on their way to a convention in San Antonio. They played poker in an intense, demonstrative way. One wore a green eye shade, another had learned to do tricks with the cards when he shuffled and another always adopted a belligerent attitude when calling in the bets. This was all obviously put on and they smiled at each other whenever one of them displayed these particular foibles.

They caught us watching them. We watched everybody quite unashamedly and when we met later for our beer and chips lunch they came over and engaged us in conversation about our journey.

After lunch they asked us if we would like to join their game. Heather looked less than happy.

'We're playing for matches.' they explained. 'And you might find it kind of interesting because as well as the poker we're trying to work out a system we can use on the guys at the convention.'

'There is no system with poker,' I pointed out. 'Skills maybe but you can't beat the fall of the cards.' I did not add that my first long train journey had been spent sharing a carriage down Africa with a man who played professional 5-Card Stud Poker on the Union Castle liners to England. I was actually quite disappointed that we weren't playing for money.

'Right,' they said, 'Right, but what we have in mind here is if we can learn our own little signals and get so as we read them it should give us an edge in the games at the convention. Like when Harry sucks his teeth I know he's got a good hand, whereas Josh here tries to look like Boris Karloff complete with bolt if he picks up anything better than a pair of twos. We have a head start in the betting on the opposition, and no cheating – a system, get it!'

'Yes,' Heather said. 'Though it would still be regarded as cheating in England.'

That earned her a few chauvinistic smiles.

'Did you ever hear of Clever Hans?'

'No,' said Heather. 'I'm surprised to hear that you play poker at your convention.'

'What else!' they laughed. 'Clever Hans was a horse that went round Europe counting. 'Cept now it has an honoured place in western psychiatry as a symbol of how we believe what we want to believe.'

'The horse could not count,' I guessed.

'Right,' they nodded, ordering more beer and chips (being English and inquisitive earned us many a free lunch on this journey) 'It could read the signals its owner was giving.'

'That's called cheating too,' Heather said, pointedly (she was, I think, still trying to keep us out of the game) 'in England.'

'No sir – sorry, ma'am – the owner didn't know he was giving the horse signals, any more than Harry or Josh here know they are. Brilliant hah? And at the convention we don't play for matches, no sir!'

'Why don't we play gin?' Heather asked sweetly.

'No sir,' I snapped.

'I don't know how to play poker,' Heather said. 'I know how to play gin.'

'You have just heard the understatement of the year,' I warned them. 'If you really want to know about Clever Hans watch her play gin.'

'Interesting,' they said.

'And I'm quite prepared to play for matches,' Heather, who had obviously not missed those smiles, said. 'If it's the money that's bothering you.'

We played for dimes and Heather, who plays excessively good gin mainly because she is a subliminal counter and likes a brisk gamble, won about ten dollars. The psychiatrists accepted all this very cheerfully and by the time we drew into San Antonio had decided to propose gin as the new game at the convention.

'Are there women at your convention?'

'Yes ma'am, some of our brightest brains are women.'

'Don't play gin with them,' Heather said caringly, picking up her winnings. 'You're all much too nice.'

'Why are you here?' they got round to asking when we were bundling their huge piles of luggage and sports gear down onto the platform in front of a beautiful station built to resemble a Spanish hacienda.

'We're going to the Alamo,' I replied. 'To see what makes America great.'

'Hot shit!' they cried with great glee. 'We're not allowed near the place.'

'Why ever not?' Heather demanded.

'It would blow our brains. The Alamo had more lunatics inside its walls than any other single location in the history of history.'

'It is not what made America great?' Heather could not hide her disappointment. 'We've come all this way for nothing?'

'Oh sure,' they conceded. 'Better, it made America what it is. And watch out for the river!'

Watch out for the river, indeed!

San Antonio (pronounced San An-Tone) is one of those towns which fate, and American get-up-and-go, decreed could be utterly changed in the interests of local prosperity. Admittedly, had it not undergone the metamorphosis from sleepy New Mexican hamlet to Disneyland film set, we and half of America would never have bothered to visit it. The only other place like it, with even less of a reason for existing, is Las Vegas. That's why everyone who goes to San Antone, psychiatrists apart, visits the Alamo.

You walk out of the fairy-tale station into a lush desert town with smart hotels, shops and restaurants lined up alongside a beautiful, sparkling river.

We had assumed that the psychiatrists' warning about the river was concerned with pollution, but this was the cleanest river either of us had ever seen, with crystal clear water running musically over a bed of fine desert sand, fringed by exotic hot-weather plants, most of them growing out of pots or tanks.

It was very civilized and we were soon settled under causarina ferns in a riverside restaurant, ordering our first Mexican meal:

frigales, re-fried beans, guacamole, tacos, enchiladas and free flies. I was just thinking what an incredible oasis this was in the wilderness of desert we had just traversed on the train, when Heather said she was experiencing a new facet of Amtrak-itis.

'Disorientation?' I guessed.

'Madness – the level of the river just dropped, by at least a foot.'

It continued to go down. We looked around but nobody else seemed to have noticed.

The waiter arrived with two bottles of superb dark beer.

'Señor,' I said. 'What is happening to the river?'

'No problem,' he smiled. 'Cleaning time.'

The San Antone river emptied before our very eyes and walking up the river bed came half a dozen garbage men with spike sticks and plastic sacks, collecting the Coke and Seven-Up-tins, broken branches, and a bloated dead cat.

Then they filled it up again while we ate our dessert.

'Isn't America great?' I insisted to Heather.

'Yes, but I've still to be convinced that it's real. If you've had enough peculiar food I think we should go to the Alamo. I wouldn't put it past them to pack this whole place up and put it away in a box for the night.'

To appreciate the greatness it helps to visit the Alamo Theatre where they give you a potted history and video show.

The Alamo was an earthwork fort where a motley group of Americans under a trio of bizarre heroes fought a suicidal last stand against the Mexican army of General Santa Ana. There was a backwoodsman in a funny hat, Davy Crockett, a street-fighter adept with the knife, Jim Bowie, and an Eastern aristocrat on the run, Sam Houston.

More simply, the Alamo provided heroes and martyrs to help fill the historical gap that has always made it difficult for America to regard itself as a nation of substance.

The Alamo martyrs did, in fact, represent all the characteristics that make America great, mainly tenacity and a unique amalgam of self-interest and the common good. Their valiant stand also usefully justified America's most vulnerable (and questionable) border and gave some credence to the prejudice espoused by most loyal Americans then, and since, that Yanks are superior to Mexs.

There is, of course, a Mexican interpretation of the Alamo legend: the fort had been established on stolen territory, General Santa Ana did his level best to get the tramps and fugitives squatting in it to give up before anyone got hurt, and he won the final battle. The fact that this is the true story matters historically not at all.

I stood in the welcome shadow of those mud walls for which men had died and realized a useful truth: the documentation of events (be it on stone, vellum or celluloid) is a contradiction in terms. It has nothing much to do with the documentation of the facts. It provides a contrived scenario of the past, precedents which justify steps forward – the building blocks of human expansion. By way of example, just think what a reaction you would get from the mighty American media if you were to offer them the story of the founding of the American south (and its most pushy state, Texas) starring a knife-throwing backwoodsman, an alleged murderer and a bumpkin with a dried raccoon on his head. Scorn? No. Not if John Wayne is available to wear the raccoon.

Apart from this momentary lapse, I had not thought television since joining the train. Heather had noticed and was delighted. 'Travel really does broaden the mind.' she approved. 'I think we should definitely go on.'

This decision had to be made because we had reached the point of no return on our Amtrak passes. If we set off back to New York from San Antone, given the need for stops which we had not initially taken into account, we would just make it back to the Big Apple before the passes expired.

To go on would inevitably mean we would have to get back to England at our own expense from much further away, or trade in the Aussie ticket and circumnavigate the globe on a budget of about a dollar a day.

We went on.

'I want to go to the Grand Canyon,' Heather said. 'It's up there on the right.'

Up there on the right resulted in an eighteen-hour journey through Texas on a Sunday, which meant the train went dry and morose on us, relieved only by one old character in a stetson waving out of the window at the miles of dun-coloured savannah, exclaiming: 'Aaarl mine, darlin', aarl mine,' a claim later confirmed by the guard who added that this elderly cattle-baron regularly rode the Sunday train to gloat over the size of his property.

Desperate for a drink we arrived in Chicago and after the great dun biscuit of Texas were delighted with the skyscrapers which are, if anything, better than those in New York. The station was another wonder of railway architecture, art deco and art nouveau stored in a great gothic box.

And it was windy, as Chicago promises in the song, so icily windy we stuck our heads up into the street and dived promptly back underground into a Polish bar-restaurant. This was a huge tiled cellar inhabited by little European-looking men in dark trilby hats drinking vodka and beer. The waitresses were all dressed as men in black trousers and waistcoats with white aprons as long as tablecloths bound round their waists and secured at the front with a bow.

One of these waitresses glanced perfunctorily at our Burberrys and Irish hats, sat us down and immediately brought us our first round of drinks – Polish beer with a little vodka chaser. We were so cold we drank the vodka first and sat sipping our beer, watching the little men eat strangely shaped lumps of meat; knuckles, trotters, whole kidneys, a boiled heart, and a wide variety of sausages. Chicago is the capital of the American meat industry and we wondered whether the little old men got the leftovers as part of their pensions.

The sausages and offally-things were delicious, as indeed were the strange vegetables served with them, particularly the sauerkraut and the little dishes of sweet and sour pickles and gherkins.

'How do you make sauerkraut,' Heather asked the waitress.

She laughed.

'You squash it in a barrel, add vinegar and stuff and leave it. I say to my regulars, for cabbage to taste this good you just have to maltreat it and neglect it. You want a vodka to finish or dessert?'

'Vodka.' We had soon to brave the winds and catch another train that would take us right across the centre of America to the Wild West.

Neither of us can remember much of this leg of the trip. Our funds were at subsistence level and we elected neither to stop nor allow ourselves the luxury of a couchette bunk. Instead we dozed in our seats and watched America slide by the windows. In the first twelve hours an entirely representative topography passed by – lakes, plains, rivers, hills, mountains and marshes.

Eventually the little guard gingerly tapped me on the shoulder to warn that Flagstaff was coming up next and we were soon decanted into a desert.

I remember the extraordinary air and light. It was very early in the morning and the air still tasted of yesterday's heat, sandwiched under the sweet-tasting morning cold. Bearded, rumpled, ravenous, I breakfasted on that morning air and was entranced by the pastel desert all around us.

We hired a little car from Dollar Rent-A-Car and drove through the painted desert to the Grand Canyon. Everything was grand and delicately painted and I could not escape the feeling that we were in a studio, that these pink and ochre views were not the backdrops for *High Plains Drifter*, my favourite cowboy movie, or that John Huston was hidden out there somewhere making the milk chocolate 'buttes' out of papier mâché.

The Grand Canyon defies the human imagination. It is too big for it. You cannot visualize a vertical mile down, or scale up the silver slick of the Columbia river as it appears from the top, to the raging torrent of reality at the bottom of the canyon.

So we decided to walk down to the bottom.

We had checked into a wooden lodge where the accommodation charge delighted us and the food was served in a vast university-like canteen, with a chunky bill of fare – 'meat, veg and a choice of a starch' and here we bought a precautionary bottle of water.

It was midday. Down we climbed. Up came the heat. We passed a little notice warning us that we should be wearing proper walking shoes, carrying ample water and that it took at least twelve hours to get to the bottom of the canyon and back up again.

I almost fell over the edge when I used binoculars on the view and allowed my eyes to pan down. The wide-angle lenses took out the ground below my feet and I only just stopped myself looping into the void as vertigo hit me.

We noticed that all the people coming up were on sure-footed mules which we had seen advertised on the top. We wondered how they had the nerve to ride an animal up so narrow a path alongside the highest drops on earth, and then we looked into their glazed eyes and realized that you will ride anything out of hell.

'I think we're being a bit daft,' Heather said after we had descended half a mile and the people on the mules were seen to shake their heads when they saw us. 'It's taken us an hour to get this far down and we haven't even started. Climbing up is going to take longer and we don't have much water.'

So we went back up, which I thought to be rather limp until we met two sturdy National Park Wardens with legs like tree trunks, wide-brimmed hats, rucksacks and water bottles, moving steadily in our direction.

One of the Wardens approached me. 'Didn't you read the notices, sir?'

'We just thought we'd take a look,' I said sheepishly.

'At this time of day?' they reproved, then in their good-humoured American way made a joke of it. 'Mad dogs and Englishmen ha?'

'Absolutely,' Heather said. 'And I want you to know I'm the English part.'

So I never did see the bottom of the Grand Canyon but I am alive to tell the tale and our best adventure was only just over the horizon.

We spent most of the rest of that day in the shower, in a bed that did not go boppedy-bop and in an orgy of starch eating – potatoes, waffles, corn. The mountain air seemed to bring on enormous appetites.

Then we drove slowly back to Flagstaff, dawdling among the pastels of the desert, visiting a very sad Indian tourist village selling rough silver and lapis jewellery made by something called the lost-wax technique. The Indians, whose claim to being Indian was confirmed by the Cherokee Chief jeeps parked behind their fake teepees, had lost their souls, it seemed, along with the wax of their jewellery.

The connection on from Flagstaff to Los Angeles was awful – four a.m. By ten p.m. we had turned in the car, had our dinner and had six hours to kill.

'Is there a café anywhere nearby where we can go till the train comes?' we asked the agent at Flagstaff.

'Nope,' he said. 'You're very welcome to make yourself comfortable in the waiting room.'

'There's a neon sign down there flicking ''bar,''' Heather observed.

'You asked whether there was anywhere I could recommend you go,' the agent sighed. 'I particularly do not recommend that joint. The guys who frequent that joint are rough, lady.'

Rough bars, I had come to learn, have the same air of challenge for Heather as the deeper holes in the earth have for me.

We went to the rough bar.

Every head lifted as we entered. Most of them were cropped or crowned with baseball caps. There were no other women there. They stared at our long white coats and high tweed hats just as the locals stared at Clint Eastwood as he rode into town in the long opening sequence to *High Plains Drifter*. Only we weren't armed. We should have been.

The bartender, a large, rangy black man with no hair at all, sang out a cheerful 'Evening folks!' as we hovered just inside the door and we went straight into his protective custody and sat at his bar on peculiar stools: metal tractor seats like huge spoons welded to short posts.

Behind us we could hear chairs shifting and the next time I looked round half the inhabitants of the room had forsaken their tables and were not occupying the remaining seats at the bar, staring mesmerized at Heather.

'Keep your hat on,' I told her.

'You bet,' she said.

'And when I say goodbye, just get up and head for the door. No stopping for anything.

'Wilco!' she grinned. 'But can we at least have a drink first?'

'What will you folks have?' the barman asked cheerfully.

'Scotch whisky please,' Heather said. I managed a nod.

Two vast scotches from an anonymous distillery were poured into shot glasses on the bar before us. It was the second scene from *High Plains Drifter*. Next Clint starts shooting from underneath his Mexican blanket.

'Those are on me,' a burly redneck in denims seated on the stool alongside Heather said thickly.

The bartender smiled at him. One big hand reached down to sit lightly on the sawn-off baseball bat which rested in open view under the liquor rack.

'No Bud,' the bartender said. 'These are on me. These folks are visitors from abroad, right?'

'England,' Heather said.

'I was in England during the war!' Bud cried. 'Do you folks know Skegness?'

'Then the next round can be on you,' the bartender said. 'Provided you stay polite to our guests here.'

And it went on from there. Bud, now a truck driver, had been a fitter with the US Air Force in 'Godawful Skegness where the bolts went rusty before you could finish doing them up,' his pal Chuck had been wounded with the US army during the Battle of the Bulge. Chuck got the next round and patted his substantial tummy. 'I lost that one you can see,' he chuckled. 'Hell, I really loved it over there in U-Rope, especially the food. Always swore I would go back, never did. What do you folks want with over here?'

'We just went to the Grand Canyon,' Heather said. 'There's nothing like that in Europe.'

'No?' They looked puzzled. Like many Americans they thought of Europe as being at least as large as the US and assumed that we would have our own rival to the Grand Canyon tucked away somewhere.

'I saw the Triumph Arch in Paris, France.' Chuck said. 'That was pretty fuckin' big.'

The bartender, who was delivering yet another round (I don't think we were allowed to pay for one) glowered at Chuck. 'You watch your fuckin' mouth, man – there's a lady present!'

He tapped the table in front of Heather.

'Any trouble ma'am, any trouble *at all*, you just call out and these bums will be eee-jected.'

'Okay Casey,' they cried. 'Be cool, man. We're just having a little wander down memory lane here. Right ma'am?'

'Absolutely,' Heather said.

'Right on,' Bud said. 'Hey Maxie come on over here and meet these folks.'

Maxie was even bigger than the rest of them, with a wide bluff Scandinavian face, rather small eyes, but a friendly smile. He bought a round and lined them up alongside the others we still had to drink.

'Maxie's the reason Casey's so jumpy,' Chuck explained. 'Casey thinks the police are keeping an eye on his place.'

'Weren't my fault,' Maxie said. 'Were an accident.'

'What happened?' Heather demanded.

'He killed his wife last week,' Chuck said. 'Right there at the bar. We all saw it. Maxie's out on bail.'

'Were an accident,' Maxie mumbled.

'Good Lord,' said Heather.

'Amen to that,' said Chuck, mistaking it for an English prayer.

'She was fooling around right in front of Maxie,' Bud confirmed. 'With this young musician person. Dancin' and stuff, getting him to play her requests.'

'I told her to quit, ma'am,' Maxie said urgently. 'They all heard me.'

'And?' I inquired reluctantly.

'Maxie gave her a little slap,' Chuck said understandingly.

'Just to straighten her out,' Maxie whispered.

'And she bounced off the bar and hit her head on one of these dumb stools. Maxie ran off with her to the hospital but she was gone.'

'That's awful!'

'Sure is,' said Maxie. 'And I miss her a lot even if she did like foolin' around.'

'It is very nearly time to beat a retreat,' I whispered to Heather.

Casey appeared at our elbow.

'Drink up folks, it seems everyone wants to buy you a round.'

'We're going to have to catch the train,' I prevaricated.

'Ain't no train till four,' Chuck said. 'I work for the railroad. You got plenty of time.'

We stayed another two hours, slowly working our way through the rounds. Casey came to our aid when we refused about the fifth lot and an ominous silence grew round the bar.

'These folks are from England,' he announced flatly. 'They probably ain't used to drinking shorts, so you lot leave them be. You don't mean no offence do you?'

'Certainly not,' Heather smiled. 'We're used to huge flat pints of bitter. We really do have to go in a minute to sort out tickets and things.'

'Whenever you're ready,' Casey said, picking up his bat. 'It will be my pleasure to escort you to the door.'

There was no way to judge the right moment. In a little while I nodded to Heather, she took the cue, we slugged back our last whiskies and stood up together.

'Goodbye,' I said. Heather stood sadly beside me.

'GOODBYE,' I said again for her benefit, but she had forgotten the retreat cue and was looking at Bud and Chuck and Maxie the Murderer and Casey with genuine affection.

'It's been a very nice evening,' she said. 'I'll be able to tell people about it in England.'

Won't you just, I thought, but only if we make it through the door.

They all stood up. Bud and Chuck fell over themselves trying to be first to open the door. Casey brushed them aside like flies and ushered us out himself. Half a dozen of them followed us outside until they saw the police car. Suddenly we were alone.

It was parked on the opposite side of the road.

'You the English people?' No friendliness here. The officer was icy-eyed, wary and stared through us at the winking bar sign.

'We're English yes,' I said.

'They're worrying about you down at the Amtrak office. It's unwise to go about this district at night.'

'We're on our way there now.'

'Stay on the lit side,' he grunted. 'We'll wait awhile. No trouble in there?'

'None whatsoever,' said Heather primly.

'You're lucky ma'am. Last week a woman was murdered in there.'

We said nothing. I knew how the truth could get bent, but am normally too remote from it to appreciate that it can affect lives. We wondered afterwards what happened to Maxie and decided he most probably would be doing time somewhere.

The police car stayed outside the bar until we entered the station and then its lights came on and it slid slowly away into the night.

The following day we rolled into the palace they built for movie people coming to the City of the Angels. Our headaches were blinding, which may perhaps account for the fact that I have always found Los Angeles a difficult town to love. Most days, given the smog, it is also a difficult town to find. Los Angeles people of course regard it and the state surrounding it, California, as the centre of the universe. It is certainly not that, but parts of it are indeed incredible. These parts house people who work in films and television.

If you study the things in which Californians believe, their passions and their cults, it is easy to come to the conclusion that they are all mad and that this derangement increases the richer you get.

My friend Bernie in New York has another view. 'Everyone has sunburnt brains out there,' he had warned me.

And almost our first experience in Los Angeles seemed to support his assessment. We were entertained by my oldest friend from Rhodesia, Tony Hitchman, and his new wife Peggy. I had been Tony's best man at his previous marriage and was godfather to his son, Paul.

Tony had obviously made good in California and looked the part, tall, bronzed, gold-chained and outfitted in pastels. Peggy was a tall friendly blonde.

He had made his money as an auditor in Scientology, a cult that had recently declared itself a church. We judged them to be very typical Californians. They took us out to a Japanese martial arts performance posing as dinner. The chef was apparently trying to commit hari-kari over the bit hotplate in front of us but the need to feed chopped prawns to the diners kept preventing him from falling on his flashing knives.

Afterwards we went back to their smart house, which they referred to not as a house but a 'home' and left us in no doubt that, be they ever so content with it, they were hoping to move on successively through ever more impressive homes until they reached the nirvana of Beverly Hills.

Tony earned vast fees by English standards practising amateur psychology. He certainly had no formal psychology training other than from the Scientologists, which in Californian sectarian terms could, I suppose, be considered as rather formal. Incomplete Californians were coming to him in droves to be improved and hopefully upgraded to superhuman 'clears.' The Scientologists having declared themselves a church, Tony was now the Rev. Hitchman.

None of this bothered me thanks to Bernie's briefing and we had a very companionable evening until Peggy mentioned that the Church of Scientology believed in re-incarnation of a very lovely type: you were reborn again at your moment of ultimate happiness.

Tony and Peggy, quite newly married, were obviously very happy together – indeed Peggy in her effusive American way had been telling us all evening how she couldn't be happier.

Heather said: 'So now's a good time to jump out of the window?'

I laughed – I had not spent all that time playing gin with her for nothing.

Peggy said: 'Beg yours?'

'One could achieve a kind of sublime immortality.'

Tony, who had been born in England, tried a laugh but Peggy was not to be patronized.

'You're suggesting I should commit suicide!'

'Pursued to its logical conclusion,' said Heather inexorably while I tried to decide whether I would boil her in oil or just have her long nails dragged out with pliers when we got out of there. 'One really should jump out of the window at each successive moment of happiness. I suppose one could say well, I was that happy before and this time I'll go on a bit and see if I can get even happier. Of course one could be topping oneself at some really rude moments . . .'

She stopped, stared at me, then at Peggy.

'You're taking me seriously,' she smiled.

'God, you English!' Peggy laughed. 'You really scared me.'

'Me too,' I said ominously, later.

'You didn't think . . .!'

'What if they had jumped?'

Heather looked at me with alarm. 'In flagrante!'

'No seriously, this is California, home of the ultimate trip – nirvana – what if they'd cried "Bliss!" and jumped?'

'Well according to their beliefs it would have been no worse than an attack of hiccups,' Heather said crossly. 'Your friend Bernie was right, it must be something in the air. I think it's time to move on.'

'But we've only been here two days, where do you want to go?'

She sighed. 'Actually I want to go home and buy an English house with a wet garden and a dustman and a milkman who I know by their Christian names.'

And that's what we did. We traded in my free ticket to Australia and went that way, skipping like a stone across the oceans dividing Hawaii, New Zealand, Australia, Thailand, Hong Kong and the Gulf. It was not as wasteful as it seems because Heather and I had made a belated but important discovery which rendered these exotic places mere diversions – there really is no place like home.

Personally, I stood back after making thirteen hours of programmes about happy eccentric people and attempted to quantify their contentment. It was quite apparent that the happiest by far were those who were at one with nature.

How do you achieve one-ness with nature – what actually is it? In a world plagued by loneliness how do special people spend months and years alone with only the company of the natural fauna and flora to inspire them. In a world of concrete jungles built to provide creature comforts why do millions of us continue to invest our leisure time in cold, muddy marshes watching (or is it envying) wild birds, walking windy moors and downs or fishing wild rivers and turgid ponds?

I had had a taste of this as a child in Africa. Via a series of natural history programmes, culminating in my series *Nature Watch* which this year completed its sixtieth episode, I came full circle and became, at the beginning of a green revolution, a wanderer in the wilderness again, lucky to the last.

Epilogue

This is not compulsory reading but I thought you might like to know what became of Bob Heller.

Soon after returning home I went to visit Bob Heller in what I was told was a mental hospital. In this hospital, without the authority of his desk, his newspapers, his special relationship with Lew Grade, Bob had reverted to a little round man, difficult to take seriously. I had never met him before.

He appeared quite sane. He explained very lucidly how he had been betrayed, how things had gone on behind his back, how he had not been given the support he needed for his most controversial project yet (a very subjective life of the Irish revolutionary-patriot Michael Collins by Hugh Griffiths), and how Lew Grade had got rid of him (admittedly still with the title 'consultant' and on full pay) but with the cruellest cut of all – an injunction that he should work from home. Deprived of the armour of his beloved job he had become ill and, he conceded, difficult to live with. He admitted that he had been overworking for years but the work had always seemed so important. He told me wryly that he and Lew Grade used to race each other into the office every morning to get to the mail first. He understood why his wife had left him.

He smiled (I had never seen such a smile before) and said he was quite happy where he was for the time being and had accepted that a period of institutionalized rest was essential before resuming his responsibilities. For this man in particular to require the balm of delusion depressed me profoundly.

When a few weeks later I heard he was dead, I must confess that I really did think that it was for the best.

Let us for a moment remember Heller, documentary-maker. His whole life had been devoted to serious television. Young, strong, ambitious sharks had swum in from the shallows and bitten off his legs. The king sharks who owed him their protection had been too busy taking over other lagoons to come to his rescue. A very dangerous and shallow business? Certainly, but I am sure much the same goes on at most places.

And just as it has always been with my movie making, this material has stubbornly refused to comply with a preconception – in this case a shark-infested custard – which may say something for integrity. There can be no dark night of the media soul because, thankfully, the public simply does not take any of us that seriously. Outside of the pages of this book, Bob Heller is a forgotten victim of a competitive business – but not much more competitive than most.

There are admittedly more sharks in television than in most established businesses but that is simply because of the nature of the material we process. Television feeds on ideas and this admits a greater flow of posers than a traditional business would allow. They don't last very long but they do a lot of biting, particularly back-biting, on their way out.

Because of television's (particularly ITV's) economic strength, it has also been possible for entrenched executives to sidestep responsibility for mediocre programmes (it being so easy to get rid of the programme-maker). These sharks also turn very nasty when challenged but their days are numbered too as better management is attracted to the commercial feeding-frenzy promised in the Tories new Broadcasting Bill.

But I hope I can claim to have stuck to the essential principle of the documentary. I have written about what there is – a lot of good intention and almost as much artistic pretension practised by an essentially well-meaning community living in cloud-cuckoo land. We even had something of an excuse because, until very recently, it really was cloud-cuckoo land.

Bob Heller's demise taught me how to recognize the dangers, the currents that could sweep you along inexorably, the reefs of executive desks, the mistake that a career in television was a way of life. He also took me from the backwoods and gave me the chance to travel to the most exciting places on earth and meet on equal terms some of the most interesting people of our time. As I write these closing lines, my daughter Tiffany who was a child in Chapter One, is leaving on a dangerous assignment to Mozambique as the Production Assistant on a Granada documentary!

For the quarter century I have been a part of this circus British television has been the best in the world. For all its shortcomings it is a tremendously valuable national asset and to allow it to be destroyed by what must surely be one of Mrs Thatcher's valedictory fits of pique would be a tragedy.

She is determined to bring British television down to earth, which is no bad thing. Her method – to let the most avaricious of the sharks loose in a commercial free-for-all that has already sharply increased the quota of soaps, game shows and old movies in peak time – is a disaster.

Inventive, investigative, quality television (drama, documentary, natural history, science, arts, opinion and good programmes for children) can only survive if they are protected by a quality clause from competition for slots with the cheaply-produced dross. Without that, then I really have been writing a requiem for the golden age of television.

Shark Infested Custard – the golden age of television?

It has an unfortunate ring of truth about it.